GOVERNANCE FOR THE E

We live in an era of human-dominated ecosystems in which the demand for environmental governance is rising rapidly. At the same time, confidence in the capacity of governments to meet this demand is waning. How can we address the resultant governance deficit and achieve sustainable development? This book brings together perspectives from economics, management, and political science in order to identify innovative approaches to governance and bring them to bear on environmental issues. The authors' analysis of important cases demonstrates how governance systems need to fit their specific setting and how effective policies can be developed without relying exclusively on government. They argue that the future of environmental policies lies in coordinated systems that simultaneously engage actors located in the public sector, the private sector, and civil society. *Governance for the Environment* draws attention to cutting-edge questions for practitioners and analysts interested in environmental governance.

MAGALI A. DELMAS is Associate Professor of Management at the Institute of the Environment at the University of California, Los Angeles, and Director of the UCLA Center for Corporate Environmental Performance.

ORAN R. YOUNG is Professor at the Donald Bren School of Environmental Science and Management at the University of California, Santa Barbara. He is also a Co-director of the Program on Governance for Sustainable Development at the Donald Bren School, and Chair of the Scientific Committee of the International Human Dimensions Programme on Global Environmental Change.

GOVERNANCE FOR THE ENVIRONMENT

New Perspectives

edited by

MAGALI A. DELMAS

*Institute of the Environment, University of California,
Los Angeles, USA*

ORAN R. YOUNG

*Donald Bren School of Environmental Science and
Management, University of California,
Santa Barbara, USA*

CAMBRIDGE UNIVERSITY PRESS
Cambridge, New York, Melbourne, Madrid, Cape Town, Singapore, São Paulo, Delhi

Cambridge University Press
The Edinburgh Building, Cambridge CB2 8RU, UK

Published in the United States of America by Cambridge University Press, New York

www.cambridge.org
Information on this title: www.cambridge.org/9780521743006

First published 2009

Printed in the United Kingdom at the University Press, Cambridge

A catalog record for this publication is available from the British Library

Library of Congress Cataloging in Publication data
Delmas, Magali A.
Governance for the environment : new perspectives / Magali A. Delmas, Oran R. Young.
p.   cm.
Includes bibliographical references and index.
ISBN 978-0-521-51938-0 (hardback)   1. Sustainable development–Government
policy.   2. Environmental policy.   3. Environmentalism–Economic aspects.
4. Environmentalism–Political aspects.   I. Young, Oran R.   II. Title.
HC79.E5D4467 2009
338.9′27–dc22
2009018065

ISBN 978-0-521-51938-0 hardback
ISBN 978-0-521-74300-6 paperback

CONTENTS

FIGURES

TABLES

CONTRIBUTORS

ARUN AGRAWAL Associate Professor in the School of Natural Resources and Environment, University of Michigan

GRAEME AULD Doctoral Student in the School of Forestry and Environmental Studies, Yale University

CRISTINA BALBOA Doctoral Student in the School of Forestry and Environmental Studies, Yale University

STEVEN BERNSTEIN Associate Professor in the Department of Political Science, University of Toronto

KEITH BROUHLE Assistant Professor in the Department of Economics, Grinnell College, Grinnell, IA

BENJAMIN CASHORE Professor of Environmental Governance and Political Science in the School of Forestry and Environmental Studies, Yale University

VIRGINIA HAUFLER Associate Professor in the Department of Government and Politics, University of Maryland

MADHU KHANNA Professor in the Department of Agricultural and Consumer Economics, University of Illinois at Urbana-Champaign

ANDREW KING Associate Professor of Business Administration, Dartmouth College, Hanover, NH

MARIA CARMEN LEMOS Assistant Professor in the School of Natural Resources and Environment, University of Michigan

THOMAS P. LYON   Dow Professor of Sustainable Science, Technology and Commerce, University of Michigan

MICHAEL W. TOFFEL   Assistant Professor of Business Administration, Harvard Business School

PREFACE

This book is a product of our collaboration in the unique setting of the Donald Bren School of Environmental Science and Management at the University of California (Santa Barbara). Unlike mainstream, discipline-based departments, which often create barriers to collaboration across the boundaries of established disciplines, the Bren School facilitates and actually encourages such collaborative efforts. So, first and foremost, we are grateful to the School for providing an academic setting conducive to our work on new developments in understanding both the nature and the role of governance in various realms.

What has made this project particularly productive for us is that new thinking about governance is developing rapidly in several different research communities that so far have had relatively little contact with one another regarding new ideas about governance. In this project, we have brought together contributors from the fields of economics, management, and political science. Lawyers also participated in the workshop on which the book is based, although none of the chapters that make up the text of the book was prepared by a lawyer.

What this effort has revealed is interesting and challenging on two counts. It is clear that there is sufficient overlap in the thinking of researchers working in these fields on the nature of governance – treated as a social function rather than a specialized organization in society – to allow for fruitful exchanges and to open up the prospect of developing a unified body of knowledge about governance. But, also, there are enough differences in the thinking of those coming from the different disciplines to provide an important research agenda for all those concerned with the creation of the governance systems needed to address a broad range of issues grouped together under the rubric of sustainable development. This is particularly good news in a period in which, as we explain in the book's Introduction, the demand for governance is rising rapidly but confidence in the mechanisms we are used to relying on to supply governance is waning.

We owe several debts of gratitude and it is our pleasure to spell them out here. The Rockefeller Brothers Fund provided a grant to the Program on Governance for Sustainable Development at the Bren School that made it possible to gather an outstanding group of researchers working in this field for a workshop held in Santa Barbara on October 12–14, 2006. The Bren School itself provided support both in cash and in kind that made it possible to navigate the transition from earlier drafts to revised drafts of the individual chapters in the book as well as facilitating the administrative tasks involved in transforming a collection of papers into a coherent book.

We are grateful to John Haslam of Cambridge University Press for taking an interest in the project and for arranging for several anonymous reviews that helped us to clarify and strengthen a number of elements of the book. We are also pleased to acknowledge the services of Peter Rooney, who prepared the index. Above all, we are grateful to Maria Gordon, the chief of staff of the Program on Governance for Sustainable Development, for an extraordinary variety of services, ranging from organizing the workshop itself to providing high-quality editorial advice regarding many aspects of the text of the book.

From its inception, this project has been rooted in a collaboration between a researcher working in the field of corporate environmental management and another specializing in environmental politics and governance. One of the major payoffs for us from the project is the opportunity it afforded us to work together and sharpen our understanding of many aspects of governance.

PART I

Central threads and analytic perspectives

~

Introduction: new perspectives on governance for sustainable development

MAGALI A. DELMAS AND ORAN R. YOUNG

We live in an era in which the demand for governance arising from human–environment interactions or, more broadly, the quest for sustainable development is growing, while confidence in the capacity of government – the conventional mechanism for handling such matters – to address problems of governance is waning. What are the sources of this paradox? What can we do to address the rising demand for governance under these circumstances? How can we expand our repertoire of mechanisms for supplying governance to avoid the onset of crises attributable to this governance deficit? These are the questions that have motivated this inquiry into the rising demand for governance and the relative merits of alternative ways to address this social challenge, with particular reference to the pursuit of sustainable development.

Our examination of this problem has yielded two broad conclusions. There is, to begin with, a critical difference between governance and government, an insight that has stimulated a lively interest in arrangements that can be characterized as governance without government (Rosenau and Czempiel 1992). In addition, there is no need to put all our eggs in one basket when it comes to meeting the demand for governance for sustainable development. Hybrid systems in which several forms of governance operate simultaneously, and even with an element of coordination, are not only possible – they are also increasingly common in the realm of sustainable development.

The paradox of rising demand and waning confidence

It is not hard to identify factors that have given rise to a growing demand for governance to address problems of sustainable development. Human actions have become a dominant force in the dynamics of large and complex socio-ecological systems (Gunderson and Holling 2002; Steffen et al. 2004). More often than not, as in cases such as climate change, the loss of biological diversity, the depletion of fish stocks, and the destruction of tropical forests, the impacts of human actions are unintended and (quite often) unforeseen. But this does not mean that we can afford to ignore the need to steer or guide human actions to prevent, or at least ameliorate, their impact on the planet's life-support systems. The need for governance to address these problems is critical if we are to avoid drastic changes in the Earth's climate system or to continue to enjoy ecosystem services on a large scale. As these observations make clear, we must address the demand for governance on a global scale. While domestic systems may have essential roles to play in experimenting with innovative approaches to governance and in implementing the overarching arrangements we create, there can be no substitute for tackling the need for new and more effective systems of governance on a global scale.

Shifting the discourse from the conventional idea of environmental protection to the new – and still contested – idea of sustainable development intensifies the growing need for governance. As the idea of the "triple bottom line" suggests, it is no longer sufficient to concentrate on protecting ecosystems in biophysical terms, leaving the economic and social consequences for others to address. We find ourselves increasingly faced with the need to consider tradeoffs between responding to looming crises such as the impacts of climate change, and coping with critical current needs such as those spelled out in the Millennium Development Goals (United Nations 2007). There are, of course, cases in which it is possible to make progress on several fronts at once. Reducing the ravages of diseases associated with extreme poverty, for instance, seems desirable on many levels. Yet the need to make tradeoffs in this realm is inescapable. As the ranks of environmental refugees swell, leading to economic and political instability and the ensuing civil strife, we will be unable to avoid making decisions about the allocation of resources to respond to immediate needs for humanitarian assistance, in contrast to addressing the underlying causes of large-scale problems such as climate change and land degradation.

So, why can we not rely on governments – social institutions and organizations specialized to address matters of public choice at various levels of social organization – to cope with the rising demand for governance for sustainable development? Although the challenge of governance is increasingly global in scope, we do not have a world government – and there is little prospect of such a government arising during the foreseeable future. Individual states are territorially defined, a feature that makes them ill-suited to addressing the need for global governance, even when they band together to devise intergovernmental arrangements, such as the growing universe of multilateral environmental agreements.

Even if it were feasible, the creation of a world government as a means of overcoming the resultant fragmentation has few supporters at this time. This is due, in large part, to a growing awareness of and concern about what are often described as government failures, a perspective that draws attention to the role of these failures as counterparts to market failures (Wolf 1988; Winston 2006). Governments are sluggish. They are often slow to respond to problems and typically make use of blunt instruments, even when they do take action to address the need for governance. Governments lack the discipline of the market; they seldom feel the pressure to seize opportunities and to perform efficiently that corporations routinely experience in competitive markets. Political leaders are typically motivated by a desire to maximize their chances of re-election, a situation that drives them to think largely in distributive terms rather than in terms of a larger concern for the public interest or the common good. Equally important, governments regularly fall prey to corruption. In extreme cases, authoritarian leaders use their power to promote their own interests, amassing fortunes held in Swiss bank accounts or other offshore locations. Even in more democratic systems, abuses of power are widespread, and accountability is limited. The role of special interests and what are often called "iron triangles" or coalitions among special interests, administrative agencies, and legislative committees has grown to an extent that breeds understandable cynicism about the capacity of governments to deal with the need for governance in more or less conventional cases, let alone the sort of situations we face today. There is no reason to expect a world government to be any more immune from governance failures of this sort than the average national government. It is not surprising that many have concluded that government can, and often does, become part of the problem rather than part of the solution, a conclusion motivating them to join movements intended to reduce both the size of governments and their ability to intervene in a wide range of issues.

The fact is that we find ourselves facing an exceptionally demanding challenge of governance with little confidence in the ability of governments to meet this challenge in an effective manner. This is a novel situation. Unlike crises in which we have turned to governments to mobilize society's resources to fight foreign wars or to intervene to reverse the tide of economic recessions or depressions at home, we now find ourselves confronting challenges on an almost unprecedented scale with little faith in existing institutions to take the steps needed to address them successfully. This is the paradox of rising demand and waning confidence. It also constitutes the central focus of this book. We have set out in search of responses to this paradox. In the process, we have sought to mine the intellectual capital of a number of disciplines to find grounds for optimism in response to this paradox, and we have discovered that many of the most promising responses to this problem involve building bridges to integrate the intellectual capital of different fields that can contribute to the development of effective responses but that are isolated from one another because they are managed by members of scientific communities who do not interact regularly with one another.

New approaches to governance

What can we do to address the paradox of rising demand and waning confidence? Are there promising developments that we can single out and nurture in this realm? More specifically, are there opportunities for productive engagement between the scientific community and the policy community as we search for a way forward in addressing the growing need for governance for sustainable development? The somewhat surprising answer, we have found, is that new ideas about the supply of governance are sprouting in many quarters. Far from being a gloomy backwater, the study of governance is a growth industry generating all sorts of new ideas about mechanisms for addressing the demand for governance. These are early times to assess the efficacy of this development; it would be premature to attempt to draw precise conclusions about the relative merits of any particular line of thought in this nascent field. But the distinction between governance and government makes it clear that we should cast our net wide in thinking about new forms of governance. Moreover, most discussions of pure forms of governance are analytic in character. To address the real problems of governance, it is often helpful to draw on several forms of governance at the same time, or even to devise hybrid systems that will seem messy to those who think in taxonomic terms but that are often better suited to getting the job done than any pure form of governance by itself.

Governance is a social function centered on efforts to steer societies or human groups away from collectively undesirable outcomes (e.g., the tragedy of the commons) and toward socially desirable outcomes (e.g., the maintenance of a benign climate system) (Young 1999a). Government, by contrast, is an organization or collection of organizations specialized to address problems of governance in a well-defined setting (e.g., a nation-state). We are apt to take it for granted that we can rely on government to take care of the need for governance. In some times and places, this natural assumption has made sense. But many governments do a poor job in meeting the demand for governance; some are more or less total failures when it comes to addressing anything but the most routine problems of governance. Conversely, organizations other than governments can, and often do, emerge as important players in efforts to meet the demand for governance. We are used to acknowledging this proposition with regard to specialized bodies (e.g., land trusts) or professional associations (e.g., scientific organizations). Yet there is clear evidence today that the idea of governance without government is spreading to other areas and is in the process of becoming a significant option in thinking about the challenges of governance for sustainable development.

Once we accept the possibility of governance without government, a variety of interesting options come into focus. There is, to begin with, the prospect of private governance, taking such forms as codes of conduct, certification schemes, and voluntary markets for permits to emit greenhouse gases (Delmas 2002). The logic of such arrangements is relatively easy to understand. Corporations – especially those that operate in a number of countries – seek clarity and predictability regarding the rules of the game applying to their operations. They often prefer well-defined rules coupled with a level playing field to a situation in which they are free to make their own decisions in the absence of regulatory rules. Civil society has also become a locus of creative initiatives for those seeking to address the need for governance for sustainable development. Whereas agents operating in civil society (e.g., environmental NGOs) once devoted their energy largely to efforts aimed at influencing the actions of governments, these players now devote substantial resources to approaches to governance that bypass governments. As confidence in the ability of governments to meet the demand for governance for sustainable development wanes, the lure of new forms of governance rises. Even at the international level, civil society has emerged as a force to be taken seriously (Wapner 1997). Any objective assessment of efforts to address the challenge of climate change, for instance, must devote at least as much attention to activities rooted in civil society as to the formalities of intergovernmental negotiations.

As this observation makes clear, there is no need to treat distinct approaches to governance as options that are mutually exclusive. A major insight we have gleaned from our research is that real-world efforts to meet the demand for governance often feature the emergence of multiple mechanisms. Sometimes these mechanisms are alternatives to one another. Voluntary codes of conduct (e.g., the CERES principles) emerge to address situations in which public regulations are either absent or inadequate. Environmental NGOs strive to bring pressure to bear on multinational corporations directly in cases where there seems little likelihood that governments will act to put effective public regulations in place. Voluntary markets (e.g., the Chicago Climate Exchange) arise in situations where participants are free to participate or not according to their own calculations. Figure 1 maps the different governance mechanisms cited in this volume, based on the actors involved in their creation and implementation. We classify actors engaged in the supply of governance into three broad categories: those belonging to the public sector, civil society, or the private sector.

However, a particularly interesting and potentially effective option, we have found, involves hybrid systems in which diverse actors seek to form coalitions that cut across different approaches to governance in the interests of meeting the growing demand for governance

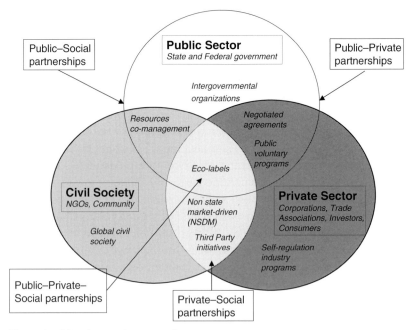

Figure 1   Mapping environmental governance systems

for sustainable development. As Figure 1 indicates, a number of the governance mechanisms identified are located at the intersection of these circles. These include public voluntary programs where the government offers technical assistance and positive publicity to firms that reach certain environmental goals (Lyon, Chapter 2, this volume; Khanna and Brouhle, Chapter 6, this volume) or negotiated agreements where firms and regulators bargain over the frame and the pollution-reduction targets set forth in the agreement (Delmas and Terlaak 2002). Co-management is an increasingly common form of collaboration between state agencies and communities (Lemos and Agrawal, Chapter 3, this volume). Eco-labeling systems (e.g., those used by the Forest Stewardship Council) often engage corporations and NGOs (Auld et al., Chapter 7, this volume); they might also engage governments.

It is too early to pass judgment on the efficacy of these hybrid arrangements in coming to terms with the rising demand for governance. But, already, we can say with confidence that the challenge of governance for sustainable development is giving rise to a variety of innovative responses on the part of those who understand that the conventional response of relying on government is unlikely to serve us well in meeting the challenges of governance arising from human–environment interactions in an era of human-dominated ecosystems.

The shape of things to come

Part I of this book consists of this Introduction together with a chapter by Oran Young that seeks to provide a common analytic framework and theoretical point of departure for the chapters to come. Chapter 1 provides a roadmap regarding ways to think about the demand for governance, major options for supplying governance, and the issues that those desiring to evaluate the effectiveness of governance systems must address in arriving at judgments about specific cases.

The three chapters that make up Part II focus on the intellectual capital that the disciplines of economics, political science, and management can provide to those seeking to address the challenge of governance for sustainable development. In Chapter 2, Tom Lyon presents a clear and comprehensive account of the ways in which economists approach the problem of governance. The emphasis here is on market failures and on the demand for governance to avoid or correct market failures, including the tragedy of the commons, the free-rider problem, and a variety of negative externalities. As one would expect, Lyon's analysis is alert to the prospect of government failures occurring as a counterpart to market failures. Maria Carmen Lemos and Arun Agrawal follow, in Chapter 3, with an account of the idea of governance from the perspective of political science. In the course of their survey, they stress the importance of approaching governance systems as socially constructed arrangements as well as the extensive experience with hybrid arrangements involving more or less complex interactions among governments, corporations, and associations embedded in civil society. In Chapter 4, Andrew King and Michael Toffel approach governance from the vantage point of business administration or management. Without denying the roles that governments play, they emphasize the importance of self-regulatory institutions. As they see it, there is a bright future for such arrangements in efforts to address important environmental problems such as climate change.

The chapters grouped together in Part III then proceed to make use of this intellectual capital to review and evaluate efforts to supply governance in a variety of real-world settings. In Chapter 5, Virginia Haufler directs attention to the role of non-state and transnational actors in addressing international and global environmental challenges. She is particularly interested in the idea that multinational corporations can become part of the solution rather than remaining part of the problem in coming to grips with issues of this sort. In Chapter 6, Madhu Khanna and Keith Brouhle review the evidence on the effectiveness of voluntary environmental initiatives from a wide range of studies. Their results are generally encouraging, although they are careful not to overinterpret the available evidence in this realm. In Chapter 7, Benjamin Cashore and several of his colleagues and doctoral students take some additional steps in developing what they call non-state market-driven governance systems (NSMDs). Here, they focus particularly on how these systems can emerge across a range of economic sectors.

Part IV consists of a single chapter – Chapter 8 by Magali Delmas – that addresses the current state of play regarding our understanding of the role of governance as a social function. Because we have sought to capture the take-home messages from our project in this Introduction, Chapter 8 does not attempt to summarize the findings of the book as a whole. Rather, this chapter examines recent achievements in this field of study, highlights several important observations about the supply of governance (e.g., the emergence of hybrid systems of governance), and identifies cutting-edge questions for research during the next phase of the pursuit of knowledge about governance. In the end, Delmas concludes that this is a highly dynamic field, giving rise to experiments with many different approaches to the supply of governance. Opportunities for productive research in helping to devise successful mechanisms for pursuing governance for sustainable development are many. We have no hesitation in recommending this field of study to our colleagues and students as a rewarding area in terms of both scientific research and policy applications during the years to come.

1

Governance for sustainable development in a world of rising interdependencies

ORAN R. YOUNG

Introduction

Governance, treated as a social function centered on efforts to steer or guide societies toward collectively beneficial outcomes and away from outcomes that are collectively harmful, is one of the great issues of every era. Thomas Hobbes, writing in the midst of the civil strife and turmoil of mid-seventeenth-century England emphasized the need to establish and maintain order (Hobbes 1660/1999). He assumed that individuals would engage in a struggle for power, concluded that life in the absence of effective regulatory arrangements would degenerate into a war of all against all, and called for the adoption of a social contract granting far-reaching authority – and the capacity to exercise it – to a central government. Writing during a period of political reform and economic prosperity in the second half of the eighteenth century, Adam Smith took a different tack (Smith 1776/1937). He started from the premise that individuals seek to enhance their own welfare and counted on the operation of the market to solve many coordination problems. Nevertheless, he assigned to governance the role of providing a stable system of rights and rules needed to allow commerce to flourish and to avoid or manage business cycles and financial fluctuations. Approaching these issues in the aftermath of the imperial wars that dominated European politics in the early years of the nineteenth century, Peter Kropotkin emphasized the dangers arising from the actions of powerful governments and came to believe in the virtues of anarchy (Kropotkin 1902/1986). But this did not lead him to deny the importance of governance. Rather, he advocated efforts to supply governance through the activities of civil society – he referred to these activities as mutual aid – in contrast with the actions of a public authority or the operation of the market. Taken together, this array of classic perspectives regarding the nature and role of governance in human societies offers an excellent starting point for a study of governance for sustainable development in today's world.

Broadly speaking, we can map contemporary views on these issues onto a spectrum of perspectives regarding the nature and role of governance. The views of those who argue that good governance is the key to economic growth and social development anchor one end of the spectrum. The argument of new institutionalists such as Douglass North to the effect that stable political institutions played a pivotal role in the rise of the West exemplifies this line of thinking (North and Thomas 1973). At the other end of the spectrum lie the views of self-proclaimed realists who assert that the exercise of power determines collective outcomes and that governance systems – or, for that matter, social institutions in general – are epiphenomena which are subject to change as the distribution of power in society shifts (Strange 1983; Mearsheimer 1994/1995). Originating in the work of thinkers such as Karl Marx during the nineteenth century (Marx and Engels 1848/1968), this perspective surfaces with some regularity in radical thinking about the role of power in society (Mills 2000).

For our purposes, however, the interesting questions pertain to the range of views concerning the role of governance that occupy the space between these extremes. Governance, on this account, is one determinant of collective outcomes in most social settings, but it is not the only driving force operating in this realm. Complex causality is the norm rather than the exception in such settings. Governance systems regularly interact with other factors, including demographic, technological, and cultural forces, so that collective outcomes are products of clusters of factors that interact with one another to produce a stream of outcomes (Young 2002a). To reach conclusions about the effectiveness of specific governance systems, it follows that analysts must ask questions about the settings in which such systems operate and be prepared to focus on the fit between actual governance systems and the distinctive features of these settings.

This way of thinking opens up a large research agenda regarding the nature of governance, the demand for governance, alternative approaches to the supply of governance, the factors that determine the effectiveness of governance systems in specific settings, and the forces that bring about changes in prevailing governance systems. Starting from the premise that governance is a social function, this chapter draws a clear distinction at the outset between governance and government treated as one approach to the supply of governance (Young 1989; Kooiman 2003). And because this analysis emphasizes interactions between governance systems and other driving forces, it assumes that efforts to design and construct effective governance systems must be sensitive to contextual conditions. A governance system that produces good results in one setting may prove ineffective in others. This suggests the need for a diagnostic approach to the development of governance systems. One size does not fit all in this realm; effective governance systems are well matched to the settings in which they operate (Young 2002b, 2008; Ostrom 2007).

Employing this functional perspective on governance, this chapter addresses the paradox of the rising demand for governance for sustainable development coupled with declining confidence in government as a mechanism for meeting this demand. The first substantive section probes the demand for governance. It couples an account of the classic arguments regarding the demand for governance with an analysis of the forces leading to a rising demand for governance in our era. The next section turns to the supply of governance. In addition to elaborating on the distinction between governance and government, it considers new approaches to the supply of governance that come into focus once we set aside the assumption that governments are required for the performance of this social function (Rosenau and Czempiel 1992). A topic of special interest is the rise of innovative efforts to meet the demand for governance without relying on governments to take the lead in doing so. The next section focuses on the effectiveness of governance systems. In addition to the familiar emphasis on problem-solving, the analysis seeks to unpack the idea of good governance and to explore the nature and significance of governance failures. The final section addresses issues pertaining to the development of a more comprehensive and policy-relevant theory of governance. What is needed to integrate various strands of thinking about governance in order to establish a common taxonomy of types of governance and an integrated research program regarding the conditions under which individual types of governance are likely to emerge and to prove successful both in terms of problem-solving and in terms of other criteria relevant to the performance of governance systems?

The demand for governance

What conditions give rise to a demand for governance? Can we group these conditions into a small number of analytically distinct categories rather than approaching individual situations in an ad hoc manner? Seeking to answer these questions, I start with a brief account of the classic approach to the demand for governance, explore several extensions of this approach, and conclude with an assessment of the proposition that the demand for governance is rising in today's world.

Solving collective-action problems

In theoretical terms, the most compelling account of the demand for governance arises from the concept of collective action. Most analysts are now familiar with the idea that actions that seem perfectly rational from the point of view of individual members of a group can lead to socially undesirable outcomes or, in other words, outcomes that are suboptimal for all the members of the group. This is the conundrum that Olson highlighted in speaking of "the logic of collective action" (Olson 1965), that G. Hardin and others drew attention to in developing the idea of "the tragedy of the commons" (Hardin 1968), and that Schelling emphasized in drawing a clear distinction between what he calls "micromotives and macrobehavior" (Schelling 1978). Much of the important thinking about governance emerging in recent decades has focused on the need to devise mechanisms to avoid the ever-present danger of falling into the traps we think of as collective-action problems (Ostrom 1990).

The dilemma of overconsumption associated with the tragedy of the commons and the free-rider problem associated with efforts to supply public goods dominate collective-action perspectives on the demand for governance. Although it is possible to model these problems in a similar fashion in purely analytic terms, it is useful to draw a distinction between them for the purpose of thinking about governance for sustainable development (R. Hardin 1982). The tragedy of the commons occurs in situations where goods (e.g., most natural resources) and services (e.g., ecosystem services including the disposal of wastes) are non-excludable but rival, and where aggregate demand exceeds supply. In the absence of governance, individuals operating in such settings will lack any incentive to conserve, and the collective outcome will be one of more or less severe depletion or overuse (Baden and Noonan 1998). The challenge of governance, under these conditions, is to introduce entry barriers (e.g., individual transferable quotas or ITQs) or to generate normative principles (e.g., the "polluter pays" principle) capable of altering the behavior of group members that gives rise to the tragedy. There are many ways to tackle this challenge, and the literature on governance is replete with protracted debates about the pros and cons of specific mechanisms for avoiding or alleviating the tragedy of the commons. But the common denominator in all these accounts is the need to influence the behavior of individual users or appropriators in such a way as to limit their use of the common pool.

The "free-rider" problem, by contrast, occurs in situations where the social benefits accruing from a public good exceed the cost of supply, but individual members of the group would prefer to enjoy the good without shouldering a share of the cost. Many environmental issues (e.g., clean air and clean water) fit this description. But so also do other environmentally relevant activities such as the production of knowledge needed to develop the tools to manage the use of natural resources or protect environmental quality. The challenge of governance here is to introduce effective cost-sharing mechanisms or to devise arrangements such as exclusive clubs, patents, or licenses that make it impossible for individual members of the group to benefit from the supply of a public good as free-riders (Sandler 1992). Whereas solving the problem underlying the tragedy of the commons is a matter of inducing appropriators to limit or cut back on their use of the relevant goods and services, solving the free-rider problem is a matter of inducing individual beneficiaries to accept responsibility for contributing to the cost of supply. As in the case of the tragedy of the commons, there are many ways to address the free-rider problem. A sizable portion of the literature on governance consists of debates about the pros and cons of various ways to influence the behavior of those expected to benefit from the supply of public goods.

Extending the logic of collective action

What makes dealing with collective-action problems central to the pursuit of governance is the fact that all members of the group stand to benefit from the creation of governance systems but that individual members are unable to bring about this change on their own. But there are other situations that bear some resemblance to collective-action problems, at least when it comes to engendering a demand for governance. What distinguishes these problems is that it is less clear that all members of the group will benefit from solving them. Yet they are similar to collective-action problems in the sense that they generate outcomes that many thoughtful members of society regard as collectively harmful – at least in the long run – and therefore as warranting the introduction of some form of governance. The most important types of situations that fit this description are social traps, externalities and unpriced ecosystem services, and issues of fairness.

Social traps are situations involving collective addiction (Cross and Guyer 1980). They occur when the members of a group adopt a form of behavior that seems beneficial at the outset but that hardens into a pattern of destructive behavior that is difficult to alter, even when circumstances change in such a way as to make the behavior collectively harmful. A prominent case in point today is the addiction of advanced industrial societies to the use of fossil fuels as a source of energy. During the earlier stages of the industrial era, the balance of benefits and costs associated with the use of fossil fuels seemed decidedly favorable. Now the balance has shifted; the costs of this practice are rising and seem likely to overwhelm the benefits in the near future, if they have not done so already. Yet sunk costs, ingrained habits, and institutional rigidity make it hard to find a way out of this social trap. The demand for governance in such situations centers on the need to identify suitable options and to alter the incentives of individuals in ways that lead to socially desirable changes in behavior.

Externalities arise when actions taken for one purpose generate side effects that are costly (or, in some cases, beneficial) to others (Cowen 1988). Classic examples include cases in which sparks from steam engines set fire to farmers' crops or pollutants from industrial activities enter nearby streams in such a way as to harm others. A related problem of growing importance today involves the use of factors of production that are available free of charge. When a factory emits carbon dioxide into the Earth's atmosphere, it is making use of the atmosphere as a repository for wastes. Waste disposal is a factor of production which, under other circumstances, the factory would need to pay for. To the extent that the atmosphere is available for such uses free of charge, producers will have an incentive to use more of it than other factors (e.g., labor, capital) that figure as costs in their benefit/cost calculations. The call for governance as a means of redressing this distortion differs somewhat from the demand for governance to solve classic collective-action problems. At a minimum, the creation of a governance system can be expected to shift the burden of protecting the Earth's climate system from the public at large to those members of the relevant group who are consumers of the products of emitters of greenhouse gases. The demand for governance in such cases arises from the failure of existing arrangements to structure incentives in an appropriate manner and the need to introduce some system of rights and rules capable of shifting the incentives of key players in a socially desirable direction.

Issues of fairness give rise to a demand for governance when there are value judgments to be made that do not lend themselves to appropriate quantification, or when relevant actors are not represented in decision-making processes (Milner 2005). For instance, if allowable harvests are insufficient to satisfy the aggregate demands of subsistence, recreational, and commercial fishers, how should catch quotas be allocated among these groups? What are the appropriate criteria for use in efforts to assess the safety of genetically modified organisms? How should we take into account the impacts of actions taken today (e.g., emissions of greenhouse gases) on the welfare of future generations? The common denominator linking issues of this sort is the inability of individual actions to produce socially acceptable answers through the operation of some sort of invisible hand. Unlike true collective-action problems, the resolution of issues of this sort will lead to outcomes that some members of society like but others dislike, at least in the short run. Even so, there is a case to be made that paying attention to the rights of identifiable groups within society (e.g., indigenous peoples) or taking into account the legitimate expectations of future generations requires the operation of some sort of governance system to produce outcomes that are collectively beneficial.

The rising demand for governance

The situations discussed in the preceding sections are generic in the sense that they can and do occur at any time and in any place. Yet there is a pervasive sense that we are currently experiencing a sharp rise in the demand for governance and, as a result, confronting a situation for which we have no precedent. The sources of this assessment encompass both changes in the material conditions facing contemporary societies and shifts in the goals and objectives that we have in mind when thinking about governance for sustainable development.

Ultimately, the demand for governance arises from the existence of interdependencies between human actors. If the actions of individual members of a group had no implications – positive or negative – for the other members of the group, there would be no demand for governance. The challenge of governance emerges when interactions among the members of the group produce collectively beneficial or collectively harmful outcomes. Such prospects clearly increase – in all probability exponentially – as levels of interdependence among a society's members rise. It is therefore important to observe that interdependence is rising rapidly and occurring at a larger scale as a consequence both of global environmental change and of global social change in such forms as globalization.

As we move deeper into an era of human-dominated ecosystems, it is no longer appropriate to assume that human actions are relatively minor factors in the operation of macro-scale biophysical systems (e.g., the oceans, the Earth's climate system) (Vitousek et al. 1997). We face, as a result, a rapid growth in the demand for governance to manage a wide range of human–environment interactions. This challenge is intensified by the fact that the speed of major changes in biophysical systems can easily exceed the rate at which it is possible to (re)construct and implement governance systems.

Somewhat similar observations are in order regarding large-scale social changes. Technological developments (e.g., advanced weapons systems, genetically modified organisms, nanotechnology) produce social interactions where none existed previously. The growth of the Internet opens up both opportunities and dangers that call for the establishment of stable rules and procedures. The emergence of a global trading system makes possible the occurrence of economic crises that erupt unexpectedly and threaten to run out of control as in the case of the global financial crisis of 1997/8. The point here is not to suggest that these large-scale social developments are, on balance, undesirable. Rather, the issue at stake involves identifying and evaluating new demands for governance arising from these developments. Just as we took steps at the domestic level to minimize the danger of a repeat of the Great Depression of the 1930s, for example, we now need to think about the establishment of governance systems designed to avoid uncontrollable fluctuations and swings in the global economy (Stiglitz 2002). There is nothing surprising or mysterious about the rise in the demand for governance associated with these large-scale social developments. But, as we shall see, there is both a lack of experience and a range of institutional impediments that make it especially challenging to devise governance systems capable of coming to terms simultaneously with global social change and global environmental change.

The second factor accounting for a rise in the demand for governance today has more to do with the way in which we frame issues than with changes in material circumstances. The essence of the matter arises from the fact that we now pursue a number of distinct goals at one and the same time. The notion of the "triple bottom line" is fully embedded in the idea of sustainable development (World Commission on Environment and Sustainable Development 1987). Economic growth that ignores impacts on the environment is no longer acceptable. Environmental protection that is insensitive to the social and cultural concerns of those living on the land is not adequate. Hanging on to social or cultural practices in ways that sacrifice the environment or result in economic stagnation is a recipe for failure. Accordingly, political leaders now strive to organize societies in ways that lead simultaneously to economic, social, and environmental progress. But this is a tall order. It is always hard to maximize with respect to two or more evaluative dimensions; a challenge intensified by the lack of a common metric for evaluating tradeoffs between or among them. Dominant solutions or, in other words, outcomes that are preferred to others on all relevant dimensions are, of course, possible. But it is easy to see that such outcomes will be rare in the domain of sustainable development.

Focusing on the triple bottom line heightens interdependencies for governance in every social setting. Evaluations that consider only one dimension make it possible to ignore or disregard a wide range of externalities or unintended side effects impacting the other dimensions. Adopting the triple bottom line as the proper yardstick for assessing collective outcomes entails an effort to endogenize side effects on a more or less massive scale. There are legitimate questions concerning the feasibility of finding an acceptable means of operationalizing the triple bottom line; the proliferation of indicators of sustainable development has so far failed to provide a well-behaved metric that can be used to determine whether, all things considered, we are making progress toward sustainable development construed as a standard encompassing economic, social, and environmental welfare (Parris and Kates 2003). But, without doubt, any effort to pursue the triple bottom line will increase the demand for governance substantially. Steering human societies toward the achievement of multidimensional goals is not a task for the invisible hand operating alone.

The supply of governance

How, then, can we meet the rising demand for governance for sustainable development? A first step in responding to this question is to highlight the distinction between governance, treated as a social function, and government, regarded as a material entity specialized to the provision of governance (Young 1999a). Even sophisticated observers are in the habit of assuming that we should look to governments to meet the rising demand for governance and that there are few alternatives to doing so. But this way of thinking is surely myopic. Most governments exhibit more or less serious limitations as mechanisms for meeting the demand for governance for sustainable development; there are other approaches to the provision of governance that bring into focus the idea of governance without government.

There is a strand of thinking about governance that runs parallel to the idea of the invisible hand in economics. On this optimistic account, exemplified in the work of Hayek, we can expect governance systems to arise spontaneously or in a self-generating fashion to meet the need for steering mechanisms in situations where all the members of a group would be better off operating within a framework of agreed-upon rules and decision-making procedures than in a setting fraught with the unpredictability associated with an absence of governance (Hayek 1973). There is an important insight embedded in this mode of thought. As we shall see in the discussion of private governance, individual actors do have incentives to support the development of rules and decision-making procedures, and there are cases in which they exhibit a capacity to develop informal social practices of some importance. Nonetheless, the idea that we can count on spontaneous processes to solve problems of governance of the sort we face today is just as far-fetched as the idea that we can count on the invisible hand to solve problems of economic coordination. Not only are difficulties arising from ignorance and high transaction costs likely to prevent progress in this realm, but also any such hopes would run full-tilt into a massive free-rider problem. What begins as an optimistic scenario for avoiding the costs of governance failures, therefore, would inevitably fail to address large-scale problems such as climate change and the loss of biological diversity.

So there is no avoiding the need to find more explicit ways to meet the rising demand for governance for sustainable development. I begin this account with the conventional response, considering the role of governments and pointing both to their resilience as a source of governance and to their inadequacies as mechanisms for meeting the challenge of sustainable development in a globalized world. This sets the stage for a discussion of alternative approaches to the supply of governance. Starting with a commentary on governance by intergovernmental agreement, I move on to consider more far-reaching alternatives including private governance, civil society as a source of governance, and various types of hybrids involving elements of different governance systems. In the process, I seek both to identify a range of plausible approaches to the supply of governance and to initiate a focused analysis of the conditions under which these different approaches are likely to prove effective or successful. The following chapters pick up this theme and examine it from a variety of perspectives.

Governance by government

It is natural, at least among those brought up in Western cultures, to assume that governments or public agencies will take steps to meet the demand for governance. Governments, in this context, are construed as material entities or organizations that have personnel, infrastructure, equipment, budgets, and legal personality. Typically, constitutions or equivalent constitutive documents assign the function of governance to specific public authorities and spell out a variety of rules and procedures to be followed by these agencies in the process of meeting the demand for governance. Most governments do expend a great deal of energy and resources on efforts to respond to myriad demands for governance. So, what is the problem? Why not simply accept the assumption that there is no need to look beyond the realm of public agencies in efforts to respond to the rising demand for governance described in the preceding section? There are a number of reasons to doubt the wisdom of this response to the rising demand for governance. Taken together, these considerations have now given rise to a burgeoning literature on alternative mechanisms for supplying governance to which the analysis returns later in this chapter.

To begin with, governments typically respond slowly to emerging demands for governance and generally find it difficult to achieve the flexibility needed to engage in the sort of adaptive management espoused by many as an important mechanism for maintaining the resilience of complex and dynamic systems (Lee 1993). As the emergence of processes generating a demand for governance has accelerated at an increasing rate in recent decades, "institutional arthritis" has become a growing obstacle to meeting the demand for governance (Olson 1982). Even looming crises (e.g., the impacts of climate change) evoke sluggish, business-as-usual responses. We are, in effect, operating in a world in which there is a growing disconnect between the demand for governance and the conventional mechanisms for addressing this demand. However, even when governments do respond to the demand for governance, success in meeting the aims for governance is by no means assured. Just as market failures can lead to outcomes that are socially undesirable, government failures can undermine efforts to supply governance in a variety of settings (Wolf 1988; Winston 2006). Those who favor privatization and deregulation generally take the view that government is a clumsy tool that seldom produces effective responses to the demand for governance. This sweeping judgment is clearly an exaggeration. But there is no doubt that government failures, in such forms as bureaucratic inertia and corruption, can and often do detract from the efforts of governments to meet the demand for governance. In addition, relying on governments to meet the demand for governance is always costly. Sometimes, this is simply a matter of efficiency and the need to prevent transaction costs from getting out of hand. More ominous, however, are the relatively common cases in which governments become oppressive and take actions that erode the rights and freedoms of their citizens.

Governance by intergovernmental agreement

As we move into a world featuring globalization and various forms of global environmental change, it is becoming apparent that the nation-state is not in a position to solve some of the most far-reaching and urgent problems giving rise to a demand for governance. The issue here centers on the fit between the defining characteristics of states and the attributes of the processes generating the rising demand for governance in today's world. Governments operate, for the most part, in association with nation-states or their subunits; their jurisdiction extends spatially over the territory of the relevant state and demographically over the citizenry of that state. But, as the previous section notes, the rising demand for governance in the contemporary world is closely associated with large-scale developments of the sort referred to in such terms as globalization and global environmental change. In efforts to address problems such as climate change or the need to take steps to avoid or control global financial crises, the nation-state and the approach to governance associated with the states system often emerge as part of the problem rather than part of the solution.

One increasingly common response to situations of this kind is to establish governance systems – or regimes as they are often called – through the negotiation of intergovernmental agreements or multilateral environmental agreements. This increasingly popular strategy has led to the creation of several hundred regimes over the last few decades, dealing with a wide range of issues from the conservation of whales to the management of the Earth's climate system. This approach to the supply of governance, which accords roles to governments, but now as players in multilateral agreements rather than purveyors of governance on their own, has become a focus of attention among policymakers and scholars alike (Young 1999a). There are a number of success stories in this realm, including efforts to protect the fragile ecosystems of Antarctica, clean up the pollution in the Rhine river, and respond to the seasonal thinning of the stratospheric ozone layer (Breitmeier, Young, and Zürn 2006a). Yet it is also clear that the creation and implementation of international regimes is a challenging task and that the performance of many regimes leaves a great deal to be desired.

The effort to take steps to come to terms with the problem of climate change offers a dramatic case in point. There is widespread agreement that stabilizing the level of carbon dioxide in the Earth's atmosphere at no more than twice the pre-industrial level will require a 60–80 percent cut in emissions by about 2050 (Intergovernmental Panel on Climate Change 2007). Yet current steps in this direction, as exemplified by the 1997 Kyoto Protocol to the UN Framework Convention on Climate Change, mandate cuts of only a few percent and have been rejected by the United States, the source of almost one-quarter of current worldwide emissions of carbon dioxide. Defenders of the Protocol argue that it is a first step in the direction of needed changes and that it may set in motion a chain of events that will gather speed with the passage of time. But it is hard to avoid the conclusion that there is a severe mismatch between the demand for governance in this realm and the conventional approach to supplying governance in situations of this sort. At best, intergovernmental agreements are apt to form slowly and to encounter a variety of problems in making the transition from paper to practice.

Private governance

Faced with these shortfalls in the capacity of governments and intergovernmental regimes to supply governance, as well as pressures to shrink the role of government through measures emphasizing privatization and deregulation, many analysts have begun to think about the prospects for meeting the demand for governance without relying on government (Rosenau and Czempiel 1992). Given the fact that over half of the 100 largest economies in the world today are associated with multinational corporations, it makes sense to direct attention to the role of corporations and industry associations in meeting the demand for governance and to inquire into the prospects for private governance (Haufler 2001). The resultant efforts take a variety of forms (Vogel 2005), including the adoption of principles or codes of conduct (Williams 2004), the development of certification and eco-labeling schemes, the creation of voluntary exchange systems (e.g., the Chicago Climate Exchange), and the rise of what some analysts call non-state market-driven governance systems or NSMDs (Cashore, Auld, and Newsom 2004; Dingwerth 2007; Pattberg 2007). But they share both the assumption that we cannot rely on governments alone to meet the demand for governance and the premise that there are circumstances under which private actors – especially large corporations – can become part of the solution rather than part of the problem in efforts to meet the rising demand for governance in today's world. Taken together, these initiatives have given rise to a discussion often referred to in terms of the umbrella concept of "corporate social responsibility" (Vogel 2005).

At first glance, this idea seems far-fetched. What incentives do profit-maximizing corporations have to create and implement the systems of rights and rules needed to address the challenge of governance for sustainable development? But it turns out that it is relatively easy to see why corporations may take ideas of this sort seriously. To the extent that the Porter hypothesis is correct, corporations that take the lead in supplying governance for sustainable development may find not only that their efforts do not impinge on their ability to make a profit but also that these efforts actually lead to financial gains (Porter and van der Linde 1995b). In some cases, corporate leaders may reason in a pre-emptive mode. In situations where intervention on the part of the state is probable, corporate leaders may conclude that it is preferable for them to introduce regulatory systems of their own devising and, in the process, to pre-empt initiatives of this sort arising either from the public sector or from civil society. More generally, there is much to be said for the proposition that corporate actors are frequently more concerned with the development of stable rules and a uniform and predictable regulatory environment than with the exact content of the resultant governance systems. Obviously, it is possible to overdo this line of reasoning; it is not good for producers of CFCs to find themselves operating in a setting that features bans on the production and consumption of ozone-depleting substances. Still, corporations are often able to pass along the costs of actions such as cleaning up hazardous waste sites or emitting greenhouse gases into the atmosphere to their customers. What they cannot do is to make rational decisions about investments in a setting where major changes in the rules of the game occur in a frequent but unpredictable fashion.

Is private governance the answer to the challenge of governance for sustainable development? We are not now in a position to answer this question in a convincing manner. But we do know quite a bit about the factors that are likely to be important in this context. Corporations themselves vary in these terms. Those in industries requiring large-scale and long-term investments will be more concerned about regulatory stability than those that have the flexibility to adjust to changes quickly. Corporations that have major operations in a number of countries and that sell their products in many markets will be more concerned with harmonization and stability than those that do not. And corporations, such as British Petroleum, that see opportunities to diversify and achieve competitive advantages resulting from the changing character of governance systems can be expected to take steps to seize these opportunities without waiting for governments to intervene.

More generally, there are relevant differences among states and markets that have a bearing on this issue. In countries such as Japan, where matters of macroeconomic policy and regulatory practices are handled through a process of consensus-building among political and economic elites, the distinction between governance by government and private governance is blurred (Schreurs 2002). In such cases, many policy initiatives emerge from the private sector, and the idea of private governance takes on a significance that it does not have in other systems. On the other hand, in countries such as the United States, where there is a sharp distinction – at least in principle – between the public sector and the private sector, the idea of private governance may take on added significance. This is not to say that the tenets of Reagonomics, emphasizing privatization and deregulation, will lead to a permanent reduction in the role of governments and their capacity to address matters of sustainable development. But the notion that governance can be outsourced to the private sector must be taken seriously in such settings.

Governance by civil society

It is a mistake to suppose that those seeking to meet the demand for governance must make a choice between governance by governments and private governance. As the growing literature on the tragedy of the commons has made clear, there are situations in which governance emerges from the actions of civil society treated as a layer of social organization above the individual and below the state (Wapner 1997). Many small-scale, traditional societies in which the role of the state is minimal, or even non-existent, succeed in establishing and implementing systems of rights and rules that govern the behavior of their individual members in such a way as to avoid severe depletions of living resources over long time periods and to produce outcomes that are generally seen as both legitimate and fair (Ostrom 1990; Ostrom et al. 2002). Questions that immediately occur in this context concern the generalizability of these findings not only among small-scale societies but, even more critically, the extent to which we can scale up such findings to apply to larger societies and even to global society (Young 2005).

We know that the idea that peoples using traditional ecological knowledge can be counted on to engage in ecosystem-based management is a myth (Fienup-Riordan 1990; Krech 1999). Rather, as many observers have pointed out, there is great variance in these terms. Some traditional societies develop effective governance systems; others do not. Moreover, some of these governance systems prove to be more resilient than others in the face of interventions on the part of exogenous, generally larger-scale, political systems. This leads directly to a search for the determinants of effectiveness with regard to governance systems arising from civil society. A large – and still growing – literature points to a variety of factors (sometimes called design principles) including clearly delineated boundaries, the existence of effective monitoring systems, and the operation of a system of graduated sanctions (Ostrom 1990). Once treated as a somewhat arcane line of analysis of interest mainly to anthropologists, this literature has become an important source of understanding regarding efforts to govern the commons.

Recently, those interested in governance have become intrigued by the role of civil society on a larger scale, and especially by the idea that we are witnessing the growth of a global civil society (Kaldor 2003; Keane 2003). With regard to the supply of governance in particular, this line of thinking has produced a rapidly rising interest in various types of networks, including constellations of public officials organized in functional terms (e.g., officials dealing with air pollution, fisheries management, or environmental compliance) (Raustiala 2002; Slaughter 2004), groupings of representatives of both state and non-state actors concerned with relatively well-defined issues (e.g., monitoring the illegal trade in wildlife) (Reinicke 1998; Reinicke and Deng 2000), and epistemic communities encompassing individuals who share both a common diagnosis of some key problem and a perspective on how to solve it (e.g., those active in the Intergovernmental Panel on Climate Change or IPCC) (Haas 1992). It is fashionable, at the moment, to set great store by the capacity of civil society to play a prominent role in meeting the demand for governance in the realm of sustainable development. But how realistic is it to rely on this response to the challenge of governance, especially at the transnational and global levels?

The growing prominence of civil society networks in contrast to intergovernmental bodies and corporate alliances seems undeniable. But this is not a basis for concluding that such networks can go a long way toward meeting the demand for governance, especially in addressing large-scale issues such as climate change and deforestation. It is hard to point to unambiguous cases of success in these realms and it seems relevant to bear in mind the findings of Putnam and others regarding the decline of civil society in domestic settings such as the United States (Putnam 1988, 2000). A more realistic expectation, at least in the short run, is to look for evidence that networks of this sort can contribute to the efforts of others to supply governance, without assuming overall responsibility for performing this social function. TRAFFIC, a wildlife trade monitoring network operated jointly by the Worldwide Fund for Nature (WWF) and IUCN, has certainly played a role in tracking trade in endangered species. The International Network on Environmental Compliance and Enforcement (INECE) has helped to develop and disseminate knowledge relating to strategies for increasing compliance with a variety of environmental regulations. The IPCC has proven effective in catalyzing the development of consensus in the scientific community on matters relating to climate change and in communicating that consensus forcefully to the policy community. Overall, the emergence of global civil society is an important development from the point of view of governance. But it will be some time before we know the full extent of the role of civil society in the supply of governance in large-scale settings.

Hybrid mechanisms

It is natural, under the circumstances, to inquire about the prospects for hybrid systems. Governance by government, intergovernmental agreements, private governance, and governance by civil society or civil governance are well-defined alternatives. But these are analytic types. In reality, efforts to meet the demand for governance in a variety of settings can, and often do, involve initiatives designed to bring two or even all three approaches to governance to bear on concrete problems. A number of countries are experimenting with negotiated agreements – sometimes called public voluntary agreements or PVAs – between public agencies and businesses dealing with regulatory issues (Delmas and Terlaak 2002; Lyon and Maxwell 2004b). The International Organization for Standardization (ISO), which is responsible for the system of environmental standards known as ISO 14001, includes national standards organizations, industry bodies, and NGOs (Delmas 2002). The International Finance Corporation (IFC) and the regional development banks often cooperate with private corporations in the interests of promoting sustainable development in the developing world. More recently, the 2002 World Summit on Sustainable Development (WSSD) highlighted the role of so-called Type II partnerships linking public agencies and private corporations in initiatives aimed at making progress toward meeting the Millennium Development Goals (Andonova and Levy 2003).

Similar remarks are in order regarding collaboration between private corporations and representatives of civil society (Pattberg 2007). The Forest Stewardship Council (FSC) operates as a coalition led by environmental NGOs but also includes a number of large corporations. For its part, the Marine Stewardship Council (MSC) was launched as a partnership linking a multinational corporation and a number of environmental NGOs. Environmental groups such as Environmental Defense have paid increasing attention to the value of collaborating with individual corporations (e.g., McDonald's) in the interests of greening the activities of major firms. Particularly ambitious cases involve the Partnerships for Climate Action that Environmental Defense has formed with a number of major corporations including British Petroleum, Shell, and Dupont, and the US Climate Action Program (USCAP) joining a collection of major corporations together with the World Resources Institute in an ambitious effort to reduce greenhouse gas emissions.

How successful are these hybrid approaches to the supply of governance likely to become? The idea has a lot of intuitive appeal. Why not replace costly adversarial relations between public agencies and corporations or between corporations and environmental NGOs with various forms of collaboration designed to produce results in an efficient manner? And proponents can point to a few apparent successes, such as the Environmental Defense Fund/McDonald's collaboration, in this realm. Yet it seems fair to conclude at this stage that the contribution of these hybrid approaches to meeting the challenge of governance for sustainable development is relatively modest. The long list of Type II partnerships contains few striking successes (Andonova and Levy 2003; Bruch and Pendergrass 2003). Environmental groups are understandably concerned about the dangers of real or apparent co-optation arising from entering into partnerships with major corporations. Public contributions to such partnerships are apt to be slow to materialize and to be subject to more or less severe corruption once they are put in place. It is clear, then, that hybrid governance is not a panacea; we should not bank on the growth of effective partnerships to satisfy the rising demand for governance in an increasingly interdependent world. Looked upon as one element in a toolkit of mechanisms for responding to the demand for governance in a wide range of situations, however, there is every reason to consider this option carefully and to forge partnerships when conditions are favorable to the success of such endeavors.

The effectiveness of governance systems

Governance is not an end in itself. We seek to create governance systems and to operate them effectively and efficiently in order to steer human societies toward advantageous outcomes and away from harmful developments. It follows that it is always important to evaluate the performance of governance systems in instrumental terms and in the context of specific challenges. Is a given governance system solving or alleviating the problem(s) that led to its creation? Is it doing so in a manner that keeps transaction costs under control and that avoids the occurrence of costly side effects or unintended consequences? Do the results conform, at least roughly, to widely shared conceptions of fairness or justice? These are issues that are of interest to scientists and policymakers alike.

Effectiveness as problem-solving

Governance systems come in two forms: relatively specific arrangements created for the purpose of solving a well-defined problem (e.g., transboundary air pollution, the management of specific fisheries, the conservation of whales, stratospheric ozone depletion) and more general constitutive agreements or constitutions intended to address a wide range of issues (e.g., national constitutions, the UN Charter, the Law of the Sea). Whereas it makes sense to think in synoptic terms in efforts to evaluate the performance of constitutions, attention focuses naturally on problem-solving in thinking about more specific governance systems. Has the system solved the problem, alleviated the problem or, at least, provided a method for managing the problem in such a way as to prevent it from getting out of hand? Do the results conform to appropriate standards of efficiency, cost effectiveness, and equity? Has the arrangement given rise to unintended side effects, and are the consequences of such effects positive or negative? Has the operation of the system generated broader consequences affecting governance in the relevant social system?

Not surprisingly, most analysts working in this field have found substantial variance in the performance of governance systems measured in these terms (Haas, Levy, and Keohane 1993; Young 1999b; Miles et al. 2002; Breitmeier, Young, and Zürn 2006a). Some systems work well; others perform poorly. Some get off to a slow start but gain strength over time; others do well at first but falter as the nature of the problem evolves or becomes more challenging. Yet it is important to note that efforts to evaluate performance in these terms are hampered by a number of methodological complications. Three are worthy of particular attention. Any effort to evaluate the performance of a governance system must address a counterfactual (Tetlock and Belkin 1996). What would have happened regarding the relevant problem in the absence of the creation and implementation of the governance system? Second, governance systems almost always operate in settings characterized by complex causality. Clusters of interactive factors, including governance systems, typically play a role in determining the content of collective outcomes in specific settings (Young 2002a). Thus, a governance system that works well in one setting may fail to solve problems in other settings, and vice versa. To make matters worse, we often find ourselves working with small universes of cases in efforts to evaluate the performance of governance systems (Breitmeier, Young, and Zürn 2006a). As a result, it is difficult in many cases to deploy mainstream statistical procedures to good advantage in studies of problem-solving. This is especially true in situations where it would be helpful to subdivide the universe of cases in order to control for one or more intervening variables.

Even so, we are by no means helpless when it comes to evaluating the performance of governance systems as institutional arrangements created to solve more or less specific problems. One approach that has proven helpful, especially in situations where small universes of cases restrict the use of mainstream statistical procedures, is to focus on the mechanisms through which governance systems and institutions more generally influence the behavior of key actors (Haas, Levy, and Keohane, 1993; Young 1999b). An important insight arising from this line of thinking centers on the distinction between mechanisms that feature incentives or the logic of consequences and mechanisms that highlight non-utilitarian sources of behavior or the logic of appropriateness (March and Olsen 1998). A more sustained effort to differentiate behavioral mechanisms and to analyze the roles they play in connection with different types of governance – governmental, private, civil, and hybrid – seems particularly promising in this connection.

More broadly, efforts to evaluate the effectiveness of governance systems have highlighted the value of employing a number of distinct methodological tools in tandem or, in other words, making use of what a number of scholars have described as a portfolio approach (Young et al. 2006). These methods include enhanced statistical procedures, natural experiments, meta-analyses, qualitative case studies, systems analyses, and simulations. When the results produced through the use of a number of methods converge, we can be relatively certain of the results of our efforts to assess the performance of governance systems. Divergent results, on the other hand, constitute a clear signal that there is a need for more research to determine what is really going on in specific cases.

Good governance

Whether or not governance systems are successful as problem-solvers, there is a rapidly growing interest in the extent to which they meet a range of normative standards often grouped together under the rubric of good governance. There is no standardized list of elements belonging to the domain of good governance, but many lists include considerations such as stakeholder involvement, accountability, democracy, respect for civil liberties, and legitimacy (Allott 1990). The implication here is that a governance system can be successful in solving one or more problems but may still receive poor marks in terms of some overall assessment of performance. Conversely, governance systems that perform well in terms of various standards of good governance may be treated with a measure of respect, even if they produce mediocre results in terms of solving the problems that led to their creation.

Many of the concerns that surface in conjunction with the idea of good governance are best thought of as matters of process, in contrast to factors determining success in problem-solving. Stakeholder involvement has to do with the degree to which a governance system allows for public participation. Accountability is a matter of the extent to which managers report to the public on their efforts to solve problems and take responsibility for the results when things go wrong. The standard of democracy is met when the system allows for regular opportunities for citizens to express their views on results; it is not a standard pertaining to the nature of the results per se. Even legitimacy is, to a considerable extent, about process. Although legitimacy is a function of a number of factors, those who feel they have a voice in the operation of governance systems and who believe that their views carry some weight in such processes are more likely to accept any given governance system as legitimate than those who feel that their views count for nothing.

The concern for good governance is on the rise in many settings and at different levels of social organization. In some settings, calls for more stakeholder involvement and accountability have achieved the status of political slogans. Criticisms of specific governance systems based on claims that they are afflicted by a democracy deficit are heard with increasing frequency. Still, it is far from clear how to apply these standards to specific cases, much less how to measure them in a manner that is objective or replicable. It is easy to count the number of comments received during public comment periods. Much the same is true regarding the production of documents that are distributed in the name of accountability. But do these yardsticks constitute useful indicators of good governance? Decision-makers may or may not take comments from members of the public seriously. Reports may be pro forma productions, even when they include large amounts of data and are widely circulated as glossy publications.

None of this is to suggest that a concern for good governance is unimportant. A particularly interesting hypothesis in this area has to do with the links between good governance and problem-solving. The underlying idea here is that governance systems that score well in terms of various measures of good governance are also likely to prove successful as problem-solvers. A belief in the accountability and legitimacy of a governance system on the part of subjects, for instance, may play a significant role in enhancing compliance on the part of a variety of actors. But it is clear that this is an area calling for much more analytic rigor. As the interest in good governance rises, the need to develop suitable tools for evaluating specific governance systems in these terms becomes a higher priority.

Macro-level consequences

So far, this discussion of effectiveness and performance has concentrated on the evaluation of discrete governance systems treated as mechanisms created to address more or less well-defined problems. But there is another important line of thinking that approaches the issue of performance at a macro-level, focusing on the roles that comprehensive governance systems, or what some call basic structures of governance, play in society as a whole (Milner 2005). This way of thinking opens up both an interesting range of questions and a set of methodological challenges that are particularly acute at this level of aggregation.

As noted in the Introduction to this chapter, some analysts see effective and resilient governance as an important determinant of economic and social success at the societal level. A particularly prominent example of this line of thinking centers on the explanation that the new institutionalists, led by Douglass North, have offered for the rise of the West and the dominant role of Western countries in international society over the past several centuries (North 1991; Eggertsson 2005). The cornerstones of this argument involve the role of governance in providing a stable political and legal playing field for the activities of private actors, and in creating a regulatory environment that provides private actors with clear incentives to invest time and resources in productive activities. Governance, on this account, is responsible for creating and maintaining appropriate structures of property rights, rules governing contracts, liability rules, procedures capable of producing authoritative interpretations of contested rules, and mechanisms capable of resolving disputes among the subjects of the system and of ensuring compliance with the outcomes. There is here a recognition of the fundamental connections between the performance of economic and social systems and the existence of good governance; a link that those responsible for restructuring institutions in the wake of the collapse of established systems (e.g., the former Soviet Union) and for encouraging growth in many developing countries frequently ignore or discount.

Another macro-level argument relating to performance centers on the role of basic structures of governance in determining who gets what at the societal level (Lasswell 1936). The perspective on the demand for governance outlined in earlier sections of this chapter focuses on collective-action problems and emphasizes the importance of steering societies in socially desirable directions. But, as many analysts have observed, governance systems exhibit a strong tendency to reflect the interests of dominant groups or classes within society, quite apart from the strategies they adopt in dealing with a variety of collective-action problems. The common metaphor that envisions representative members of society coming together to negotiate the terms of a mutually agreeable social contract diverts attention from the distributive impacts of governance systems. Yet it does not require sophisticated methods of analysis to see that such systems can, and often do, favor the interests of some over others (Bullard 1990). Voting rules limiting the franchise to owners of property or to individuals having a certain level of assets are classic examples. But other cases abound. They range from the impacts of appointments to high courts to provisions granting corporations legal personality and on to rules that make it easy for wealthy individuals to use their resources to influence the outcomes of elections (Weaver and Rockman 1993). It is important to distinguish these distributive effects from the ability of governance systems to provide the stable expectations needed to spur socioeconomic development. Needless to say, basic structures that produce distributive consequences that are completely out of bounds are likely to run into trouble in other realms. Even so, as the growth of inequality in the United States and the privileged position of elites in China make clear, governance systems can prove effective in providing the institutional substructure needed to facilitate economic growth even when they produce distributive consequences that are hard to justify in terms of any reasonable standards of fairness or distributive justice.

Appealing as it is in many respects, the shift from a micro-level perspective on discrete governance systems as mechanisms for handling well-defined problems to a macro-level perspective on basic structures and their impacts on society as a whole poses additional methodological challenges. Although the universe of cases available to draw on in analyses of problem-solving is generally small, the analysis of basic structures often involves a universe of one. Although cross-national comparisons are possible, the existence of a host of socioeconomic and political differences between and among countries makes such comparisons suspect from the outset. And when we come to the international level, the only opportunity for serious comparative analysis involves a consideration of basic structures operating during different time periods.

As numerous observers have pointed out, globalization reinforces this point by increasing interdependencies both in spatial terms and across levels of social organization. It is virtually impossible today for countries, or even remote communities, to operate in a manner that avoids the profound impacts of activities occurring elsewhere. This does not mean that there are no opportunities for rigorous analyses of macro-level consequences of basic structures of governance. Essentially parallel problems facing researchers endeavoring to understand the behavior of the Earth's climate system have not posed insurmountable barriers to the conduct of scientific research. Research on the climate system has moved forward through a combination of simulations (e.g., the various global circulation models or GCMs) and empirical observations intended to verify the projections of the GCMs regarding the trajectory of the Earth's climate system over time (Steffen et al. 2004). A parallel effort to model large-scale structures of governance and to compare projections generated by the models with observed behavior might prove equally rewarding.

Governance failures

Just as economists emphasize the idea of market failures and devote time to thinking of ways to avoid such failures or overcome them once they occur, those interested in governance systems must pay attention to the prospect of governance failures (Wolf 1988; Winston 2006). Here, too, there is much to be said for organizing our thinking at two levels: the micro-level of governance systems created to solve a specific problem and the macro-level of basic structures of governance. Failures are common at both levels, but they call for somewhat different modes of thinking, especially when we want to consider the relative merits of alternative ways to avoid or respond to such failures.

At the micro-level, the major categories of governance failure are easy enough to identify. Many arrangements reflect ideological preferences rather than a careful assessment of the defining characteristics of the problem at hand. Bargaining processes can make governance systems incoherent, and problems of implementation can turn them into dead letters. Special interests may find ways to manipulate arrangements to serve their purposes, and individual governance systems may become corrupt, sluggish, and incapable of adapting to the changing nature of the problems they address. Overall, the need for leadership is apparent at every stage in the process, but the likelihood that ambitious individuals will make use of the roles they play to further their own careers rather than to solve or manage the problems at hand is always present. There are no simple cures for these problems; the best advice is to remain vigilant at all times and to devise self-correcting mechanisms, such as the discipline of electoral politics, that offer some opportunities to hold those responsible for administering governance systems accountable to the public.

At the macro-level, the situation is both different and more challenging to address. As political analysts at least since the time of Aristotle have observed, all political systems have two phases, a virtuous phase and a degenerate phase (Aristotle 1962/1992). Thus, monarchy can degenerate into despotism, aristocracy into oligarchy, and democracy into mob rule. Much of the effort of those concerned with good governance over the past several millennia has gone into efforts to understand the conditions controlling these relationships and into the creation of mechanisms designed to strengthen virtuous systems and minimize the likelihood that those systems will flip over into their degenerate forms. Nowhere is this issue more important than in efforts to meet the challenge of governance for sustainable development. Major problems in this realm involve the predatory behavior of despots concerned mainly with amassing wealth and power, the greed of oligarchs who care little about the common good or social welfare over the long run, and the mindless materialism of ordinary citizens who are unable or unwilling to grasp the seriousness of environmental problems likely to produce far-reaching crises in the foreseeable future. There are no easy solutions to these problems. Human societies have been struggling with them for millennia; they have failed to devise viable solutions for a sizable proportion of that time. But, as insightful thinkers such as Reinhold Niebuhr have argued, there is no alternative to engaging in an ongoing effort to address problems of this kind, even when we are well aware that our efforts can, and often will, fail (Niebuhr 1944).

Research frontiers

We are in the midst of what amounts to a paradigm shift in our thinking about governance. Approaching governance as a social function rather than focusing on the behavior of governments severs the analytic link between thinking about the demand for and supply of governance and a reliance on the intellectual capital of the discipline of political science. Of course, political scientists will continue to be leaders in the development of systematic thinking about governance. But now we can also expect to receive important contributions from many others who have backgrounds both in other social science disciplines and in fields of study that focus on complex and dynamic systems. This is good news, especially in an era marked by the paradox of a rising demand for governance coupled with declining confidence in governments as suppliers of governance. But it also raises conceptual and methodological issues that we must pay attention to in order to produce contributions to understanding governance that are cumulative rather than degenerating into a cacophony of discordant voices.

The fact that those working on issues of governance bring a wide range of backgrounds to this endeavor highlights the need to operate on the same page with regard to conceptual and definitional matters. Most important is the acceptance, as a point of departure, of the proposition that governance is a social function centered on steering human groups, and the distinction that follows between governance and government. This conceptual move not only opens up a research agenda featuring analyses of the efficacy of relying on governments as primary suppliers of governance; it also allows us to direct attention toward a variety of other mechanisms that can and do emerge as suppliers of governance under specific conditions. This is good news for those who take seriously the paradox of the rising demand for governance coupled with declining confidence in governments as suppliers of governance. It provides a basis for optimism for those struggling to devise effective governance systems to address macro-level problems such as climate change and land degradation. But, at the same time, it increases the probability of communication failures among those who have a common interest in governance but find themselves talking past one another because they define key concepts in different and even incompatible ways.

Assuming that we make the effort to operate on the same page with respect to conceptual and definitional matters, there is much to be said for adopting a portfolio approach in selecting methods suitable for making progress in answering questions about the demand for and supply of governance for sustainable development (Young et al. 2006). The mainstream of research in this field relies on case studies. The best work of this sort integrates carefully selected case studies to investigate theoretically grounded hypotheses (Young 1999b; Miles et al. 2002). A second, narrower stream seeks to bring the analytic resources of economics and public choice to bear on issues relating to the supply of governance in a variety of settings (Barrett 2003). The application of the two streams to individual cases (e.g., the long-range transboundary air pollution regime in Europe) has generated some interesting conundrums that deserve to be examined systematically. Although small universes of cases are hard to avoid in this field, there are also opportunities to make good use of quantitative data in examining issues relating to governance for sustainable development (Breitmeier, Young, and Zürn 2006a). Future work in this field may well make progress using other methods, such as qualitative comparative analysis and simulations (Stokke 2004). But the basic message is clear. Using multiple methods to analyze common questions can lead to increased confidence in the conclusions when the answers we generate using two or more methods converge; diverging answers, on the other hand, help to bring into focus those analytic puzzles that require more sustained analysis.

As is the case in other fields, we can draw a distinction in analyses of governance between pure science and applied science. Much research on questions relating to governance is curiosity-driven; we simply want to understand why a given governance system works in one setting but not in another, or why a governance system that worked well in the past produces results that are unacceptable today. Nonetheless, there are compelling reasons to adopt an applied perspective in conducting research on governance today. The paradox of rising demand and declining confidence makes it imperative to devise new approaches to governance capable of addressing large-scale issues such as climate change or the loss of biological diversity. This is good news in some respects. It highlights the relevance of research on questions relating to governance, and it facilitates mutually interesting exchanges between those in the scientific community studying governance and those in the policy community responsible for creating and administering governance systems. But a word of caution is in order here. One size does not fit all situations when it comes to meeting the demand for governance. In fact, simple solutions (e.g., prescriptions to privatize, deregulate, and let the market solve the problem) are almost always inadequate to meet the demand for governance in complex and dynamic settings. What is needed is an approach that starts with a systematic diagnosis of the problem in hand and proceeds to devise a governance system that is both politically feasible and carefully tailored to the principal features of the problem (Young 2002a, 2008; Ostrom 2007). This approach, which has much in common with more familiar applied work on the part of architects, engineers, and physicians, is not likely to yield broad generalizations pointing to conditions that are necessary for the development and implementation of effective governance systems in a wide range of settings. But it can yield agreement about institutional designs that are well suited to making progress in addressing specific problems.

Concluding remarks

Questions pertaining to governance are among the great issues at all times and in all places. In this respect, our current situation is no different than that of those facing the challenge of governance in other times and places. Yet there are some extraordinary features of the demand for governance for sustainable development in today's world that merit special attention. Dramatic increases in the scope and intensity of the impact of human actions on large-scale biophysical systems (e.g., the Earth's climate system) have given rise to an era of human-dominated ecosystems in which we must expect changes to be nonlinear and often abrupt, irreversible, and nasty, at least from the perspective of human welfare. Yet our confidence in conventional mechanisms for responding to the demand for governance (e.g., government actions, intergovernmental agreements) is declining. We face what amounts to a global crisis of confidence with regard to meeting the challenge of governance for sustainable development. In many ways, this is a daunting prospect. But it also amounts to a period of opportunity. Once we shift the discourse via conceptual moves such as introducing a clear distinction between governance and government, new approaches to governance come into focus. The challenge before us today is to press forward vigorously to explore these new approaches and to put well-crafted governance systems in place quickly enough to steer societies away from the worst effects of human domination of the Earth as a system.

PART II

Governance for solving environmental problems:
perspectives from economics, political science,
and management

2

Environmental governance: an economic perspective

THOMAS P. LYON

Introduction

From an economic perspective, it is natural to think of the "demand for" and "supply of" environmental governance. The demand for governance comes from individuals concerned about the quality of the environment. They may express this demand in their roles as citizens, consumers, investors, or members of nongovernmental organizations (NGOs). The supply of governance is generally thought of as coming from government in the form of legislation and regulation, outcomes of the political process. However, as pointed out in Chapter 1, it may also come from direct negotiations between NGOs and corporations, a process sometimes referred to as "private politics." In addition, environmental governance may come about through the workings of the marketplace, as consumers demand environmentally friendly products or investors show a preference for environmentally friendly companies. Some of the most intriguing forms of modern environmental governance result from the interplay of all three of these processes, as will be illustrated throughout the course of this volume.

The conventional wisdom of neoclassical economics had little to say about environmental governance. "Externalities" arose when market transactions affected third parties and led to "market failure." It was the job of government to "internalize the externalities" through the imposition of Pigouvian taxes set equal to marginal external costs. Although this may have been a reasonable prescription for a Platonic philosopher king, it completely obscured the processes by which governance might be achieved in the absence of such a convenient being.

As in many fields of economics, the seeds of a new perspective on environmental governance were sown by Ronald Coase. In his 1960 paper, "The problem of social cost," he argued that externalities could be internalized through direct negotiation in a world without transaction costs.

Since neoclassical economics implicitly assumed that transaction costs were zero, its prescription of Pigouvian taxation was internally inconsistent. The way forward lay in a new form of economic analysis that explicitly recognized the presence of positive transaction costs.

The "new institutional economics" (NIE) that has arisen in the wake of Coase's insights has gone a long way toward developing a new research approach to industrial organization and public utility regulation (Williamson 1985), public choice (Mueller 1989), and economic history (North 1990). However, for the most part, the NIE has not focused on environmental governance. Exceptions to this rule include Elinor Ostrom's work on common-pool resources (Ostrom 1990) and Oran Young's work on international environmental governance (Young 2002b).

This is a propitious time for building a unified theory of environmental governance. Although the NIE has been surprisingly slow to expand into environmental governance, it and several other strands of economic research provide valuable tools that can be applied to the task. This chapter attempts to provide an overview of economic research that is relevant to environmental governance, and to point the way toward a more unified theory. The remainder of the chapter is organized as follows. The next section gives a brief overview of the "economic approach" to research, for the benefit of scholars from other disciplines, such as political science and sociology. In the following section (Environmental economics), I survey the relevant portions of mainstream environmental economics, focusing on the literatures on instrument choice and monitoring and enforcement. The next section (The political economy of environmental policy) turns to the rapidly growing field of political economy, followed by a section entitled "Voluntary approaches to environmental protection," which reviews the relatively recent literature on "voluntary approaches" to environmental protection. The next section (The new institutional economics of the environment) briefly discusses the work of Ostrom and her colleagues on small-scale common-pool resources, and the work of Young and his colleagues on international regimes. The concluding section summarizes and suggests some directions for future research.

The economic approach to environmental governance

Economics is often thought of as "the study of the allocation of scarce resources," but this gives hardly any more insight than the smug insiders' definition that "economics is what economists do." Gary Becker has provided a more helpful perspective, defining economics by its approach to understanding social phenomena, rather than its content. According to Becker (1978, p. 5), "The combined assumptions of maximizing behavior, market equilibrium, and stable preferences, used relentlessly and unflinchingly, form the heart of the economic approach as I see it."

Applying "methodological individualism," economists typically begin their analyses with individual entities (either individual people or individual organizations such as firms), which are assumed to have objectives that they set out to achieve.[1] The traditional assumption that individuals maximize their utility is so broad as to be adaptable to almost any situation. It does not require that people are purely selfish, nor that they are perfectly informed, have infinite cognitive capacities, or never make mistakes. It is an approach rather than a demonstrable hypothesis. It parallels the assumption that corporations act to maximize value to their shareholders, although the latter is a hypothesis that is testable and for which there is substantial evidence.

In the political domain, identifying objectives is more challenging. It is common for political economists to model politicians as maximizing the probability of re-election. In the literature on public utility regulation, regulators are often modeled as maximizing a weighted average of consumer surplus and producer surplus. Which of the two they favor may depend upon whether they seek a job in the regulated industry after leaving the regulatory commission, or instead seek to run for public office. In environmental economics, less attention has been paid to the objectives of regulators. Environmental regulators are often modeled as maximizing environmental quality with no concern for the prices that consumers pay for products or for the value of firms. This is an assumption that makes sense only in a political setting where the regulator has been delegated a strict environmental mandate and is well insulated from any other political pressures.

The objectives of NGOs are poorly understood, compared with those of individuals, firms, or politicians. It does not seem unreasonable to model NGOs as desiring to maximize environmental quality, subject to the need to raise funds and maintain membership. Their attempts to obtain the required resources, however, may lead them to adopt strategies that conflict with environmental protection. Indeed, there is a growing chorus of criticism of some large environmental NGOs, who are accused

---

[1] There is a large and fascinating literature on the theory of the firm, which probes the inner structure of corporations, but it is beyond the scope of this chapter. For an introduction, see Holmstrom and Tirole (1989).

of devoting themselves to currying favor with the wealthy and powerful, rather than focusing on their own missions.[2] This is an area where further research is clearly needed.

Some imagination is needed to generalize the notion of market equilibrium – as Becker has done – to such areas of human behavior as the family, crime, and politics. However, John Nash's (1951) concept of equilibrium in non-cooperative games is general enough to be applicable to virtually any social situation, properly formulated. Much research in political economics takes a game-theoretic approach in which each player maximizes his or her own objective function, given what all the other players are doing – in other words, a Nash equilibrium is used as the solution concept.

The assumption of stable preferences is not meant to apply to the specific set of goods and services on offer at any particular place and time. Instead, it refers to more "fundamental aspects of life, such as health, prestige, sensual pleasure, benevolence or envy" (Becker 1978, p. 5). Its primary purpose is to prevent the scholar from explaining puzzling social phenomena by the expedient of positing a convenient change in preferences. As mentioned above, more research is needed to clarify the preferences of various actors in environmental governance, particularly NGOs and environmental regulators.

Taken together, the above building blocks have allowed economists to tackle a very broad range of phenomena using a single basic paradigm. Their strength is in their parsimony, clarity, and generality. They have provided economists with tools for building elegant mathematical theories with interesting, substantive, and falsifiable implications. However, they can be difficult to apply to certain topics. For example, social movements are difficult for economists to analyze because they focus on social aggregates whose objectives are difficult to specify. Even in this area, however, economists have made progress by applying their standard tools with the assumption that individuals possess imperfect information, and that mass protests, for example, may be a way of conveying that information to policymakers.[3]

Economists test their theories in a variety of ways. The most common is through the application of statistical methods to large datasets. Typically, the data are generated not through experiment but through the processes of daily life. A host of clever techniques have been developed to cope with the limitations of this kind of non-experimental data. A second approach

---

[2] See, for example, the concerns raised by Bosso (2005) and Chapin (2004).
[3] For a formal model of this theory, see Lohmann (1993).

to testing, which has grown enormously more popular in recent years, is the use of laboratory experiments. Pioneered by Vernon Smith, experimental economics has yielded many insights into collective action, social norms, and the functioning of market mechanisms (Smith 1962, 1982). A third approach to bringing theory into contact with reality is the use of case studies. These are not well suited to the direct testing of formal hypotheses, but can be extremely helpful for inductive reasoning and the generation of new theories. If conducted with care, especially as part of a broad attempt to gather representative field data, case studies can also be useful for hypothesis testing, as Ostrom (1990) has shown.

Environmental economics

Mainstream environmental economics is a Hobbesian project, built upon the foundation of a Leviathan that uses its monopoly on coercion to strictly enforce environmental regulations.[4] This perspective is captured perfectly in Garrett Hardin's famous solution to the tragedy of the commons: "mutual coercion, mutually agreed upon."[5] As mentioned in the Introduction, this neoclassical approach is simplistic and obscures many of the mechanisms of governance. Nevertheless, it provides an excellent starting point for the study of governance. In a sense, it presents an upper bound on society's ability to solve its environmental problems, similar to Becker's (1968) analysis of crime and punishment, in which the efficient solution is to impose the most severe punishment possible. Economists frequently employ similar reasoning when thinking about what could be accomplished by a "boiling in oil" contract, which imposes a punishment severe enough to deter most undesirable behavior, providing that it can be imposed with certainty and with accurate knowledge of who committed which actions.[6]

In a sense, the entire field of environmental governance can be conceived as a study in what happens when the conditions for "perfect coercion" fail. Perhaps most important, there may not exist the political will to pass legislation creating the requisite coercive power. This is starkly evident in international relations, where there is no overarching political body granted coercive power. Lacking the "stick," international governance must be conducted solely with "carrots," which vastly reduces what

---

[4] See Hobbes (1660/1999).   [5] See G. Hardin (1968, p. 1247).
[6] Clearly, suicide bombers pose a challenge to this paradigm.

is possible in this domain.[7] Similar forces are at work in domestic politics. At the time of writing this, the United States has adamantly refused to pass federal legislation that would impose mandatory limits on greenhouse gas emissions ("sticks"), preferring instead to offer a collection of voluntary approaches ("carrots") such as funding for research and development, the Department of Energy's voluntary greenhouse gas registry, and the "Climate Leaders" program offered by the Environmental Protection Agency.[8]

The conditions for perfect coercion can fail in other ways too. First, in most democratic countries, the death penalty and the use of torture are prohibited.[9] More relevant for environmental policy, penalties for violating environmental laws are often so small as to provide firms with little incentive to comply. Second, information about environmental violations is often woefully inadequate. When emissions come from a small number of large polluters, it is possible to monitor them carefully. However, when emissions come from a multitude of small or "non-point sources," as is the case with perchloroethylene emissions from small dry-cleaners or pesticide residues from agricultural runoff, it becomes extremely difficult to determine who is causing environmental degradation. Furthermore, information about the transmission of pollutants through the air or water is often imperfect, as is knowledge of the human health impacts of various contaminants. The net result is that environmental governance must often be conducted under severe informational limitations. Third, the transaction costs of imposing coercive solutions are often so high as to make such solutions impractical. In the USA, the legal costs of implementing the death penalty through a sequence of court appeals may be greater than the costs of imprisoning a criminal for life. The costs of monitoring and enforcing toxic chemical regulations on small dry-cleaners similarly make such a strategy questionable.

To summarize, coercive solutions to environmental problems are often constrained by lack of political will, weak penalties, imperfect information, or high transaction costs. When some or all of these conditions

---

[7] For a deeply insightful analysis of the optimal use of sticks and carrots in repeated games, see Abreu (1988).

[8] See Lyon and Maxwell (2003) for a formal model of the role of public voluntary programs when the political will for mandatory programs is lacking.

[9] The USA is relatively unusual in its ongoing use of the death penalty, and the Bush Administration's policy toward enemy combatants has been viewed in many other countries as a violation of accepted prohibitions on the use of torture.

are present, other institutions for environmental governance must be developed.

Despite the foregoing caveats, mainstream environmental economics has much to say about environmental governance, especially regarding the most efficient form of regulatory intervention to use for specific environmental problems. The literatures on instrument choice, and monitoring and enforcement, are particularly relevant for building a unified theory of environmental governance. To a large extent, these literatures, including much of environmental economics, retain the traditional neoclassical perspective of the welfare-maximizing regulator. Nevertheless, they provide powerful insights into the problems that arise due to imperfect information, and, to a lesser extent, limitations on available penalties. These literatures will need to be broadened somewhat to play a more useful role in a positive theory of environmental governance, but their basic ideas are quite general and robust.

Instrument choice

Instrument choice has to do with a government's choice between alternative policy "instruments" such as effluent fees, subsidies, standards, tradable permits, or mandatory information disclosure. Familiar textbook treatments show that in simple, static, deterministic settings of full information, where monitoring and enforcement are not a problem, any of a range of instruments can be used equally effectively to internalize an externality. However, when one relaxes these restrictive assumptions, the choice between alternative policy instruments becomes interesting and important. For example, environmental taxes provide stronger incentives for innovation than do standards, since standards offer no reward for going beyond compliance. Taxes also allow society's environmental goals to be met more cheaply than standards, since a tax induces more abatement from firms with the lowest costs of emissions reduction. Sterner (2003) provides an excellent introduction to the issues.

The seminal paper in this area is Weitzman's (1974) analysis of "prices vs. quantities" as alternative policies when the marginal benefits and/or marginal costs of abatement are not known with certainty. Loosely speaking, Weitzman showed that prices (e.g., effluent taxes) are preferred when marginal benefits are relatively flat, and quantities (e.g., an emissions standard) are preferred when marginal costs are relatively flat. Intuitively, if marginal benefits are flat, then errors in setting an emissions tax will lead to small deviations from social efficiency, and if marginal costs are flat then an error in the quantity constraint will also have a small social cost. Roberts and Spence (1976) showed that a "hybrid" that combines a quantity constraint with a "trigger price" that caps compliance costs performs even better than either policy alone.

An instrument of growing interest is the use of tradable emissions permits. Initially proposed by Dales (1968), and further analyzed by Montgomery (1972), such permits are attractive because they allow the use of a quantity instrument but also allow firms to trade abatement burdens until marginal abatement costs are equalized across emitters, thereby minimizing social costs. Tradable permits are also attractive from a political perspective, since politicians can dole out initial permit allocations to favored constituents, thereby increasing the political acceptability of the policy. Permit trading finally became serious business when the United States 1990 Clean Air Act Amendments created tradable permits for sulfur dioxide emissions. The success of the SO_2 trading program has led to the use of tradable permits in other contexts, such as nitrogen oxide trading in southern California and carbon trading in the European Union.

Instrument choice becomes increasingly interesting as one introduces additional constraints on the capabilities of the political process. For example, politicians may be unable to commit to future policies, and it may be impossible to prevent regulators from colluding with firms to distort the information that reaches the public. In fact, Boyer and Laffont (1999) show that, in certain cases, crude command-and-control regulations can perform better than sophisticated incentive regulations. They consider a situation where political majorities may fluctuate over time, leading to instability in policy. Restricting the available instruments reduces policy instability, and can increase welfare.

Solving some environmental problems, such as global warming, requires substantial research and development (R&D). It has long been recognized by economists that environmental standards provide poor incentives for innovation, since firms are not rewarded for going beyond the statutory requirement. Environmental taxes perform better in this regard, since firms have direct financial incentives to continuously reduce emissions. Nevertheless, designing policy instruments to induce desired levels of R&D is a challenging task. One reason is that R&D has some of the characteristics of a public good: knowledge can be shared without being used up, and it is hard to exclude rivals from learning about one's latest breakthroughs. As a result, markets will tend to underinvest in R&D, even when environmental taxes internalize externalities. In the area of climate change, Popp (2004) finds that combining R&D subsidies with a carbon tax is better than either policy alone, and that if one can only implement a single policy then a carbon tax is more beneficial than R&D subsidies alone.

When high transaction costs, weak political institutions, or a lack of information on pollution damage makes it hard to implement traditional regulations, regulators increasingly turn to mandatory information disclosure programs. The best known of these is perhaps the Toxic Release Inventory (TRI), mandated by the USA's Emergency Planning and Community Right-to-Know Act of 1986, which requires reporting on releases of hundreds of toxic chemicals. However, similar programs exist in various other countries, including Canada's National Pollutant Release Inventory. The aim of such programs is that citizens will make use of the reported data to directly pressure toxic emitters to reduce their emissions, avoiding the need for more costly government regulations. Unfortunately, it is difficult to conduct empirical analyses of the impact of information disclosure programs, since there are typically no data on corporate performance prior to the onset of reporting requirements. Nevertheless, there is some evidence that mandatory disclosure programs can drive environmental improvements. For example, Delmas, Montes-Sancho, and Shimshack (2009) found that electric utilities reduced emissions after being forced to report information on their polluting behavior to consumers via monthly bill inserts. Blackman, Afsah, and Ratunanda (2004) found that the worst polluters in Indonesia reduced their emissions after the country implemented a program to rate firms' environmental performance. Similarly, Powers et al. (2008) found that the worst polluters in India's pulp and paper industry improved their performance after the Centre for Science and the Environment, an environmental NGO, began rating them publicly.

Information disclosure is not always driven by government regulation. As discussed in detail in Chapter 7, NGOs may create certification programs encouraging firms to disclose their environmental performance, as in the Forest Stewardship Council (FSC) program for timber harvesting. In other cases, industry creates its own certification programs, such as the Sustainable Forestry Initiative (SFI), offered as an alternative to FSC certification. These nongovernmental programs are especially important in forest products, since this industry engages in much international trade that cannot be controlled by any single nation. Fischer and Lyon (2008) have developed an economic model of competing environmental labels, in a setting where consumers cannot determine the environmental quality of individual products on their own. They allow for an NGO to set an environmental standard and create a certification program for firms wishing to meet its standard, and also allow for industry to do the same. Not surprisingly, they show that an NGO has incentives to create a more environmentally stringent label than does industry. Furthermore, when the two labels coexist, industry has incentives to weaken its label below the level it would choose if it operated alone. Whether multiple labels help or hurt environmental quality is impossible to determine in general. In some cases, environmental damages can be worse when both labels co-exist than if there were only an NGO label, but in other cases the addition of an industry label can actually improve overall environmental quality.

Instrument choice in developing countries is an area that is just be-ginning to attract serious academic attention. Many developing countries have weak political institutions, which render traditional policy instru-ments ineffective. For example, Bell and Russell (2002) question whether markets for tradable emissions permits make much sense in developing countries, which may lack the political infrastructure to make permit systems viable. Blackman, Lyon, and Sisto (2006) argue that voluntary programs may play a useful role in developing countries when regulatory capacity is weak.

Monitoring and enforcement

Corporate compliance with environmental regulations provides an inter-esting vantage point from which to view environmental governance. Regulatory authorities typically lack the resources to ensure that laws are enforced with full compliance. Indeed, environmental economists have long puzzled over business motivations for compliance with environ-mental regulations, since it is generally agreed that environmental audits are too infrequent and penalties for noncompliance too small to deter firms from defying environmental regulations. For example, Harrington (1988) pointed out that, between 1978 and 1983, the average penalty assessed for water discharge permit violations in the state of Connecticut was a mere $363. Yet, compliance rates among regulated entities remain high (Cohen 1999).[10]

---

[10] Magat and Viscusi (1990), for example, reported that the average level of compliance in the US pulp and paper industry between 1982 and 1985 was on the order of 75 percent. Harrington (1988) cited US Environmental Protection Agency (EPA) studies that put compliance rates for some sectors at 90 percent or higher.

Much effort has gone into explaining this apparent contradiction. For instance, Harrington (1988), Russell (1990), Harford and Harrington (1991), and Harford (1991) have developed dynamic models that illustrate firms' incentives to comply today so as to avoid more aggressive regulatory enforcement (i.e., intensive inspection scrutiny and higher penalties for noncompliance) tomorrow. Indeed, the empirical record suggests that inspections, or at least the threat of inspections, do positively influence firms' compliance.[11] Other studies have looked for nonregulatory costs to explain high compliance rates. Konar and Cohen (2001) investigated a sample of S&P 500 firms and found that a firm's asset value is reduced by about $380 million (or 9 percent of the replacement value of a firm's tangible assets) as a result of poor environmental performance. This finding suggests that investors can serve as an environmental governance mechanism. Further research is needed in this area, however, since financial markets may simply be reflecting the punishments expected to be imposed upon poor environmental performers by other governance devices. Furthermore, in recent years, there has been a regulatory shift toward higher fines and holding corporate officers and directors personally liable for environmental damages. Both of these trends may be driving better compliance, and merit detailed empirical investigation.

A good compliance record may pay dividends in a variety of ways. Decker (2003) has shown that a poor compliance record can significantly lengthen the time it takes for a firm to receive a permit to build or a permit to discharge pollutants. Boyd, Krupnick, and Mazurek (1998) cite case study evidence that production delays can cost up to $1 million a day in lost revenues. Such figures can easily swamp any expected regulatory penalties from noncompliance. Considerably more research is needed to deepen our understanding of what really motivates environmental compliance.

Inducing compliance becomes increasingly difficult as the number of firms covered grows. For "non-point sources" of pollution such as agricultural runoff or small sources of greenhouse gases or toxic chemicals, monitoring and enforcement may be prohibitively expensive. In these cases, good environmental governance may need to rely on community norms or so-called "voluntary" methods of environmental protection.

---

[11] See, for instance, Laplante and Rilstone (1996), Gray and Deily (1996), Nadeau (1997), and Weil (1996).

The political economy of environmental policy

As mentioned in the Introduction, economists have long cited market failures as a justification for government regulation, and for years they have offered market-oriented policy prescriptions to regulators. Seldom have economists' incentive-oriented proposals been implemented as proposed, however. Indeed, many critics have argued that environmental regulation, in practice, is often highly inefficient.[12] In response, economists have devoted more effort toward a positive understanding of the political economy of environmental protection. Using the economic approach to human behavior, they argue that politicians and bureaucrats have objectives that they attempt to maximize, such as getting re-elected. The analysis then seeks to understand the nature of political competition and the resulting equilibrium outcomes.

In the 1960s, led by James Buchanan and Gordon Tullock, economists associated with the Virginia School of public choice developed a body of work that uses economic principles to study collective choice processes. As presented in Buchanan and Tullock (1962), they emphasized the application of competitive market models to understand the supply and demand for policy. Central to their analysis is the idea of "rent-seeking" behavior, through which interest groups attempt to capture the economic rents created by the application of the state's monopoly on the legal use of force.

In the 1970s, economists associated with the University of Chicago developed an economic theory of regulation, complementary to that of the Virginia economists, which attempts to provide a general theory of regulatory behavior. In fact, its formulation of political decision-making is so general as to not really distinguish between legislative and regulatory behavior, thereby rendering it what might be called an economic theory of politics. In this literature, political action is driven by interest groups that form to advance their own agendas. The optimizing politician chooses a policy that balances, at the margin, the political support offered by all the different groups.

Political economy sheds new light on topics such as the choice of policy instruments. For example, Buchanan and Tullock (1975) present a positive analysis of the differences between pollution taxes and output restrictions. Output restrictions drive a wedge between price and marginal cost, and induce new firms to enter the industry and incumbents to surreptitiously expand output. Thus, direct regulation imposes a greater

---

[12] See, for example, Peltzman (1991).

enforcement burden on the government. If government successfully enforces the rules, incumbent industry members will prefer the output restriction to a tax, since the latter forces the industry to pay for a resource (the environment) it would otherwise be able to use for free. Even though the rest of the community prefers a tax, since it generates tax revenues, the small, concentrated, and intensely interested industry may carry the day politically. Indeed, it may even gain from the output restrictions imposed by the environmental regulation.[13]

The work of the Virginia and Chicago Schools revolutionized the way in which economists think about political processes, and opened up a vast new area of research. However, much of this work has tended to focus on the demand for policy by pressure groups and rent-seekers. It often glosses over the "details" of how policy is actually supplied through political institutions.

More recently, political economists have begun to develop game-theoretic models of political processes and institutions. These include voting models, analyses of campaign contributions, studies of the way in which interest groups recruit majorities for the passage of desired legislation, empirical analyses of the drivers of regulatory decisions, and sophisticated analyses of how legislators use administrative procedures to constrain the discretion of regulators. Of particular interest for environmental governance is the growing formal theoretical literature on special interest groups (SIGs) and their influence on policy. Grossman and Helpman (2001) provide an outstanding introduction to this body of research. They consider the role of SIGs in voting and elections, in transmitting information to policymakers, and in providing campaign contributions. Although much of the book studies situations with a single SIG, the authors also extend the analysis to the situation of multiple SIGs. This is important in environmental politics, where there are many well-established environmental groups vying for influence.

Somewhat surprisingly, there is little economic work that examines the organization of the spectrum of groups that form the backbone of the environmental movement, such as the Sierra Club, the National Audubon Society, the Worldwide Fund for Nature, the Environmental

---

[13] Maloney and McCormick (1982) extend the analysis of Buchanan and Tullock (1975), deriving sufficient conditions for environmental regulation to raise industry profits. They go on to present evidence that two recent regulatory initiatives actually raised industry profits. Similarly, Pashigian (1985) showed that the Clean Air Act's "prevention of significant deterioration" (PSD) rules benefited northeastern urban areas and harmed southwestern rural areas.

Defense Fund, and Greenpeace. It would appear that many of the tools of industrial organization could be applied to provide new insights into how these groups compete and cooperate. Bosso (2005) provides a descriptive treatment of many of these issues from the perspective of a political scientist, though he does not develop formal models of their behavior, or test hypotheses using statistical techniques.

Voluntary approaches to environmental protection

In recent years, a new literature has emerged that attempts to explain why corporations engage in environmental protection that goes beyond what is required by law. This literature is positive in nature, and is motivated by the growing number of examples of voluntary initiatives by corporations, industries, and regulators. Large companies such as Dupont and Alcoa have made – and kept – voluntary pledges to reduce their greenhouse gas emissions. Companies including McDonald's and Federal Express have worked with environmental NGOs such as the Environmental Defense Fund to reduce their packaging waste and the fuel consumption of their vehicle fleets. The chemical industry has created its "Responsible Care" program to encourage companies to reduce their emissions of toxic chemicals. The US EPA has created numerous partnership programs inviting – but not requiring – industry to work with government to reduce environmental impacts. Similarly, as Harrison (2001) describes in detail, Environment Canada has actively promoted voluntary programs, such as the Accelerated Reduction and Elimination of Toxics (ARET) challenge, which in 1994 invited industry to reduce emissions of thirty key toxic chemicals by 90 percent by the year 2000, and to reduce emissions of another eighty-seven toxics by 50 percent by the same year.

This new emphasis on voluntarism makes little sense within the conventional neoclassical framework. Because pollution control is costly, firms are expected to avoid it whenever possible, and governments must impose penalties large enough to compel compliance. Even from the public choice perspective, voluntary programs are anomalous: while some firms or industries may prefer to become regulated to restrict competition, the strategy works by invoking the coercive power of the state to raise rivals' costs, not by voluntarily raising one's own costs. The seemingly sudden shift to voluntarism initially seemed puzzling to economists, and warranted further research.

In the last decade, there has been a groundswell of academic interest in voluntary approaches to environmental protection. The topic provides an excellent point of departure for the study of environmental governance, since it encompasses all avenues of governance that go beyond traditional regulation. Chapter 6 provides a detailed assessment of the application of these new approaches to environmental governance. There have been several surveys of this new literature, including those by Khanna (2001), Lyon and Maxwell (2002), and Alberini and Segerson (2002). In addition, Lyon and Maxwell (2004b) provide a rigorous book-length treatment of this new field of study. They argue that these alternative approaches to governance cannot be understood in isolation from traditional regulation; indeed, many voluntary actions actually occur under threat of regulation, while others are taken precisely because the threat of regulation is weak. A complete theory of environmental governance must incorporate the economics of instrument choice, and monitoring and enforcement, as well as the political economy of environmental policy.

Most voluntary approaches fall into one of three categories: corporate self-regulation, public voluntary programs, and negotiated agreements. Corporate self-regulation involves firms (often as part of an industry trade association) initiating a public pledge to improve their environmental performance. Under public voluntary programs, participating firms agree to make good-faith efforts to meet program goals established by the regulatory agency; in return, they may receive technical assistance and/or favorable publicity from the government. In a negotiated voluntary agreement, the regulator and a firm or industry group jointly set environmental goals and the means of achieving them; such agreements consequently tend to be heterogeneous in nature.

I discuss each of these forms of voluntary environmental activity below.

Self-regulation

Several rationales have been offered for the recent surge of corporate environmental activity. Perhaps pollution is symptomatic of broader production inefficiencies, and pollution reduction and cost reduction go hand-in-hand to create "win/win" opportunities in today's economy.[14] Perhaps a new generation of "green" consumers is willing to pay higher prices for clean products, and firms are simply responding to that shift.[15] Both explanations offer the hope that markets are gradually supplanting

---

[14] For an exposition of this perspective, see Gordon (2005).
[15] For a recent analysis of green electricity programs, see Kotchen and Moore (2007).

regulation as the driver of environmental improvement. Alternatively, perhaps business has simply become savvier about the workings of the political system, taking proactive steps to avert political conflict rather than reacting to public pressure after the fact. Each of those theories has some merit, but the evidence suggests the roles of cost-reduction and green marketing are modest.[16] Instead, it is the opportunity to influence public or private politics that makes corporate environmentalism profitable.

Corporate non-market strategy, which focuses on strategy in the political arena, is a rich area of inquiry.[17] A number of different corporate environmental strategies have been identified in the academic literature. I discuss three such strategies here: (1) pre-empting tougher government regulations or NGO boycotts; (2) influencing forthcoming regulations, in situations where full pre-emption is impossible; and (3) reducing the extent of monitoring by regulatory agencies.

Maxwell, Lyon, and Hackett (2000) present a model of pre-emptive self-regulation in which political action is costly for citizen/consumers to undertake.[18] The political costs faced by consumers drive a wedge between the consumer benefits of voluntary abatement and the benefits of mandatory abatement, and firms can take advantage of this wedge to pre-empt regulation. As consumer costs of gaining political influence fall, the model predicts that corporate self-regulation will intensify. In other words, an increasing threat of government regulation induces firms to voluntarily reduce pollution. The authors find empirical support for the theory using data on toxic chemical emissions, and show that emissions reductions were greater in states with high initial levels of emissions and high environmental NGO membership. They also show that regulatory pre-emption is welfare-enhancing: it reduces political transaction costs, while leaving intact the protective threat that consumers will organize if the pre-emptive measures are deemed insufficient.

---

[16] For example, Kotchen and Moore (2007) find that when electricity customers are offered the opportunity to pay a modest premium for electricity from green sources, only about 3 percent elect to do so.

[17] See Baron (2005) for a thorough introduction to the area of non-market strategy.

[18] Individuals must inform themselves of the implications of pollution control for their well-being, and of the efficacy of various feasible policy remedies. Individuals of similar interests must then coordinate on a mutual strategy for gaining political influence. Even after individuals are organized, they must incur expenses to wield political influence, which might be attained through a variety of means, including lobbying activities, election campaign contributions, and tolerated forms of bribery such as revolving-door arrangements, junkets, and honoraria.

Often pre-emption requires coordinating the actions of numerous firms within an industry. Maxwell, Lyon, and Hackett (2000) show theoretically that free-rider problems make pre-emption more difficult to achieve the larger the number of firms in the industry is, and they find empirical evidence in support of this prediction. King and Lenox (2000) study the chemical industry's Responsible Care program, created in the wake of the Bhopal chemical disaster, allegedly to pre-empt the emergence of new chemical regulations. They find substantial evidence of free-riding; in fact, Responsible Care did accelerate environmental improvement in the industry, but only among non-members! One theory consistent with this finding is that NGOs naively took Responsible Care membership as a signal of good behavior by a company, and focused their efforts on firms that did not join the program.

Baron and Diermeier (2007) examine pre-emptive self-regulation in the context of private politics; that is, direct interaction between an NGO and a company, that is not mediated through the legislative or regulatory process. They show that firms have incentives to self-regulate in order to pre-empt the threat of a consumer boycott initiated by an NGO, and illustrate the theory using the example of Rainforest Action Network's campaign against Home Depot, which convinced Home Depot and other retailers to reduce their procurement of hardwoods that are unsustainably harvested. A key difference between pre-emption of public and private politics is that in the former, activism is typically aimed at regulating an entire industry, while in the latter it targets a specific company.

In some cases, pre-emption of government regulations may be impossible, but the voluntary actions of firms may influence the regulations subsequently set by government. For example, the Clean Air Act Amendments of 1990 identified 189 toxic chemicals which were to be subjected to maximum available control technology (MACT) standards by the year 2000. Because the details of the standards were not specified by Congress, firms had the chance to influence the standards that are actually set through their own actions. Similarly, Hoffman (2005) argues that many businesses are undertaking voluntary reductions of greenhouse gas emissions as a way to obtain a "seat at the table" from which they can influence future regulations. Lutz, Lyon, and Maxwell (2000) study this type of setting using a model that includes both "green" consumers and a welfare-maximizing government regulator who sets environmental standards. They show that a firm can weaken future regulations (and reduce social welfare) by committing today to a level of environmental performance beyond today's standards but below what the regulator would desire in the future.

A third way that corporate environmentalism interacts with public policy is by reducing the stringency with which the firm is treated by regulators. Maxwell and Decker (2006) argue that a firm may engage in voluntary environmental investments in order to commit to higher levels of compliance with existing regulations and may, in return, win a lower monitoring rate or laxer permitting scrutiny from regulators. If a firm makes an irreversible investment to lower its future costs of regulatory compliance, and if the regulator can observe this investment, then it can infer that the firm is less likely to violate the standards in the future, and will naturally pursue a laxer monitoring policy, since the returns to monitoring have been reduced.[19]

In sum, there are numerous channels through which corporate self-regulation can profitably influence the political behavior of citizens, regulators, and activists. Some of these are welfare-enhancing, and some are welfare-reducing. A robust theory of environmental governance must encompass this full range of channels.

Public voluntary programs

An increasingly popular instrument for solving environmental problems, especially in the United States, is the "public voluntary program" (PVP), in which government offers technical assistance and positive publicity to firms that reach certain environmental goals. The United States Environmental Protection Agency (US EPA) offers dozens of these programs, which it refers to on its website as "partnership programs."[20] Among the better known of these are the 33/50 program, Climate Leaders, and WasteWise.[21] According to the US EPA, "Governments promote voluntary initiatives for a variety of reasons, including the pilot testing of new approaches and *the absence of legislative authority*

---

[19] Decker and Pope (2005) extend this theory of voluntary investment to explicitly include multiple firms. They show that firms can take observable pro-environmental actions that convince regulators to focus their monitoring and enforcement efforts *on other firms*.

[20] The EPA's partnership programs are described in detail at www.epa.gov/partners/.

[21] The 33/50 program, which ended in 1995, encouraged firms to reduce their toxic chemical reductions by 33 percent in 1992 and 50 percent in 1995, relative to a 1988 baseline. See Khanna and Damon (1999) for details.

to establish mandatory programs."[22] This new generation of regulatory programs has been celebrated by some as a superior, low-cost instrument that can be used in preference to traditional, inefficient, regulation. Alternatively, however, one can see them as weak "carrots," used when political opposition makes the "stick" of environmental regulation infeasible.

Lyon and Maxwell (2003) have developed an economic model of PVPs in which a regulator has the option to propose an environmental tax or create a public voluntary program. They show that the tax is inherently a more powerful instrument, and that the regulator is better off imposing a tax rather than a PVP unless political opposition to the tax is high. Their chief normative findings are surprising: PVPs can reduce welfare by increasing industry resistance to socially beneficial tax proposals and by reducing industry incentives to engage in welfare-enhancing self-regulation.

In a sense, self-regulation and PVPs represent opposite ends of a spectrum: the former is adopted by companies when the threat of regulation is strong, while the latter are adopted by regulators when the threat of regulation is weak. Perhaps not surprisingly, the empirical evidence on the effectiveness of PVPs is mixed. Khanna and Damon (1999) find that the EPA's 33/50 program had a measurable effect in accelerating toxic emissions reductions, but Darnall and Carmin (2005) argue that the design of many PVPs is so lax as to make them ineffective.

Negotiated agreements

Negotiated agreements are more common in Europe and Japan than in the USA, perhaps because of the corporatist structure of many of these countries, which allows industry to negotiate as a unit with government. In addition, the parliamentary structure of the democracies of Europe and Japan ensures that the legislative and executive branches of government are of the same political party, potentially making legislative threats more credible.

Segerson and Miceli (1998) present a model of negotiated agreements. In their model, a new piece of environmental legislation mandating pollution reductions is forthcoming with some probability. The welfare-maximizing regulator cannot unilaterally impose new binding regulations, but is delegated the authority to offer the firm a voluntary

---

[22] Environmental Protection Agency (2001, p. 173), emphasis added.

agreement calling for a greater level of pollution reduction; if the firm accepts the offer, the regulator can eliminate the background threat of legislation. Both the firm and the regulator face lower transaction costs under a voluntary agreement, so the unique equilibrium of the game is for the regulator to offer a voluntary agreement and for the firm to accept. Depending on the parameters of the problem, the voluntary agreement may or may not embody the first-best level of abatement. The first-best level is feasible when the probability of legislation is high and voluntary compliance is significantly cheaper than mandatory compliance. Glachant (2003) extends this model to the case where the probability that proposed legislation will pass is determined by a rent-seeking competition between industry and a green lobbying group. Recognizing that passage of the bill becomes more difficult when the bill's requirements are tighter, the regulator strategically weakens the legislative proposal to increase the chance that it will pass.

Like self-regulation, negotiated agreements raise issues of industry coordination and free-riding. Negotiated agreements are typically negotiated by an industry trade association, which then implements the agreement by allocating the burden of abatement across its members. When all firms in the industry are identical, this allocation process is simple. When firms differ in their size or in their cost of abatement, however, allocation becomes a more delicate task. The most efficient outcome would be for firms that can abate cheaply to take on a larger share of overall abatement, perhaps with some form of side payments from other industry members. If side payments are impossible, though, it will be more difficult to convince efficient firms to shoulder what may seem to them an unfair share of the overall burden, and free-riding may become a serious problem.

Voluntary approaches: a summary

The literature on voluntary approaches to environmental protection has generated a number of new insights for the study of environmental governance. First, it demonstrates that a theory of environmental governance is inherently political: even in the absence of environmental regulation, corporate environmental behavior is strongly influenced by political forces, perhaps most importantly by the perceived threat of regulation. Second, it shows that government, as well as industry, can benefit from devising alternatives to traditional regulation, although the value of voluntary programs to government depends upon the background threat of regulation. Voluntary agreements reached under a strong threat of regulation may reduce the transaction costs of governance, and hence be more efficient than regulation. However, voluntary programs may also be instituted because the threat of regulation is weak, in which case voluntary programs are likely to be relatively ineffective. In this regard, the work of Harrison and Antweiler (2003) offers a cautionary tale: they find that most of the toxic emissions reductions reported through Canada's National Pollutant Discharge Inventory were due to conventional regulation of a small number of very dirty facilities, and that voluntary reductions have played a minor role. Third, the literature shows that corporate environmental strategy can influence public policy through a variety of channels, some welfare-enhancing and some welfare-reducing; all of these alternative forms of influence need to be understood in order to develop a satisfactory theory of environmental governance.

The new institutional economics of the environment

As mentioned earlier, the new institutional economics (NIE) has not focused on issues of environmental governance, with the exception of the work of Elinor Ostrom and her colleagues on small-scale common-pool resources, and the work of Oran Young and his colleagues on international environmental regimes. This section briefly reviews these streams of work.

Arguably the most systematic work to date on environmental governance is that of Elinor Ostrom and her colleagues at Indiana University's Workshop in Political Theory and Policy Analysis. The books by Ostrom (1990) and Ostrom, Gardner, and Walker (1994) are probably the best-known presentations of this work. Through a unique combination of game theory, economic experiments, and field case studies, Ostrom's research program has provided a rich theory of the governance of common-pool resources such as fisheries, pastures, and groundwater reservoirs. In sharp contrast to Hardin's view that government coercion is needed to solve the "tragedy of the commons," Ostrom finds numerous examples of common-pool resources that have been successfully governed by local people without reliance on government policy.

By combining theory, experiment, and field research, Ostrom has laid the foundations for a theory of environmental governance that includes such elements as bounded rationality, altruism, and social capital, topics that are at the frontiers of economic research today.

Economic experiments have forced scholars to recognize that individuals deviate systematically from the stark predictions of simple models of *Homo economicus*. For example, in the "ultimatum game," one player proposes to another how they should divide a fixed sum of money, and the second has only the option to accept or reject the proposal. Standard game theory predicts that the first player will claim effectively all of the pie, and that the second player will accept any crumbs he may be offered. In the laboratory, however, it is common for the second player to reject offers that are viewed as manifestly unfair. Such observations have led experimental economists and game theorists to begin introducing social norms into their models. Ostrom (2000) provides an overview of the evolution of social norms and how they enable collective action.

Research on social norms has led to a deeper recognition of the importance of "social capital" for solving environmental governance problems. Pretty (2003) presents a concise overview of this topic. In recent years, economists have become particularly interested in social capital, and it remains a research area that is growing rapidly. For a skeptical perspective, see Sobel (2002).

While Ostrom and her colleagues have focused on small-scale environmental systems, Oran Young (e.g., 1999a, 2002b) and his colleagues have focused on large-scale systems, with a primary emphasis on international environmental regimes. They have considered environmental "problem sets" such as the tropospheric ozone layer, tropical forests, the Arctic, and global climate change. Young has emphasized that the effectiveness of international environmental governance varies widely from one problem to the next. This is well illustrated by comparing the Montreal and Kyoto Protocols, which represent classic efforts at creating international agreements between nation-states. Perhaps the most successful international agreement ever created is the Montreal Protocol for the reduction of ozone-depleting compounds, signed on September 16, 1987, which has been documented in detail by Parson (2003). By 2007, 191 nations had ratified the Protocol, and the production of chlorofluorocarbons had been essentially eliminated. In contrast, the Kyoto Protocol on greenhouse gas emissions, which came into force on October 22, 2004, with Russia's ratification, attempts to address a global challenge that will endure for centuries with a treaty that extends only until 2012 and that has not been ratified by the USA or China, the world's largest emitters.

In light of the manifest limitations of formal governments in dealing with environmental problems, Young has argued strongly for the importance of other forms of international environmental governance, which provide complements (or possibly substitutes) to formal international agreements. Among these are environmental management systems such as ISO 14001, discussed in detail in Chapter 4, and environmental certification programs such as the Forest Stewardship Council (FSC) and the Marine Stewardship Council (MSC), discussed in detail in Chapter 7. Environmental management systems are especially interesting in the international context, since multinational corporations increasingly require their upstream suppliers in developing countries to certify with ISO 14001. This provides a mechanism through which the environmental standards of rich countries can be transferred to developing countries, even if the developing countries lack strong capabilities for regulatory enforcement. In a related vein, certification programs such as FSC and MSC allow the environmental preferences of "green" consumers in wealthy countries to translate into environmental performance on the ground in developing countries. These varying forms of certification offer valuable complements to formal agreements between nation-states, and offer excellent examples of the hybrid forms of environmental governance that are emerging around the world.

Unfortunately, there has been surprisingly little cross-pollination between groups working on micro- and macro-scale environmental governance. Dietz, Ostrom and Stern (2003) identify a set of factors that are required for successful environmental governance at any scale: providing information, dealing with conflict, inducing rule compliance, providing infrastructure, and being prepared for change. As described in earlier sections, most of these factors have been the subject of considerable economic research, but they have not yet been combined into a full theory of environmental governance, even for small-scale common-pool resources, much less for global environmental problems such as climate change. Young (2005) issues an urgent plea for greater efforts to bridge the gap between micro- and macro-level research, and makes a series of concrete proposals that might improve matters.

The research programs of Ostrom and Young and their colleagues provide valuable cornerstones for building a more complete theory of environmental governance. This work will require careful attention to the roles of communities, corporations, NGOs, nation-states, and international agreements, with particular emphasis on the many interesting hybrid forms of governance that are possible. The following section offers a number of suggestions for ways to proceed with this task.

Directions for future research

Although significant progress has made in the economics of environmental governance in recent years, many questions remain. In this concluding section, I mention just a few of the topics needing further work.

1. Although the commitment power of government shapes the effectiveness of voluntary programs, this dimension has not yet received adequate research attention, from either a theoretical or an empirical perspective. Lyon and Maxwell (2005) present a model that unifies the negotiated agreement model of Segerson and Miceli (1998) and the self-regulation model of Maxwell, Lyon, and Hackett (2000). They show that the key difference between the two models is that the negotiated agreement is assumed to remove the threat of future legislative action, while self-regulation does not. The most striking implication of this difference is in how the two approaches respond as the regulatory threat (i.e., the probability of legislation) increases. The level of abatement under the negotiated agreement rises smoothly with the probability of legislation. Self-regulation, however, displays a nonlinear pattern, with voluntary abatement at low and high levels of legislative likelihood, and no action for intermediate levels. It remains to be seen whether these predictions are borne out in empirical data. In addition, more research is needed into how the political structure of different countries affects their commitment powers, and the effectiveness of their voluntary agreements.

2. There is a need for much more research into the performance of voluntary approaches when information is imperfect. Government information disclosure programs such as the US Toxic Release Inventory bring governance issues to the forefront, as shown in work by Bui (2005), but we are far from having a good understanding of how these programs produce results. Concerns are frequently voiced that voluntary programs are mere "greenwash," but this epithet is often used in a vague and sloppy manner, and it has received little academic study. Lyon and Maxwell (2006) build on the literature on financial disclosure to build an economic model of greenwash and examine the efficacy of NGO strategies that attempt to eliminate it. Lyon and Kim (2006) find empirical support for the theory in the participation behavior of electric

utilities in the US Department of Energy's Voluntary Greenhouse Gas Registry, but far more research is needed in this area. The role of the media more generally also warrants much more economic research. Baron (2004a) presents a model in which an activist and an industry compete to influence public sentiment by providing information to the media, and Baron (2004b) shows how such competition can result in persistent media bias. Dyck and Zingales (2002) provide empirical analysis of the effects of media coverage on corporate social responsibility but, again, more research is needed.

3. The impact of socially responsible investors on business decisions is often alluded to, but there is little empirical evidence upon which to ground such assertions. Margolis and Walsh (2003) review the academic research on the correlation between financial and social performance, concluding that while most writers find a positive correlation between the two, nobody has been able to establish the direction of causality. Do high-performing firms have the luxury of indulging in environmental protection, or does environmental protection lead to improved profits? Research that answered this question with some degree of finality would be extremely worthwhile.

4. We need a better understanding of how environmental NGOs target corporations in the domain of private politics, and how these groups decide when to cooperate and when to compete. This new research area might be thought of as the "industrial organization" of NGOs. Despite some initial theoretical work by Baron and Diermeier (2007), and some intriguing empirical work by Eesley and Lenox (2006) and Sam and Innes (2008), much more remains to be done. The descriptive work by political scientists such as Bosso (2005) may provide a helpful point of departure for those interested in building more formal models. Work that links private and public politics would be particularly interesting. I believe it is important to join the insights of sociologists studying social movements, political scientists studying interest group mobilization, and economists studying non-market strategy in order to produce a robust theory.

5. Environmental governance in developing countries with weak political institutions is an important area that needs more work. Pargal and Wheeler (1996) present intriguing empirical evidence of "informal regulation" in Indonesia, and show that there is less pollution in areas where residents are wealthier and have higher levels of education, but they provide no theory of how this process works. The role of social capital, e.g., norms of behavior and social networks, may be particularly

important in the developing-country context. Woolcock (1998) provides a useful point of entry into this line of research. Blackman, Afsah, and Ratunanda (2004) use survey research to probe how the Indonesian PROPER program of pollution disclosure has achieved its results, linking the literatures on developing countries and on information disclosure programs.

In summary, environmental governance is an exciting area of scholarly work that draws upon a variety of strands of economic research. The time is ripe for an interdisciplinary dialog that brings these insights together with those from political science, law, sociology, and strategy.

3

Environmental governance and political science

MARIA CARMEN LEMOS AND ARUN AGRAWAL

Introduction

This chapter reviews the literature on environmental governance using a political science lens to examine how writings on governance have attempted to address some of the most pressing environmental challenges of our time – for instance global climate change, ecosystem degradation, biodiversity loss, and the like (Young 1994; Dietz, Ostrom and Stern 2003; Millennium Ecosystem Assessment 2005). Our review suggests that a significant proportion of writings on the subject has tended to emphasize a particular agent of environmental governance as being the most effective – typically market actors, state actors and, more recently, civil society-based actors such as NGO-based and local community actors. However, a broad array of hybrid environmental governance strategies are today in practice. It is also clear that even seemingly purely market, or state, or civil society-based governance strategies have always depended for their efficacy on support from other domains of social interactions.

The ensuing discussion uses insights from a review of the literature to focus especially on emerging hybrid forms of environmental governance. Of significant interest to our review are soft governance strategies that try to align market and individual incentives with self-regulatory processes, and co-governance, which is predicated on partnerships and notions of embedded autonomy across state–market–society divisions (Evans 1996; Sonnenfeld and Mol 2002). These innovations in environmental governance can potentially be extended to engage multiple types of environmental problems and conflicts. The chapter begins with a discussion of the significant promise of hybrid forms of environmental governance for coupled human and natural systems, and provides a close examination of some of the critical problems to which these forms remain subject. Especially crucial to the success of these partnerships is the extent to which constituent actors in the partnerships are able to overcome problems of coordination, political asymmetries, and issues of trust.

It is important to strike a note of caution at the outset. One of the prime difficulties in attempting to review the contributions of political science to environmental governance is, of course, the limited interest that political scientists have shown in environmental issues, despite the overwhelming evidence that the Earth systems upon which humans depend for their survival are in danger of being seriously disrupted by human actions. Consider an anecdote. Twelve recent past presidents of the American Political Science Association recently conducted a conversation about the blind spots, research accomplishments, and necessary directions for the discipline. Entirely absent from the conversation was any mention of the word "environment" (Agrawal and Ostrom 2006). It would be an astonishing revelation to those outside the discipline that when political scientists contribute to questions related to the environment, they do so despite their discipline. We therefore adopt a relaxed set of criteria in determining whether a scholarly contribution uses a political science orientation. Writings that use institutional approaches to investigate environmental problems, that focus on power in trying to explain environmental processes and outcomes, or that highlight the unequal distribution of environmental hazards, costs, and benefits fit our definition of contributions that use a political science lens on the environment.

We begin this chapter with a definition of environmental governance, a few reflections on its historical roots, and some fruitful ways in which to explore governance. To investigate emerging trends in environmental governance in a way that is both sufficiently general for a review and that reflects ongoing changes in the world of governance, we focus on three themes around which some of the most interesting writings on environmental governance cluster. The ensuing discussion first reviews the scholarship on globalization, decentralized environmental governance, and market-oriented governance instruments to identify how the conventional roles and capacities of important actors and institutions are getting reconfigured. This discussion leads us to a framework through which approaches to environmental governance and the terrain of environmental governance can usefully be explored. In developing this framework, we attend closely to the argument in the Introduction to the volume about the importance of environmental governance partnerships. We apply insights from this framework to two sets of consequential environmental problems: global climate change and ecosystem degradation. We identify important limitations of hybrid forms of environmental governance, and conclude with a discussion of some of the implications of ongoing developments related to environmental governance, with a special focus on the importance of power and politics in relation to partnerships.

Defining environmental governance

Environmental governance is the use of institutionalized power to shape environmental processes and outcomes. This definition accomplishes three objectives central to our review: it foregrounds the relationship of power to governance, it directs attention to institutions and suggests that they are basic to governance, and finally, it suggests that governance seeks to influence both what happens to the environment and the means through which these effects are generated. Thus, for the purposes of this chapter, environmental governance is synonymous with interventions aiming at changes in environment-related incentives, knowledge, institutions, decision-making, behaviors, and identities.

Although the origins of governance can be traced as far back as the history of human organization into groups and kinships, the same can scarcely be said for studies of governance. Thus, studies of the origins of the state often identify early forms of governance – conscious authoritative actions taken to shape social outcomes – that evolved into the modern state through a more explicit definition of the bureaucratic apparatus, more efficient appropriation of productive surplus, and the consolidation of territorial sovereignty (Spruyt 2002; Agrawal 2005). In addition, the historical analysis of different forms of governance has been more the focus of disciplines such as anthropology and sociology than of political science, which has focused on government rather than governance for the most part. This relative lack of attention to governance can be partly explained by the distrust that mainstream political science has of approaches that fail to provide "either a social-scientific explanation of historical variations in government or a historical interpretation of the construction of political institutions" (Brisbin 1999, cited in Muhll 2003, p. 136).

It should be clear then that governance is not the same as government, especially as the latter is conventionally understood in political science. For most political scientists, government properly concerns the formal decision-making apparatus of the state at multiple levels – national, provincial, and local. Governance, however, includes the actions of states, and in addition encompasses actors and mechanisms such as communities, businesses, NGOs, and supranational organizations. Key to different forms of environmental governance, therefore, are the political–economic relationships that institutions embody, and which shape identities, actions, and outcomes (Gibson 1999; Jagers and Stripple 2003). International accords, national policies and legislation, local decision-making structures, transnational institutions, and environmental NGOs are all examples of the forms through which environmental governance takes place. Because governance can be shaped through non-organizational institutional mechanisms as well, for example when it is based on market incentives and self-regulatory processes, there is no escaping it for anyone concerned about environmental outcomes. Environmental governance is varied in form, critical in importance, and near ubiquitous in spread.

Indeed, to anchor governance in the use of institutionalized power is to take advantage of the insights of the vast and growing literature on institutions and institutional change, and thereby connect it to a domain of solid theoretical advancement in political science in the past three decades. Institutionalist arguments in political science have been central in advancing the understanding of common-pool resources (Ostrom 1990; Schofield and Sened 2006), democracy (Bates 1989; Tilly 2007), development policies (Keohane and Ostrom 1995), international regimes (Lipschutz 1996), the origins and impacts of property rights (North 1990; Hirst and Thompson 2002), and other similar social phenomena. They also offer significant theoretical insights, especially concerning the relationship between governance strategies and individual incentives, the aggregation of individual actions through institutions, and the relationship between individual behavior and social outcomes, for those interested in environmental governance.

Studies of institutions can conveniently be divided into those that focus on the emergence of new institutions and institutional forms, and others that focus on institutional outcomes. Young's focus, in Chapter 1, on the demand for and supply of governance concerns the origins of new forms of governance. His methodological caveat about the need to attend to problem structure/socio-ecological context when trying to understand how governance arrangements work directs attention toward the need to understand the effects of governance mechanisms more rigorously. In both these domains, the work of the new institutionalists constitutes an exciting avenue for the exploration of common interests by those concerned with environmental governance and its connection to political science's more mainstream interest in institutions. The study of environmental governance mechanisms as both causes and outcomes of environmentally interested actions, depending on the temporal perspective and analytical interests of scholarship, has the potential to make the links between political science and the study of environment stronger, more durable, and more integral. Developing such links can only benefit the two parties in the relationship – scholars of environmental governance, and political scientists interested in institutions and institutional analysis.

Pressures toward hybrid forms of environmental governance

We suggest that three major sources of pressures are preparing the ground for the hybridization of environmental governance strategies: globalization, decentralization, and marketization. Individually and in combination, these shifts in the nature of social and governmental interactions are making environmental action by individual agencies and actors less effective. They are increasing the need for greater attention to cross-scale issues in efforts to govern the environment, and making the shortcomings of any single governance agent more evident. They are also, in consequence, leading to more vociferous calls for collaborative forms of governance, as political actors in state agencies, corporate offices, NGOs, and other civil society organizations seek to distribute the costs of environmental action.

Globalization describes an interconnected world across environments, societies and economies. Multiplicity, diversity, interdependence, and flows of influence and materials are common themes associated with globalization, even if there is little agreement about its definition, implications, impacts, and even usefulness as a concept (Clark 2000; Nye 2001). Although globalization produces both negative and positive pressures on governance, its most consequential impact is to intensify the flow of energy, materials and organisms in a manner that "couples the actions of people in one place with the threats and opportunities faced by people long distances away" (Eakin and Lemos 2006). It thereby broadens the range of problems that national governments are called upon to address, straining the resource basis of nation-states at the same time as it contributes to socioeconomic stresses, and possibly inequalities (Haas 1989).

Even when globalization produces positive impacts on the environment as, for example, by enhancing the depth of participation and the diversity of actors shaping environmental governance, it broadens the array of potential governance strategies, making it difficult for any single actor to shape what happens to the environment. By introducing new ways of organizing, interacting with, and influencing governmental processes, globalization can help increase the social and political relevance of non-state actors such as NGOs, transnational environmental networks, and epistemic communities – defined as networks of knowledge-based expertise (Busch, Jorgens, and Tews 2005; Heijden 2006). More accessible and cheaper forms of communication improve access to knowledge and technology and enhance the rate of information exchange, speeding up the dissemination of both technological and policy innovations (Jordan, Wurtzel, and Zito 2003; Ruggie 2003). At the same time, greater access to global capital for corporate actors, and the emergence of extraordinarily large multinational corporations create the prospects of more drawn-out confrontations in oppositional versus cooperative interactions.

Even if early writings on international environmental problems tended to focus on the role of international and multilateral organizations, more recent works have been motivated by perceived deficiencies of international regimes and a desire to identify new governance institutions, partnerships, and mechanisms that could be more inclusive. Such a set of governance mechanisms holds the promise not only of innovative governance strategies, but also of expanded cooperation among social actors that were previously outside the policy process: corporate interests, social movements, and nongovernmental organizations (Haas 2004). The fragmentary nature of the sources of complex environmental problems such as global climate change, and the reluctance or inability of nation-states to regulate the sources of these problems mean that non-state actors and organizations may be able to play an essential role in mobilizing public opinion and generating innovative solutions (Papadopoulos 2003). It is for this reason that scholars of environmental governance, such as Peter Haas, have proposed multilevel, non-hierarchical, information-rich, loose networks of institutions and actors as an alternative to ineffective state-centric international regimes (R. Hardin 2002).

If climate change, globalization, recent socio-political transformations, and the challenges they pose for environmental processes have been the major concerns occupying many of the scholars who have written and talked about environmental governance, it is at least equally true that some of the most important pressures toward changes in environmental governance are occurring at the subnational level. They are leading to new efforts to better incorporate finer-scale governance units and social groups into formal processes of environmental governance. Until as recently as the late 1970s and early 1980s, those concerned about loss of biodiversity, soil erosion, desertification, deforestation, decline of fisheries, and other environmental phenomena used to call for more elaborate and thorough-going centralized control. But today we witness an increasing loss of faith in state agencies as the ultimate custodians of nature and natural processes. In addition, there are very real practical reasons that have prompted a shift away from centralized state apparatuses where environmental governance is concerned. Economic pressures on states, resulting both from greater integration of economic activities across national boundaries and a decline in aid flows, have been supplemented by fiscal crises in many developing countries. In addition, a shift toward more democratic political processes throughout much of the developing world has facilitated the move toward alternative forms of governance that rely on higher levels of participation and greater involvement of citizens.

Since the mid-1980s, decentralization of authority to govern renewable resources such as forests, irrigation systems, and inland fisheries has gathered steam. Indeed, it has become a characteristic feature of late twentieth and early twenty-first century governance of renewable resources, even if nonrenewable resources continue to be held by state authorities in a tightfisted grip (Hutchcroft 2001; Johnson and Forsyth 2002; Watts 2005). National governments across the developing world have advanced strong claims about the imperative to establish and strengthen partnerships in which local administrative and organizational arrangements complement or substitute for more central efforts to govern environmental resources (Bagchi 2003). In many cases, they have backed these claims with changes in renewable resource policies. Whether these changes have occurred because of the alleged advantages of decentralized governance or because of the significant flows of aid funds tied to decentralized governance is difficult to judge, but the shift in favor of decentralization has produced alternative means and brought new political claimants to the fore as nation-states attempt to reclaim governance through partnerships with local organizations.

When successful, decentralized governance of natural resources can be seen as effecting three sets of changes in politico-environmental relationships: how decision-makers in lower level units of governance in a territorial-administrative hierarchy relate to those at higher levels; how local decision-makers relate to their constituents; and how subjective relationships of people with each other and with the environment also change. The goal of these changes it to make the exercise of institutionalized power both more thorough and more economical. Decentralization disperses multiple points of political leverage throughout an administrative structure, and makes them available to central decision-makers (Cashore 2002; Wilks 2005). It does so by encouraging the systematic creation of legal codes and performance standards that are specified through the exercise of legislative or executive authority, and adherence to which is the price of inclusion in decision-making processes. In addition to helping effect fiscal economies, decentralization also serves political and strategic considerations to the extent to which dissatisfaction with governance can find local points of authority against which to protest rather than seeking to engage centralized authority.

The decline of the state associated with globalization and decentralization has also propelled a variety of market-based environmental governance strategies to the fore. Instead of relying on hierarchically organized, regulatory control, or even purely participatory structures, market- and agent-focused instruments aim to mobilize individual incentives in favor of environmentally positive outcomes through a careful calculation and modulation of costs and benefits associated with particular environmental strategies. They differ from more conventional regulatory mechanisms along a number of dimensions, including the source of their legitimacy and authority. Cashore (2002) suggests that the strength of these instruments lies in their utilization of market exchanges and incentives to encourage environmental compliance.

Market instruments encompass a broad range: eco-taxes and subsidies based on a mix of regulation and market incentives, voluntary agreements, certification and eco-labeling, and informational systems are some of the major examples. Although some of them – energy taxes, tradable permits, voluntary agreements, and eco-labeling – were introduced as early as the 1960s in a number of Western countries, their adoption has gathered steam especially since the 1990s (Engel, Lopez, and Palmer 2006). These instruments are founded upon the bedrock of individual preferences and assumptions about self-interested behavior by economic agents. A strong claim advanced in their favor is their superiority in terms of economic efficiency related to implementation. Although an emerging literature focuses on the extent to which process-oriented evaluative criteria such as popularity, responsiveness, legitimacy, transparency, and accountability may also be associated with market incentive-focused instruments, the extent to which they meet these criteria needs much greater exploration.

Some of the drivers of market-based policy instruments in the developed world are analogous to those motivating decentralized environmental governance in much of the developing world (Durant et al. 2004). Dissatisfaction with regulatory control by state agencies and the bureaucratization associated with their growth plays an important role in the expansion of the forms of market incentive-based instruments, and their adoption across sectors and national boundaries (Bartley 2003).

Difficulties in implementation of traditional regulatory instruments provide a partial explanation of the willingness of governments to experiment with market-oriented efforts. High costs of compliance with environmental regulations and increasing awareness of environmental issues among consumers are other parts of the explanation.

The success of market instruments depends significantly on the internalization of positive environment preferences among relevant stakeholders, most importantly citizens and consumers. Not surprisingly, corporate and industry actors are less likely to adhere voluntarily to new environmental standards to the extent that they prove more costly in comparison to a situation where such standards are absent or weak. Indeed, efforts to induce voluntary compliance by economically motivated actors have been found to be vulnerable to free-riding behavior when effective mechanisms to deter free-riding are not in place (Cochran and Wood 1984; Delmas and Keller 2005). Other research focusing on corporate social responsibility examines the extent to which environmentally oriented actions of market actors are tied to their expectations about consumer preferences – both those specific to their products, and "green preferences" more generally (Alchian and Demsetz 1972).

Citizen preferences expressed in the form of a greater willingness to purchase green products, and policy environments in which superior environmental outcomes are prized, are an important driver of the success of new market- and agent-focused instruments of environmental governance. These considerations suggest that the growing popularity of market incentive-based instruments should not lead to the conclusion that governments are being replaced by governance. A conclusion more broadly supported by the existing evidence would be that there is a complex relationship between governments and governance. Governments are the source of credible threats of regulatory action that would require costly compliance. Such threats encourage the adoption of voluntary agreements on environmental standards. They also constitute the monitoring authority to which appeals regarding violations of environmental standards can be made.

The terrain of environmental governance

The elaboration above of environmental governance-related changes and challenges related to three different themes shows that there are intriguing parallels across them despite the many (and expected) differences in how governance is getting reconfigured as a result of globalization and decentralization, and the increasing importance of cross-scale governance market instruments and individual incentives. Perhaps the most obvious of these parallels relate to the emergence of alternative institutional forms of governance. Some of the new forms of governance are innovative hybrids between the conventionally recognized social roles that markets, states and, more recently, communities play. Others are the result of a clearer appreciation that the effectiveness of what was conventionally understood as a pure form of governance, based in the market or the state, may be the result of existing relationships among market, state, and civil society actors. Figure 2 presents a schematic structure to classify strategies of environmental governance as they are founded upon the actions of the three different social mechanisms.

The triangle connecting states, markets, and communities constitutes the core of the figure. The emphasis in the figure on these social mechanisms is a reflection of early conversations related to the environment that viewed environmental governance strategies as being especially

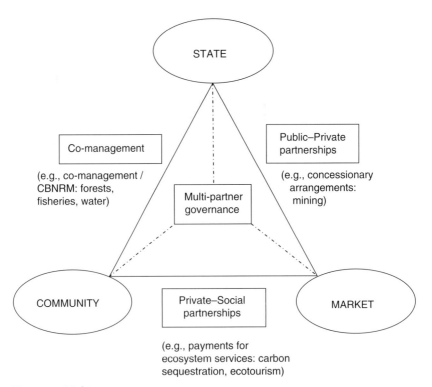

Figure 2   Multi-partner governance

necessary to address the externalities stemming from the public goods nature of environmental resources and processes. To overcome these externalities, some writers saw state action as necessary; others, surmising that externalities could lead to market failure, advocated clearer definition of property rights to allow functioning markets to emerge (G. Hardin 1978; Ostrom 1990). Arguments advanced by scholars of the commons engaged these policy prescriptions and identified communities as a third potential locus of environmental governance (Ostrom, Schroeder, and Wynne 1993). These efforts, championing state-, market-, and community-based governance strategies, were built around perceived strengths of the particular social arena being considered: the capacity for action across jurisdictions backed by state authority; the mobilization of basic human incentives through market exchanges; and the deployment of solidaristic relationships and time-and place-specific knowledge embodied in communities (Agrawal 2005).

In the past decade and a half, however, an exciting array of research has identified opportunities for more nuanced arguments regarding hybrid forms of collaborations across the dividing lines represented by markets, states, and communities. The four major forms we identify in Figure 2 – co-management (between state agencies and communities), public–private partnerships (between state agencies and market actors), private–social partnerships (between market actors and communities), and multi-partner governance (involving all the different types of agents) – each incorporate joined action in at least two of the social arenas in the core triangle, and correspond to literally scores of specific experiments in which constituent social actors find differing levels of emphasis. They simultaneously illustrate the dynamic and fast-changing nature of contemporary environmental governance. The emergence of these hybrid forms of environmental governance is based upon the recognition that no single agent possesses the capabilities to address the multiple facets, interdependencies, and scales of environmental problems that may appear at first sight to be quite simple.

The hope embodied in hybrid mixed forms of environmental governance is evident in each case. They seek simultaneously to address the weaknesses of a particular social agent, and to build upon the strength of the other partner. Thus, the involvement of market actors in environmental collaboration is typically aimed at addressing the inefficiencies of state action, often by injecting competitive pressures into the provision of environmental services. In the same vein, market actors are viewed as enabling greater profitability in the utilization of environmental resources. The addition of community and local voices to environmental governance is seen as providing the benefit of time- and place-specific information that may help solve complex environmental problems, at the same time allowing a more equitable allocation of benefits from environmental assets. Higher levels of participation by different stakeholders and the blessings of state authorities can help overcome the democratic deficit and lack of legitimacy that are often associated with market-focused instruments. Moreover, state actors, ostensibly, create the possibility that fragmented social action by decentralized communities and market actors can be made more coherent and, simultaneously, more authoritative.

A second obvious parallel across the discussion of the different themes related to environmental governance is that, within hybrid strategies, we can discern a mobilization of individual incentives that had initially been the core of market-oriented instruments and is now becoming increasingly common. Thus, contemporary co-governance strategies, in contrast to their historic counterparts, focus on how the individual subject will respond to efforts at governance. Through such a calculation of individual responses, decentralized environmental governance aims to elicit the willing cooperation of those subject to the goals of governance (Rhodes 1996; McCarthy 2004). The emphasis on willing cooperation has even prompted some scholars of incentive-based governance strategies to term them "governance without government" (Bennett 2000, p. 652).

In view of the extent to which an appeal to individual self-interest is a part of new environmental governance strategies, it is reasonable to conclude that a pervasive attempt to restructure agent-level incentives and attitudes toward the environment underpins governance instruments related to civil society-based solidarities, market-based policies, and voluntary compliance mechanisms (Ashford 2002; Robertson 2004). The same is true for public–private and social–private partnerships, each of which is enabled by a level of valorization of corporate entities and market actors that would have been quite unimaginable in the 1970s (Sanderson 2002; Ribot and Peluso 2003; R. Hardin 2006). It would be no exaggeration to suggest that the logic of efficiency, which is the hallmark of capitalist organization of production, is also coming to colonize the goal of environmental conservation and sustainable development.

Limitations of hybrid governance strategies

We identify three major limitations of hybrid governance strategies. The first concerns the extent to which they can be effective in addressing the shortcomings of other forms of governance in which a single actor is dominant. The second is equally basic, and concerns the public versus private aspects of governance. The third focuses on the power differentials among the actors that are part of any environmental governance partnership.

The reconfiguration of environmental governance so that the state is no longer the only actor viewed as capable of addressing environmental externalities has enormous implications, not all of which have found easy acceptance among those concerned about environmental outcomes. The focus on individual incentives, the creation of new property rights and markets in relation to water, carbon, or ecosystem services, and the encouragement to the corporate sector insofar as the policy environment enables more extensive public–private and social–private partnerships have been construed by some scholars as moves toward increasing democratic deficit and higher levels of inequality in the allocation of environmental resources. Those who are able to exercise greater access and expertise in relation to these new mechanisms are more likely to derive greater benefits from them (Liverman 2004). Other scholars have expressed significant concerns about the extent to which the incorporation of market actors in a more thoroughgoing manner into environmental governance is likely to lead to what Liverman (2005), among others, has called the commodification of nature. Greater efficiency in the utilization of natural resources, for many, is equivalent to higher rates of extraction and, thereby, brings up issues of intergenerational equity.

For others, especially those coming from a radical political economy perspective, there is no new approach to global environmental governance; rather, the supposed new mechanisms of governance are little more than a natural evolution of traditional regime politics, because outsiders and disempowered groups continue to have little opportunity to participate in contemporary efforts at governance despite the greater incorporation of civil society actors (Lipschutz 1996). The key difference between models of new global environmental governance and older conceptions of regime theory is the role and importance accorded to members of global civil society – understood as a sphere of voluntary societal associations located above the individual and below the state as well as across state boundaries (Lipschutz 1996; Ford 2003). However, Ford (2003) argues that the rhetoric of societal participation introduced by the Brundtland Report did little to affect regime politics, since it failed to democratize the negotiation process itself.

New forms of global environmental governance, therefore, can be viewed simply as reflecting the existing distribution of power despite the incorporation of new players and as not having changed anything fundamental. Indeed, new forms of environmental governance can arguably be viewed as being integrally connected to the near-ubiquitous acceptance of neoliberal economic principles and practices which have become hegemonic in the neo-Gramscian sense (Falkner 2003). In this sense, new hybrid forms of environmental governance are allegedly part of a broader agenda to achieve corporate interests that economic globalization is all about (Paterson, Humphreys, and Pettiford 2003). In a world of weak states, deterritorialized action, and concentrated power, corporate interests and multilateral organizations can control and re-frame environmental action as a means to legitimize their preferences in terms of developmental models (Paterson, Humphreys, and Pettiford 2003). In this view, the very actors responsible for environmental degradation are also the ones defining the terrain of environmental governance and the terms of environmental protection. "Governance from below," represented by the role of social movements and protests against organizations such as transnational corporations, the World Trade Organization (WTO), the World Bank, and the International Monetary Fund (IMF) may be the only recognizable challenges to this hegemony (Papadopoulos 2003).

In the case of horizontal governance networks including a wider array of social actors such as private and corporate interests, a major argument in their favor is the need to guarantee that veto players, whose "voice" or "exit" can jeopardize public action, agree with policy choices. Here, if these elite actors are provided with a privileged space for participation, they will have no incentive to exert their veto power or obstruct the decision-making process. The rationale behind the legitimacy of horizontal networks is both that they work and that the outcome justifies compromise for the "greater good." However this is hardly a justification for legitimacy (Manor 2005). Moreover, the mere inclusion of more social actors does not necessarily make governance systems more democratic (Papadopoulos 2003). On their part, advocates of new forms of governance argue that even if these approaches are characterized by a democratic deficit, they are no worse than traditional representative democracy (Jessop 2002). Still, critics point out that they fail to meet normative models of deliberative democracy whose fairness is grounded on the equal participation of all stakeholders. Finally, the opacity of governance networks may prevent the mass public from identifying and evaluating the role of specific agents such as experts who play prominent roles in the building of relevant issues and action agendas. For example, in cases of environmental problems with potential catastrophic impacts (e.g., global climate change), the predominance of "less than democratic" expert politics is justified because of the urgency and severity of the problem (Lemos 2008).

But governance from below may be too timid a remedy and the "greater good" not enough justification for what is essentially the superimposition of new governance "technologies" – in the form of hybrid partnerships – on top of local realities fraught with inequalities that often define the problems that environmental governance mechanisms are seeking to solve. The deployment of hybrid governance mechanisms without attention to the distributional inequalities related to income, education, power, and so on that underlie the different practices of different environmental actors may be tantamount to putting a new roof on top of a house with decaying foundations. Without addressing the root social and economic causes of environmental problems, the adoption of new environmental governance strategies may lead only to short-term fixes and long-term ineffectiveness.

Another problem with market-based instruments and multilevel governance frameworks concerns their effects on state capacity, particularly in relation to environmental problems. In multilevel governance systems, the role of the nation-state is reconfigured in that the "denationalization" of statehood, reflected empirically in the "hollowing out" of the national state apparatus [that is, the loss of state authority and capacity to upper (globalization) and lower (decentralization) levels of governance], has reorganized state capacities both territorially and functionally (Pelkonen 2005). Indeed, globalization and subnational challenges have led to the emergence of a re-scaled state that simultaneously transfers power upwards to supranational agencies and downwards to regional and local levels (Painter and Pierre 2005), changing the way in which policymaking capacity is distributed. This transfer of power to different levels of decision-making may have already affected the policy capacity of the modern state in a negative way (Jayasuriya 2005). In the context of the shrunken state and the emergence of new governance partnerships, public administration theory also needs adjustment. For example, Jayasuriya (2005, p. 21) proposes that capacity-building for policy design and implementation under these new conditions requires a new theory that goes beyond the definition of capacity attributes (e.g., resources, professional and competent bureaucracies, etc.) to include the relationships between the state and those new actors with whom the state cooperates. Paradoxically, the hollowing out of the state replaces the limited scope of government with the much broader level of resources of governance. Indeed, hybrid modes of environmental governance and emerging partnerships across conventional divisions suggest that the state is neither the only, nor even the most important, partner in environmental co-governance (Lowi 2002). Yet, advocates of a bigger role for the state contend that, especially in cases where redistributive policymaking becomes necessary (e.g., adaptation to climate change), it is unlikely that either the market or hybrid forms of governance will be able to accomplish it (Foucault 1978/1991).

An equally fundamental set of criticisms of new forms of governance concerns the ways in which the idea of governance finds a place in the work of poststructuralist scholars, many inspired by Michel Foucault's idea of governmentality. For scholars of governmentality, the problem of government exceeds that of governance in that it includes the ways in which individuals and their private lives are also shaped by the exercise of power. The distinction between the private and public realms of human existence is undermined in a very substantial way in this approach to thinking about government since the creation of and changes in public institutions affect what happens to individuals in their private lives, and understanding these changes is also an objective of an analysis of government.

Foucault's (1978) initial use of governmentality or governmental rationality focused on macropolitical relations and identified it as a new form of exercise of power in modern, liberal democratic societies in contrast to disciplinary or sovereign forms of power. Many of the scholars who have used his ideas have applied them to social processes related to education, family, insurance, risk management, welfare, criminality and policy, space and architecture, and security (Patton 1989; Dean 1999). The goal of these analyses is to understand and describe how modern forms of power and regulation achieve their full effects, not by forcing people toward some state-mandated goals but by turning them into accomplices. This radically divergent understanding of power as a positive means to shape individuality and individual subjectivity is what distinguishes poststructuralist analyses of government from more social-scientific attempts to understand and analyze governance.

According to Foucault, the explosion of the problem of government occurs when one of the functions of state powers becomes the administration of life. The regulation of life – both the life of the population and that of the individual – raises with particular intensity the problem of "how to govern oneself, how to be governed, how to govern others, by whom the people will accept being governed, how to become the best possible governor ..." (Foucault 1978/1991, p. 87). This problem of government is concerned with examining how new subjects of power come into being through adopting certain actions, gestures, and desires over time. In talking about the constitution of subjectivity, Foucault is concerned with practices and knowledges that have a historical dimension: "New techniques for examining, training, or controlling individuals, along with the new forms of knowledge to which they give rise, bring into existence new kinds of people" (Miller 1992, p. 264).

Power, in a positive sense, plays a critical role in three different ways in which new subject positions come into being. Subject creation occurs through scientific inquiries that focus on and help identify particular types of subjects as their target – for example, the productive and the laboring subject of economics, the speaking subject of philology and linguistics, or the subject/citizen dichotomy of normative political theory. Subject formation also takes place through disciplinary practices that instantiate distinctions such as those between the sane and the insane, the sick and the healthy, or the author and the reader. Finally, the ways in which a human being turns him/herself into a subject, by following certain practices and modes of thought in response to new forms of exercise of power, constitutes a third, practical, mode of making subjects. It is this third way in which new subjects come into being that is of relevance to environmental governance, particularly for analyses that take market-based mechanisms and individual incentives seriously.

Indeed, writings on governmentality can supplement and help further the analytical sharpness of works focusing on environmental governance in at least three distinct ways.

1. Instead of taking power as the fixed property of some agent(s), they suggest that it is more fruitful to examine how power is generated by and located in different strategies of governance. No particular agent or person can then be seen as being located in a permanently more powerful political position vis-à-vis another. Instead, one can begin to ask why some strategies of government work in certain ways and with what effects.
2. Governmentality as an optic also orients attention toward the careful study of the techniques, forms, and representations of knowledge that are related to new means of governance. Statistics, maps, numerical tables, and their collation in specific formats can become the basis for producing new forms of knowledge that make some actions seem naturally more appropriate in comparison with others as an invaluable aid to the process of government. In other instances, models,

equations, instrumentation, and predictions can become the means to new knowledge that justifies new forms of governance.

3. Studies of governmentality bring to the forefront questions about the relationship between government and self-construction. If the literatures on institutional analyses, public policy, and the state treat the process of subject formation and identity change as lying outside their legitimate domain, the study of governmentality is about integrating institutional and other social changes with changes in subjectivities.

This last point is particularly important. In talking about technologies of government, Foucault broadly divided them into two sets: technologies of power and technologies of self. In attending primarily to technologies of power and their effects – through rules, enforcement, and externally accepted norms – nearly all the work on governance in political science and most of the other social sciences has focused too narrowly on the public exercise of power through institutions. Gary Miller (1992), drawing upon the work of Bengt Holmstrom (1974), argues how attempts to induce compliance, when based solely on enforcement threats in hierarchical organizations, are either prohibitively expensive or ineffective. There is a lesson here for those interested in governance. Institutional forms of enforcement and environmental governance are probably inadequate as means to promote effective forms of sustainability, and their relationship with changes in people's subjectivities and orientations toward the environment is also critically important in order to understand which strategies of governance are more likely to be effective.

Not all governance is equal: North-South tensions

As mentioned above, the deployment of new forms of governance is not without tension, especially with regard to the unequal power relations among the actors involved in a partnership. The three-fold classification of the types of actors in joint governance strategies is admittedly simplistic. Nonetheless, it points toward issues that it would be necessary to consider in any type of partnership among organizations with unequal power and political relationships that are asymmetric in many, if not most, instances. The impact of politically asymmetric relationships can be considered with respect to both the resources and strategies of partners.

Among the three broad sets of partners involved in joint governance efforts, it is more than likely that civil society actors such as NGOs, community groups, federations of voluntary organizations and so forth have fewer resources to bring to a partnership in comparison with corporate actors, who can draw on their own capital assets and also on market-based strategies of raising resources as necessary, and government agencies – who would typically rely on the capacity of the state to act authoritatively. What civil society actors offer to environmental governance partnerships are perceptions about their legitimacy, and the faith that publics often have in their sincerity and trustworthiness. The greatest leverage of civil society actors in mobilizing such resources typically exists in the initial stages of a partnership. Furthermore, these resources are in the nature of step goods – they cannot be rationed. Either an NGO or a civil society actor is part of an environmental governance partnership, or it is not.

On the other hand, government agencies and corporate actors can use their resources – authoritative action and material resources – in more finely calculated and diverse ways. Depending on their level of commitment, they can bring more or less of their resources to the partnership, and reduce or increase the initial amounts with far greater flexibility than can civil society actors. These differences between the resources and strategies of different sets of actors suggest that civil society actors are inherently in a weaker position in governance partnerships than are market and state actors. Unequal power relations between countries and groups within countries are also equally fundamental to thinking about environmental governance partnerships.

Between more and less developed countries (LDCs), this tension is never more salient than when the definition of governance includes power distribution and the unequal relationships between the North and the South. Tensions in the implementation of hybrid environmental governance strategies emerge along (but are not limited to) two different dimensions.

1. The relationship between LDCs and developed countries is far from static. Informed both by a history of distrust and conflict, and shaped by colonialism, it has also been marked by the strengthening of economic, political and social ties between countries in the context of increased post-colonial globalization.
2. While tensions informed by a history of contentious state–society relations also arise within LDCs, they have been modulated by the emergence of new forms of association made possible in the wake of democratic reform in the majority of Latin American but also in a number of African and Southeast Asian countries.

Historically, environmental conflicts between LDCs and developed countries have had their roots in the pattern of occupation and exploitation of natural resources, begun during the colonial period. This relationship not only defined the division of work between exporters of natural resources in the South and consumers in the North (Lipschutz 1996) but also produced, as one of its legacies, a striking devaluation of natural resources beyond their immediate economic import. It also resulted in high levels of inequality in the distribution, regulation and consumption of natural resources between North and South. Although these inequalities have been tempered by a growing awareness of the interconnectedness of environmental conservation and degradation at the global level and by the growth of transboundary environmental activism (Chalmers, Martins, and Piester 1997), tensions remain on what constitutes appropriate regimes for environmental governance – internationally as well as subnationally. For many developing countries, there is little indication that new forms of governance are not "more of the same" in that the "weaker" partner in the South fails to reap the benefits of natural resource exploitation while having to bear the brunt of the negative impacts of both environmental degradation and the costs of environmental protection. Protected areas, as a strategy of environmental governance that combines the efforts of environmental NGOs and governments, are a case in point. Because most of the world's terrestrial and marine biodiversity is located in the tropics, the costs of conserving biodiversity have typically fallen on citizens of the developing world. According to various estimates, between 1 million and 4 million of them have been displaced from their homes and livelihoods as a result of the implementation of diverse environmental governance strategies (West, Igoe, and Brockington 2006).

Similarly, within LDCs, tensions around new forms of governance are critically informed by the past history of state–society relations, especially between traditionally privileged elites (including state actors) and less powerful groups who often depend on the same resources for their livelihood that the elite seek to protect and conserve. The relationship between state officials and community actors has been the product of asymmetric political relationships marked by repression, clientelism, co-optation, and rent-seeking (Collier and Collier 1991). Neocorporatist relationships in Europe may be defined as a win/win situation in which state and society come together and negotiate by means of dialog to find solutions through which the common interests of diverse constituencies can be met. In developing countries, corporatist negotiations still remain a form of unequal representation of interests (Schmitter 1971; Lemos and Oliveira 2004). Thus, in countries where both mistrust and confrontation have been the staple characteristic of state–society relations, hybrid forms of governance, especially those seeking to involve communities, face extra barriers.

However, an emergent literature on environmental governance in developing countries has begun to showcase positive accounts of relationships between citizens and public officials in the context of progressive local governments (Evans 1996). In environmental policymaking in particular, scholars have identified successful cases of policy implementation and natural resources management in which urban and rural actors as well as neighborhood associations, natural resource management councils, and communities play a role. In some cases, such relations can create a policy environment in which positive interactions between citizens and public officials across the private–public divide can flourish (Eakin and Lemos 2006). This new trend, in the form of what Chalmers, Martins, and Piester (1997) call "associative networks," is an alternative to earlier, more exclusionary forms of representation. And even if new associational forms are unevenly distributed, they bode well as a background for the dissemination of hybrid forms of governance in both developing and developed countries.

Applications: climate change and ecosystem degradation

The sources of pressure for new forms of environmental governance that we highlighted above, and the framework for viewing emerging hybrid mechanisms of environmental governance are visible in the major problem areas related to the environment. Two significant arenas in which these themes and hybrid governance strategies are especially evident are global climate change and ecosystem degradation. An examination of these areas of environmental concern and crisis provides useful indications about the extent to which contemporary and emerging environmental governance approaches have the capacity to help address major problems.

Global climate change

Among the factors that challenge environmental governance structures, global climate change promises to be one of the most critical. As the need to design policies to respond to the negative impacts of climate change increases, more attention has been paid to emerging modes of environmental governance: how they can increase the capacity of economic, social, and cultural systems to help humans mitigate and adapt to climatic change. Considering that climate is one of many stressors, the resilience of already overextended economic, political, and administrative institutions may decrease rapidly, especially in the more impoverished regions of the globe (Hempel 1996). Some signs of how environmental stresses may exacerbate governance challenges related to poverty, violence, and authoritarianism are already visible. Among expected casualties of governance breakdown as a result of climate change may be economic growth, democratic institutions, and sustainable livelihood conditions for many.

Responses to global climate change fall broadly into two main categories: those seeking to curb or stabilize the level of emissions of greenhouse gases into the atmosphere (mitigation) and those seeking to boost natural and human systems resilience to prevent, respond to, and recover from potential impacts of a changing climate (adaptation). Although, at this point, adaptation may be inevitable, its magnitude and range depend on how much mitigation is successfully implemented to prevent and avoid the most dangerous interference to the climate regime.

Many of the factors that make global climate change unique also make it complex. Global climate change is the quintessential multi-scalar environmental problem: because greenhouse gases mix equally in the atmosphere, the costs of the negative effects of climate change are socialized at the global level but the effects are likely to be felt at the local level. The fragmented and highly politicized nature of the causes of climate change means that it is extremely difficult to assign blame and to target offenders. Effective responses to climate change are likely to require a diversity of actors and organizations across the state–society divide. The high level of uncertainty still involving the definition of the magnitude and character of the impacts of climate change in different human and natural systems, and the fact that they might not be felt for years, also make it a politically and financially costly problem (Adger 2001). Finally, the differences between those causing climate change (large producers of greenhouse gases) and those likely to be most negatively affected by it, including the global poor and natural and biological systems, make it unique in terms of the distribution of costs and benefits and bring up a whole host of equity and environmental justice questions (Brooks, Adger, and Kelly 2005). For example, while mitigation actions are likely to fall upon the countries and sectors mostly responsible for the production of greenhouse gases, such as polluting corporations and developed countries, adaptation will mostly be realized by affected groups such as the poor living in less developed countries or agencies entrusted with the task of building generic adaptive capacity to climate change, such as NGOs and aid organizations. In the burgeoning literature on adaptation, most of the efforts to compare differential vulnerability have identified already-stressed countries and regions in Africa and South Asia, and Small Island States as the most vulnerable (Skjaerseth 1992; O'Brien et al. 2004). However, the primary burden of mitigation falls on developed countries and greenhouse gas producers in the context of international regimes to curb their emissions, such as the Kyoto and Montreal Protocols (IPCC 2001; Streck 2004).

Mitigation

The IPCC defines mitigation of global climate change (GCC) as "an anthropogenic intervention to reduce the sources or enhance the sinks of greenhouse gases" (Socolow et al. 2004). Mitigation of greenhouse gas emissions has been organized at the international level primarily through the entering into force of the Kyoto Protocol, and realized at the national level through regulation and implementation of new governance mechanisms across the public–private divide. Mechanisms to mitigate global climate change range from technological fixes to the design of institutions that curb carbon emission practices. Five categories of strategies to mitigate carbon emissions are available: energy conservation, renewable energy, enhanced natural sinks, nuclear energy, and fossil carbon management. Yet the magnitude, complexity and urgency of the climate change problem suggest that the implementation of any (or a combination) of these strategies would require tremendous amounts of financial, human, and political capital (Kates 2004).

Not surprisingly, the lack of capacity of nation-states to implement such strategies – exemplified by the lackluster accomplishments of the Kyoto agreement so far (Nelson and Jong 2003) – and the general lack of confidence that this capacity will improve dramatically in the near future suggest that a broader array of hybrid modes of governance is necessary in order to address global climate change. Co-management and public–private partnerships in the implementation of Kyoto's Clean Development Mechanism, and social–private partnerships to develop community-based carbon sequestration projects are a promising start (Klooster and Masera 2000; Gulbrandsen and Andresen 2004). Carbon taxes and joint development of fuel-efficient technology (e.g., FredomCar, California Fuel Cell Partnership) are also examples of initiatives involving both public and private actors. Yet, despite the promise of effectiveness of hybrid modes of governance, many question their ability to address mitigation as fast and as broadly as is necessary to defuse many of the most negative impacts of global climate change.

Already, in the implementation of mitigation policy, NGOs and businesses have played a particularly important role in influencing both the design and the implementation of climate governance mechanisms. While business interests have mostly focused on flexible mechanisms for carbon trading and the achievement of fuel efficiency (as well as also playing an oppositional role to the implementation of emission curbing strategies), NGOs have played a broader role in monitoring implementation and compliance of regulation, lobbying, raising equity issues, and providing scientific and technical knowledge (Corell and Betsill 2001; Gough and Shackley 2001; IPCC 2001; Streck 2004). One of the most effective ways in which NGOs have influenced the global climate change policy process has been through their role as knowledge producers, as members of information networks, and as epistemic communities seeking to affect the response process.

Adaptation

The IPCC defines adaptation as "the degree to which a system is susceptible to, or unable to cope with, adverse effects of climate change, including climate variability and extremes." Vulnerability, in turn, is "a function of the character, magnitude, and rate of climate variation to which a system is exposed, its sensitivity, and its adaptive capacity" (Brooks and Adger 2004). Adaptive capacity, the third concept important for understanding vulnerability to global climate change, is the "potential and capability to change to a more desirable state in the face of the impacts or risks of climate change" (Brooks, Adger, and Kelly 2005). It is the ability of a system to adjust to global climate change and to moderate GCC-related damage. It takes into consideration the entitlements, assets, and resources inherent to a system that improve its ability to resist, cope with, and recover from a given hazard.

In contrast to mitigation policy, building adaptive capacity has been mostly defined at the national scale both because it is the appropriate level at which to make policy decisions and because it allows for the comparison of vulnerability across countries (Adger, Arnell, and Tompkins 2005). Similarly to mitigation policy, the reality of building adaptive capacity involves cascading decisions across scales and a diversity of private and public agents and organizations (Eakin and Lemos 2006). However, because of the redistributive character of adaptive capacity-building, the bulk of the action is expected to fall on nation-states (Brooks 2003).

At the local level, global climate change critically intersects with decentralization, not only in the assessment of different levels of vulnerability within countries but also in the design of policy to enhance adaptive capacity. Vulnerability assessment (e.g., participatory vulnerability mapping) holds the promise of a more accurate understanding of the "character" of the vulnerability of specific social and human systems (Adger 2001). At the global level, the main implication for adaptation policy refers to the role that institutions such as the United Nations Framework Climate Change Convention (UNFCCC) play in coordinating international action and advancing rationales for compensation and preparation for future impacts (Liverman 2005; Millennium Ecosystem Assessment 2005).

The panoply of governance strategies related to global climate change is clearly difficult to view as being centered on any single category of social agent as depicted in Figure 2. Although it might have been argued a decade ago that nation-states are the only actors who can generate effective measures to address climate change, it is evident that, although their involvement is necessary to deal with climate change, they are not adequate to the task by themselves. The willing cooperation of civil society and market actors and changes in individual-level actions are critically important to the successful implementation of the set of governance strategies that might have some prospect of being effective.

Ecosystem degradation

Like climate change, ongoing and fundamental alterations in the relationships between humans and ecosystems pose a complex set of challenges for environmental governance. Ecosystems and their services are the basis upon which human lives and all human actions are founded, thus it is not surprising that when examining human impacts on the environment, the Millennium Ecosystem Assessment (MEA) focused on ecosystem services. In this section, we draw upon this comprehensive assessment of ecosystems to pursue our arguments about changing forms of environmental governance. The Millennium Ecosystem Assessment (MEA 2005) categorized the range of benefits available to humans from ecosystems into "*provisioning services* such as food, water, timber, and fiber; *regulating services* that affect climate, floods, disease, wastes, and water quality; *cultural services* that provide recreational, aesthetic, and spiritual benefits; and *supporting services* such as soil formation, photosynthesis, and nutrient cycling" (MEA 2005, p. v, emphasis in original).

The Assessment concludes that human beings have altered ecosystem services more comprehensively in the past half-century than at any previous comparable period. Although these alterations in the relationships between humans and ecosystems have led to substantial net gains in economic development and well-being, 60 percent of ecosystem services are being degraded or used unsustainably. Not only are current use and management patterns unsustainable, they also increase the likelihood of non-linear and irreversible changes such as disease emergence, the collapse of fisheries, alterations in water quality, and regional climate shifts. Finally, the costs of ongoing changes are being borne disproportionately by the poor, thereby contributing to growing disparities.

To address these changes, the Assessment evaluates a range of potential responses, and focuses especially on those that would (a) lead to institutional changes and governance patterns that can manage ecosystems effectively, (b) align market incentives better with the real costs of environmental services, (c) focus on particular social behavioral obstacles to better utilization of ecosystems, (d) promote more efficient technologies, (e) provide better knowledge about what is happening to ecosystems, and (f) improve the efficacy of environment-related decision-making. Throughout the discussion of these responses, it is evident that the authors of the Assessment simultaneously define the terrain of environmental governance rather narrowly and extremely broadly.

On the one hand, they identify a specific set of responses – those having to do with institutional and governance-related changes – as properly the domain of environmental governance. Such responses would include the integration of ecosystem goals into existing sectoral strategies (for example, in the poverty reduction strategies encouraged by the World Bank), increased emphasis on international environmental agreements and target setting, and greater accountability of environmental decision-making.

On the other hand, they treat environmental governance too narrowly in restricting its scope to specifically institutional responses. In fact, the entire set of responses they identify in relation to markets, social behaviors, technological innovation, and monitoring capacity is contingent on changes in governance. Indeed, without comprehensive changes in contemporary national policies, the basis on which market exchanges are organized, and the incentives on which individuals act, there is little reason to think that the real costs of negative environmental outcomes will be incorporated into economic decision-making. Similar arguments are not difficult to advance in relation to desired technological changes, social behaviors, or cultural processes. Although we may, in part as a result of a particular division of social-scientific labors, view the world as being divided into economic, social, political, and cultural domains, shifts in human actions in all of these domains require a reconfiguration of the costs and benefits of given actions; in the absence of changes introduced through shifts in governance patterns, there is little likelihood that humans will change their economic, political, social, or cultural behaviors.

Precisely because of the social interconnections across what we view as local, regional, national, and global levels and what we categorize as the economic, political, social, and cultural domains, successful environmental governance strategies will require heightened cooperation of many different actors across these levels and domains. Thus, not only is it the case that human beings will be able to introduce manageable changes in ecosystems only through significant transformations in environmental governance strategies, it is also very likely that successful outcomes will hinge on environmental governance approaches that are founded upon heightened cooperation involving all actors in all three social locations identified in Figure 2: market, state, and community.

Conclusions

Our review of the changing terrain of environmental governance has emphasized four elements.

1. We suggest that environmental governance signifies a wide set of regulatory processes, not just international governance mechanisms and their impacts at the international level, or just the state and its agencies at the national and subnational levels. Along with the Introduction to this volume, we suggest that the emergence of multiple forms of governance is not only a fact, it is also necessary in order to address the multiform environmental problems and crises that beset societies in different parts of the world. Familiar forms of social and economic change, coupled with new types of social and economic interactions concomitant with globalization, faster developmental processes, and in many cases social confrontations and violence, make older modes of environmental governance inadequate. Even as state-centric governance regimes continue to be necessary to address many environmental problems, it has become crucial to imagine and create additional mechanisms and strategies that can do justice to the variety

of environmental difficulties that currently plague different human societies.

2. We highlight the hybrid, multilevel, and cross-sectoral nature of emerging forms of governance. Our review examines, in particular, how environmental governance has changed since the 1960s. From a focus on specific agents of change such as state and market actors, advocates of effective environmental management came to view communities and local institutions as important actors to be involved in governance. Especially in the past decade and a half, new sets of instruments of environmental governance have emerged. We identify three broad terms that denote these partnerships: co-management as the form of collaboration between state agencies and communities; public–private partnerships between market actors and state agencies; and social–private partnerships between market actors and communities.

3. We describe how emerging forms of environmental governance that have become increasingly popular since the mid-1990s rely on the one hand on partnerships, and on the other hand on the mobilization of individual incentives that is characteristic of market-based instruments of environmental regulation. Because they seek to gain the willing participation of a range of actors who would be subject to their regulatory effects, they are viewed by many observers as being more efficiently implementable. Once again, in focusing on the importance of partnerships and joint approaches to governance, our chapter re-emphasizes one of the central thrusts of the Introduction to this volume, which focuses on the increasingly important role of partnerships in environmental governance. Such partnerships are important, on the one hand, because of the opportunities for cooperation and collaboration they afford across the conventional divisions of state-market-civil society – divisions that have perhaps always been no more than analytical fictions. But, on the other hand, they are also important because they help to bring the significant capacities of new partners to bear on problems. For any given problem, civil society actors may not only bring an aura of legitimacy to the partnership but may also be able to act with greater flexibility in terms of defining goals and strategies. For the same problem, market actors may be more able to raise resources and create efficiencies than either state or civil society actors. Finally, state agencies may be able to act with greater authority and assertiveness. The coupling of these different capacities may be precisely the leverage needed to address environmental problems effectively in any given context. At the same time, it is worth pointing out

that partnerships inevitably require greater coordination, investments in building trust and social capital, and willingness to give up some of the functions that an actor may have treated as its own preserve prior to the partnership.

Greater efficiency in the design and implementation of environmental governance instruments is undoubtedly a major concern of state authorities, who may be under fiscal pressures and who may therefore find partnerships with market actors highly desirable. A partnership with private actors may also appear attractive to civil society actors and communities historically strapped for funding. However, a number of observers of changing environmental governance have raised concerns about the degree to which increasing recourse to market actors and processes undermines social goals related to higher levels of democratic participation, creates problems of unequal access to resources, and raises the specter of lack of accountability.

4. This chapter also explores valid concerns about the unanticipated consequences of emerging forms of environmental governance that have been expressed by important observers. An ethical concern for democratic participation and more equitable outcomes in environmental governance represents a welcome development as part of the emerging form of environmental governance that emphasizes collaboration across what were conventionally considered pure forms of governance: markets, states, and civil society. Nonetheless, an exclusive focus on greater efficiency in emerging efforts at environmental governance, especially where natural resources are concerned, may yield the unanticipated outcome of increasing the commodification of nature. The fact that human interventions in ecosystem processes are already leading to the unsustainable use of more than 60 percent of ecosystems suggests that, together with greater efficiency, it is equally necessary to work toward restraint in the human use of major ecosystems. The mobilization of individual incentives and their incorporation into innovative strategies of environmental governance are critical for efficient governance. However, effective environmental governance will additionally require the incorporation of knowledge about limits on the aggregate availability of environmental resources into strategies of environmental governance.

4

Self-regulatory institutions for solving environmental problems: perspectives and contributions from the management literature

ANDREW KING AND MICHAEL W. TOFFEL

Introduction

What role can business managers play in finding solutions to environmental problems? For many years, the business management literature proposed that managers could help their firms discover win/win opportunities that protect the environment while simultaneously increasing profits (Porter and van der Linde 1995b; Hart 1995). This is an attractive suggestion, for it implies that environmental protection can be accomplished with little pain, and that environmental problems are caused not by defects in our institutions but by failures in our insight or perception.

The literature on when it might "pay to be green" has advanced our understanding of how and when firms achieve sustained competitive advantage. What this literature has failed to do, however, is demonstrate that "win/win" opportunities will be sufficient to bring about meaningful environmental improvements. "I used to think that all we needed was a few managers to 'get it,'" remarked Matt Arnold, founder of the Management Institute for the Environment and Business. "Now I think that the problem goes much deeper."[1]

If managers who "get it" cannot find ways to profitably protect the environment, then, given the magnitude of today's environmental problems (UNEP 2002; Worldwatch Institute 2006), the rules of competition must be changed to make environmental responsibility more profitable. North (1991, p. 97) defines these rules, which he terms "institutions," as the "humanly devised constraints that structure political, economic, and social interaction." Institutions come in many forms: formal or informal, private or public, centralized or decentralized (North 1981; Ingram and

---

[1] Matt Arnold, personal communication with Andrew King, March 2, 2004.

Clay 2000). For-profit firms, the subject of most management research, are examples of private, centralized institutions. They are categorized as private because participants can choose whether to opt in or out. They are defined as centralized because they usually include an authority that sets and enforces internal rules.

When and why economic tasks are organized within a firm hierarchy as opposed to within markets (i.e., exchange between firms) is a classic and enduring theme in the management literature. The "theory of the firm" proposes that transactions are internalized in firms when particular features (e.g., uncertainty or specificity) are problematic with respect to market exchange, and the magnitude of the problems exceeds the disadvantages of organizing within firms (e.g., bureaucracy costs, "low-powered" incentives) (Coase 1937; Williamson 1985).

From its earliest days, this literature has had direct relevance to environmental problems. When the cost of negotiating and enforcing a mutually beneficial outcome is low, the theory goes, institutional controls are not needed (Coase 1960; Stigler 1989). Those who desire to protect a natural (environmental) resource can directly negotiate improvements with those who might harm it. For example, in the early 1990s, the nonprofit Environmental Defense Fund worked with McDonald's to help it develop and adopt packaging that caused less pollution.

When the costs of negotiating and enforcing such solutions are high, however, a single firm might take control of both the resource and the potential polluter in order to facilitate a better outcome (Coase 1937, 1960). For example, to help manage land as both a source of timber and a preserve for endangered species, International Paper and The Conservation Fund set up a new independent corporation to manage an important tract of land in Texas.

When neither negotiation nor firm control is feasible, governments can provide regulatory solutions to environmental problems. For many environmental problems, however, government lacks either the will or the authority to develop a regulatory solution. Pollution and invasive species do not stop at regulatory boundaries, much of our planet lies outside the territorial waters of any nation, and the earth's atmosphere is a commons shared by all. In a handful of instances, such as the Montreal Protocol regulation of chlorofluorocarbon (CFC) emissions, governments have coordinated regulatory solutions to important environmental problems. In some cases, governments have established non-binding institutions but have proven unwilling to add "teeth," even when faced with mounting evidence of their ineffectiveness. For example, Auld et al. (Chapter 7, this volume) describe how governments were unwilling to move beyond forming a non-binding international institution to address forest destruction despite evidence of its ineffectiveness in curbing defor-estation. Stringent, rigorously enforced international conventions are the exception rather than the rule, despite a plethora of transboundary and global environmental problems.

Can management scholarship provide insight into how firms might help resolve important environmental problems that lie within or span political and regulatory boundaries?

In the absence of government regulation, solutions to environmental problems might require that actors "self-regulate." Scholars have long been skeptical that, unmediated by a central authority, actors would be able to agree upon and enforce better rules of competition. Scholars from William Forster Lloyd (1833) to Garrett Hardin (1968) have employed "the tragedy of the commons" as a powerful metaphor for the problems inher-ent in self-regulation. Although each actor shares in the benefits derived from the conservation of common resources, each actor also directly profits by consuming more of the resource. Thus, according to Hardin (1968), "the inherent logic" of any commonly held resource "remorse-lessly" leads to ruin. The logic of commons problems can be extended to the self-regulation of any shared problem. As Schlager (2002, p. 804) observes, the mutual benefits afforded by self-regulation generate a new, "second-order," commons problem.

By cooperating and adopting sets of rules that coordinate use of and con-tributions to a common-pool resource, appropriators can solve the first-order dilemmas. However, the sets of rules themselves might be thought of as public goods. Once provided, they benefit all appropriators, whether or not all appropriators contributed to their creation. Appropriators are thus faced with an incentive to free-ride off the efforts of others who have attempted to resolve the first-order dilemmas.

Such a history of skepticism would seem to imply that self-regulatory institutions should be rare, but empirical observation suggests otherwise. Self-regulatory institutions exist in industries as diverse as accounting, electronics, computer software, agriculture, and banking (Furger 1997). Some of these, such as the Motion Picture Association of America's movie ratings system and the chemical industry's Responsible Care program, are well funded and visible.

Inspired by scholars such as Elinor Ostrom, Robert Keohane, and Oran Young, management scholars have begun to investigate prominent examples of self-regulatory institutions, with an emphasis on those that address environmental problems.[2] Early work in the business and environment literature sought simply to categorize the numerous sponsors of self-regulatory institutions, including corporations, trade associations, international organizations, and other stakeholders (see, e.g., Nash and Ehrenfeld 1997). Some, such as the Marine Stewardship Council, were formed through the collaboration of corporations and stakeholder groups (Reinhardt 2000). Others were created by international organizations such as the International Organization for Standardization (ISO). Programs developed by regulators, industry associations, and other nongovernmental organizations feature "almost equivalent program designs [regarding] environmental, administrative and conformance requirements" (Darnall and Carmin 2005, p. 84). These sponsors often seek and incorporate input from an array of stakeholders to enhance the legitimacy of the self-regulating institution (Carmin, Darnall, and Mil-Homens 2003).

Research on environmental self-regulatory institutions has both contributed to and drawn inspiration from research on self-regulation of other types of problems. Studies of knowledge-sharing organizations (Furman and Stern 2006), developer communities (Harhoff and Mayrhofer 2007), open-source software (Alexy and Henkel 2007), and interconnectivity standards (Farrell and Simcoe 2007) are, in concert with research on the self-regulation of environmental problems, advancing our understanding of self-regulation.

In this chapter, we review the growing literature on self-regulatory institutions for solving environmental problems. Our focus is on private institutions, which means that firms and other actors choose whether or not to participate. Many are decentralized, lacking a central authority that can administer sanctions. Scholars have examined the circumstances under which self-regulatory institutions that exhibit these characteristics arise, how they gain power and participants, and whether they are effective at influencing behavior.

Drivers of self-regulation in modern industries: when do self-regulatory institutions arise?

Many management scholars have been influenced by Elinor Ostrom's path-breaking work on the self-regulation of commonly held water,

---

[2] For excellent reviews of the theoretical and empirical literature on government voluntary environmental programs, see Khanna and Brouhle (Chapter 6, this volume), Khanna (2001), and Lyon and Maxwell (2007).

forests, and fishery resources (Ostrom 1990; Ostrom, Gardner, and Walker 1994). Several leading examples of self-regulation institutions over these types of commons issues, including forests and tropical ornamental fish, are described by Auld et al. in Chapter 7 of this volume. Yet, the common-pool resource problems that Ostrom studies are not immediately apparent in many modern industrial settings (see Khanna 2001). What might drive self-regulation in these industries? Some authors have tried to explain the emergence of self-regulatory institutions in industries that do not share a common physical resource by arguing that common problems can arise from interaction with other institutions or institutional actors. Other scholars have suggested that self-regulation might be a response to market inefficiencies caused by asymmetric information.

Common sanctions

Several scholars have argued that the blunt application of force by governments or stakeholders can create a shared fate that encourages collective action (King, Lenox, and Barnett 2002; Dawson and Segerson 2005). For example, if the decision to regulate an industry is determined by its collective performance, a classic social dilemma is created in which individual firms want others to improve but have little incentive to do so themselves (Maxwell, Lyon, and Hackett 2000; Dawson and Segerson 2005). A risk of common sanctions can also be occasioned by consumers' or activists' inability to differentiate between the performance of different firms. For example, the Earth Island Institute initiated a boycott of all albacore tuna even though some companies sourced from locations where porpoises were not put at risk by tuna fishing (Reinhardt and Vietor 1996). Auld et al. mention (in Chapter 7, this volume) how European retailers sought to shield themselves from boycotts opposing tropical deforestation by working with nongovernmental organizations to develop a certification and labeling scheme to differentiate paper and wood products sourced from sustainably managed forests.

A number of studies have quantified this industry commons problem by investigating how the behavior of one firm might influence the perceived value of another firm in the industry. Research has demonstrated, for example, that an accident at one firm can lower stock prices of other firms in its industry (Hill and Schneeweis 1983), and that recalls of pharmaceuticals and automobiles reduced the value of competitor firms in those industries (Jarrell and Peltzman 1985). The magnitude of this "common sanctions" problem increases the more similar the firms are (Blacconiere and Patten 1994).

Dawson and Segerson (2005) observe that the risk of common sanctions can drive the formation of self-regulatory institutions by helping to coordinate collective improvements that might forestall government regulation. There are many examples of firms coordinating to avoid increased regulation. The US rechargeable battery industry responded to a regulatory threat of landfill bans and end-of-life take-back requirements by establishing the Rechargeable Battery Recycling Corporation (Toffel 2004). After the US Environmental Protection Agency (EPA) proposed tighter regulations on their waste management practices, firms in the pulp and paper industry worked through their trade association to negotiate a voluntary agreement with the EPA (Delmas and Terlaak 2001). Seeking to pre-empt legislation relating to climate change, the US electric utility industry worked with the EPA to develop the Climate Challenge program (Delmas and Montes-Sancho 2007).

Hoffman (1999, p. 366) notes that major accidents and spills, as well as exogenous events such as the publication of Rachel Carson's *Silent Spring*, can change the perception of industries "suddenly and unpredictably." Hoffman and Ocasio (2001) argue that such events have greater impact when they violate existing norms and frames. Indeed, many prominent environmental self-regulatory institutions were born in the wake of accidents or controversies that raised the threat of common regulatory or stakeholder sanctions.[3] The threat of more stringent regulation following the Three Mile Island accident, for example, prompted nuclear power industry executives to create the Institute of Nuclear Power Operation, a "private regulatory bureaucracy" charged to "develop standards, conduct inspections, and investigate accidents" (Rees 1997, p. 478). Similarly, the Exxon Valdez tanker accident encouraged the development by the petroleum industry of the "Valdez principles," later renamed the CERES

---

[3] An example of another domain in which a self-regulatory institution emerged in response to the threat of common sanctions is the Classification and Ratings Board created by the Motion Picture Association of America "in response to a national cry for some kind of regulation of film content" (www.mpaa.org/Ratings_history1.asp, accessed April 16, 2006). Similarly, prompted by the perceived ongoing regulatory threat posed by Congress and the Federal Trade Commission, the three major alcoholic beverage industry associations operate under voluntary advertising codes that include guidelines for preventing the marketing of alcohol to minors. When the Distilled Spirits Council announced that it would end its 50-year-old voluntary ban on television and radio advertising, the beer and wine industries were concerned that the move would lead to more regulation of *all* alcohol marketing (Beaver 1997).

principles (Nash and Ehrenfeld 1997); a smuggled video of dolphins being caught and tortured on tuna boats provided impetus for the creation of the Dolphin Safe certification system (Reinhardt 2000); and the chemical industry developed its Responsible Care program following a deadly accident in Bhopal, India that spurred calls for increased regulation of chemical manufacturers (Gunningham 1995). With regard to the latter incident, Nash and Ehrenfeld (1997) described the threatened common sanction as follows: "The Bhopal disaster crystallized the *public's image of the chemical industry* as indifferent to environmental and safety concerns and as sealed off from public scrutiny" (p. 498, emphasis added).

Asymmetric information

Since Akerlof (1970), scholars have recognized that asymmetric information can cause a collective problem by creating an inefficient "market for lemons" in which only low-quality products can be sold. Such inefficient markets are a common cause of environmental problems because the environmental attributes of goods and services are usually hidden. For example, customers cannot determine by inspection whether or not the cotton in a pair of trousers was grown in an organic manner or whether a pound of coffee beans was grown under a natural forest canopy. Solving asymmetric information problems can improve the welfare of both producer and consumer. When an unobserved quality has an impact on the environment, solutions to inefficiencies caused by asymmetric information can also provide environmental benefits.

A commonly proposed solution to the problem of asymmetric information is for the party with superior information to make visible those expenditures that would only be rational if its claims of superior quality were truthful. Signaling models suggest that, on some hidden quality dimension, participants should perform better than nonparticipants.[4] A classic example is expenditure on brand advertising; such investments are thought to be profitable only to firms with higher-quality products that will generate sufficient rents to cover the advertising expenditure.

Signaling is particularly important in experience goods (for which some important attributes are unobservable before consumption) and

---

[4] Later in this chapter, we review the empirical literature that tests the signaling story by examining the extent to which environmental self-regulating institutions (a) attract participants that exhibit superior ex ante environmental performance, or (b) lead participants to develop superior environmental performance.

credence goods (for which some important attributes remain unobservable even after consumption). Environmental goods and services are often credence goods. Consider the two examples above: even after purchasing and "consuming" the trousers and coffee, the consumer will never be able to directly ascertain whether the cotton was organic or the coffee "shade-grown." In such cases, it might be possible to resolve information asymmetry only by creating institutions that send knowledgeable outsiders to inspect and certify characteristics that are unobservable at the point of sale (Darnall and Carmin 2005). Scholars have proposed that self-regulatory institutions that require changes in behavior as well as certification of these changes help firms to communicate unobserved attributes of their products or processes to customers (King, Lenox, and Barnett 2002).[5]

Sources of power: why do firms participate in self-regulatory institutions?

How environmental self-regulatory institutions gain the power to influence behavior has been the subject of much research. Why do organizations follow their rules rather than free-ride? Scholars' responses have emphasized two broadly differing perspectives: institutionalization and strategic interests. According to the former perspective, an institution's power derives from becoming "institutionalized" in social settings. Agent cognition and choice are thereby constrained, inhibiting opportunistic behavior. The latter perspective presumes organizations to continue to have the freedom to behave opportunistically, but to be constrained by self-interest from doing so. Management scholars have explored these two perspectives by way of investigating the factors that lead firms to participate in self-regulatory institutions.

Institutionalization

From the perspective of institutional theory, self-regulatory institutions represent pre-conscious or post-conscious constraints on strategic behavior. Pre-conscious constraints occur because institutions include taken-for-granted elements that create powerful schema or frames for

---

[5] Several examples of private certification schemes that govern forest management, coffee production, and the tropical ornamental fish trade are described by Auld et al. in Chapter 7 of this volume.

decision-making (Berger and Luckmann 1966). These elements influence what decision-makers perceive and what choices they consider. Post-conscious constraints "directly or indirectly divert design adoption away from the proposed dynamic in transaction cost economics (i.e., comparative efficiency) and toward the dynamic of legitimacy" (Roberts and Greenwood 1997, p. 355). Thus, institutionalism emphasizes "factors which make actors unlikely to recognize or act on their interests" and that causes "actors who do recognize and try to act on their interests to be unable to do so effectively" (DiMaggio 1988, p. 5). Hoffman (1999) argues, for example, that in the chemical industry, frames of perception evolved as metaphors of pollution shifted from being a regulatory compliance problem to a feature of corporate strategy and profitability. As shared frames of perception changed, responses included more strategic considerations, and firms' interactions with stakeholders assumed new forms.

A number of authors searching for evidence of the pre- and post-conscious constraints applied by self-regulatory institutions have investigated whether cognitive, normative, or coercive pressures lead organizations to participate in self-regulatory institutions. Delmas (2002, p. 91) concludes that they do, as she finds that "regulatory, normative, and cognitive aspects of a country's institutional environment greatly impact the costs and potential benefits of the ISO 14001 [Environmental Management System] standard and therefore explain the differences in adoption across countries."

Several studies have found that coercive pressures influence organizations to adopt self-regulation programs. Empirical studies have found firms' decisions to adopt the ISO 14001 environmental standard to be influenced by, for example, coercive pressure from wealthy local stakeholders, civil society, and customers in Europe and Japan (Christmann and Taylor 2001; Neumayer and Perkins 2004). Other authors have found that government pressure or support influences firms to participate in self-regulatory institutions (Rivera 2004; Rivera and de Leon 2004; Shin 2005; Chan and Wong 2006; Rivera, de Leon, and Koerber 2006; Short and Toffel 2008).

Researchers have also found evidence that normative pressure causes firms that participate in one self-regulatory program to participate in others. For example, several researchers found that firms that had adopted the ISO 9000 Quality Management System standard were more likely to adopt the ISO 14001 Environmental Management System standard as well (King and Lenox 2001; Corbett and Kirsch 2004; Marimon Viadiu, Casadesús Fa, and Heras Saizarbitoria 2006).[6]

---

[6] For an exception, see Melnyk, Sroufe, and Calantone (2003).

Recent work has begun to develop a contingency theory of institution-alism that explores why organizations subjected to common institutional pressures nonetheless participate in different self-regulating institutions. Hoffman (2001, p. 138) argues that such decisions reflect the interaction between institutional pressures and internal organizational factors such as "organizational structure and culture." In their empirical analysis, Delmas and Toffel (2008) found evidence of such interactions. They found organizations with corporate marketing departments influential on environmental matters tend to adopt ISO 14001 to distinguish their environmental status to customers. On the other hand, those with more influential legal departments are more likely to adopt government volun-tary environmental programs to distinguish themselves to regulators.

Strategic choice

The strategic choice perspective maintains, in sharp contrast to the insti-tutionalism perspective, that self-regulatory institutions represent nothing more than the outcome of strategic interactions. Drawing on the theory of cartels and clubs, scholars have developed many formal models of self-regulatory institutions (Barrett 1994; Dawson and Segerson 2005; Potoski and Prakash 2005b). In most of these models, actors propose rules for the group to which the group responds by deciding whether to participate and how to behave. In making these decisions, each actor considers how all the others will behave, and how different options will influence the deci-sions of other actors. By considering this process in detail, scholars iden-tify one or more equilibria in which each actor will be making the best decision (given what they expect everyone else to do). The "institution," as it is observed in business practice, is the expression of this equilibrium.

To empirically investigate the extent to which strategic opportunism drives firms' decisions on whether to participate in self-regulation insti-tutions, several authors have looked for standard signs of opportunism. These authors have predicted that programs without strict entry rules or robust monitoring systems will fall victim to "adverse selection." For example, participation in the chemical industry's Responsible Care program required firms to sign a paper "commitment" to adopt the program's principles and practices. Launched without any other entry requirement, without any required objectives or timetables, and with no monitoring system, the program suffered from adverse selection: participating firms tended to pollute more than comparable firms in the same industry (King and Lenox 2000). Studies of other self-regulatory programs with weak enforcement have also exposed telltale signs of strategic opportunism. For example, Rivera and de Leon (2005) found no evidence of superior environmental performance on the part of participants in a hotel "eco-label" program in Costa Rica. They also found the environmental performance of participants in the self-regulatory Sustainable Slopes program for ski areas to be inferior to that of non-members (Rivera and de Leon 2004).

Overlapping oversight by different institutional actors in the maritime shipping industry promoted the monitoring of conformance to that industry's self-regulatory safety institutions, according to Furger (1997), who explains that sanctions and rewards from insurance companies provided incentives to conform to agreed-upon standards. Self-regulatory institutions lost the power to control behavior, he observes, when market pressure and new industry entrants eroded these conditions.

The ISO 14001 Environmental Management System standard is one of a handful of self-regulatory institutions that impose a robust entry requirement – namely, third-party certification – as a condition of participation. A number of studies have suggested that organizations adopt ISO 14001 to signal their superior environmental management or performance. King, Lenox, and Terlaak (2005) found that firms obtain ISO 14001 certification to overcome information asymmetries that tend to be particularly acute when dealing with distant or foreign exchange partners. Welch, Mori, and Aoyagi-Usui (2002) found that decentralized organizations are more likely to adopt ISO 14001, which might imply that facility managers use adoption to signal to corporate officers the (unobservable) quality of facility processes. They also found that adopters are subject to more local regulation, which might imply that some organizations use adoption to signal to regulators their serious commitment to compliance. The extent to which these signals should be viewed as credible remains unclear: one empirical study found that, on average, organizations that adopted ISO 14001 exhibited superior environmental performance (Toffel 2006); another found no distinction between adopters and non-adopters (King, Lenox, and Terlaak 2005).

Others have looked beyond stringent monitoring to the threat of sanctions to mitigate opportunism. Lenox and Nash (2003), for example, argue that self-regulatory institutions that have demonstrated a serious commitment to expel noncompliant members are less likely to suffer from adverse selection. Their empirical analysis found that a forestry trade association's self-regulation program, which featured a credible threat of expulsion, attracted a disproportionate number of participants that exhibited superior environmental performance ex ante, but no evidence that a similar provision of a chemical distribution association was effective in such screening.

Integrating the two perspectives

A few researchers have begun to integrate the institutional and strategic perspectives. Jiang and Bansal (2003, p. 1047), for example, make an important distinction between participation in the underlying technical aspects of self-regulatory programs and the use of symbolic association with such programs. They find that "institutional pressures and market demand often motivate firms to adopt the technical aspects of programs" and that the tendency to seek visible association with the institution (e.g., by obtaining third-party certification) is driven by "task visibility and environmental impact opacity." King, Lenox, and Terlaak's (2005) empirical test of this idea in a larger setting corroborates these results. They found that different factors explained the propensity to adopt versus certify an environmental management system. Pressure from waste handlers encouraged adoption of the management system, whereas the need to communicate improvement to distant or foreign product buyers tended to lead to certification.

Empirical evidence of power: assessing the effectiveness of self-regulating institutions

As the long-standing skepticism about the potential for self-regulation has given way to a sense of possibility, scholars have begun to explore when and where such institutions can be effective. Early work expressed excitement and optimism that these institutions represented a general advancement in human attitudes and social organization. For example, Nash and Ehrenfeld (1997) concluded a major review of self-regulation programs by noting that:

> The human tragedy of Bhopal and the environmental disaster of the Exxon Valdez oil spill intensified public pressure on industry to change not just its practices but its underlying values. ... This review suggests that codes have culture-changing potential. Codes include elements that may be establishing a closer connection in people's minds between their activities and the natural world. Codes may also be increasing managers' sense of responsibility to surrounding communities (p. 525).

In the ensuing decade, a small but growing literature has examined the extent to which self-regulatory institutions are actually delivering on their promise to mitigate environmental damage. We review several program evaluations that investigate the implications of participating in particular self-regulatory institutions. These studies have focused on two types of dependent variables: process metrics such as the adoption of particular management practices; and outcome metrics such as pollution levels and environmental regulatory compliance. Researchers have focused on monitoring and sanctions as potential mechanisms for bolstering program effectiveness.

Early evaluations focused on the Responsible Care program, which lacked implementation requirements (it required only a "commitment") as well as monitoring and sanctions mechanisms. Empirical researchers found that participation provided "a poor indicator that any particular standard practices will be followed" (Howard, Nash, and Ehrenfeld 2000). Worse, the program apparently suffered from "moral hazard," as participating firms exhibited less environmental performance improvement than nonparticipants (King and Lenox 2000). Similarly, Rivera, de Leon, and Koerber's (2006) evaluation of Sustainable Slopes, another self-regulatory institution that lacks independent monitoring and enforcement provisions, found that, even five years after its inception, participants still had not overcome their initial deficit in environmental performance relative to nonparticipants.[7]

In contrast, evaluations of self-regulatory institutions that feature independent monitoring have found evidence suggesting that they facilitate performance improvement. Recent studies have found, for example, that plants that became certified to ISO 14001 subsequently improved their environmental regulatory compliance (Dasgupta, Hettige, and Wheeler 2000; Potoski and Prakash 2005b) and reduced their pollution levels faster than plants that had not adopted the standard (Potoski and Prakash 2005a; Toffel 2006). Another empirical evaluation found that plants that were certified to the ISO 9000 Quality Management System standard subsequently reduced waste to a greater extent than did non-adopters (King and Lenox 2001).[8]

---

[7] According to the US EPA, the program has "non-binding obligations" and "no consequences … if resorts do not employ suggested actions or do not report annually" (Rivera, de Leon, and Koerber 2006, pp. 202–3).

[8] For an exception, see Terlaak and King (2006).

Scholars have noted that some self-regulating institutions bolster their internal monitoring and enforcement provisions by operating in the shadow of the regulator (Rees 1994; Short and Toffel 2008). For example, Rees (1994) notes that the Institute of Nuclear Power Operation, a self-regulating institution created by the nuclear power industry, could support its internal sanctions with a threat to reveal noncompliance to the Nuclear Regulatory Commission. Indeed, Rees (1994) attributes the success of self-regulation among nuclear power plant operators to their ability to use the threat of sanctions from government regulators to discourage free-riding. Furger (1997) argues, in a similar vein, that self-regulatory institutions in maritime shipping could enforce compliance by revealing information to insurance companies or regulators. Only a few of the many voluntary environmental programs developed by government agencies contain provisions that impose a risk of penalties on participants that fail to obey the rules (Short and Toffel 2008).

Signaling models of self-regulatory institutions also suggest that participants should benefit financially. Because ISO 14001 has been adopted by relatively few facilities (at least in the USA), scholars have turned their attention to its close cousin, the ISO 9000 Quality Management System standard. Terlaak and King's (2006) finding that certification is associated with a moderate increase in production suggests that it helps to attract marginal customers, and Corbett, Montes-Sancho, and Kirsch (2005) found ISO 9000 certification to be associated with substantially higher financial returns.

Equilibrium models of cartel-like self-regulating institutions are much harder to test. Depending on the precise structure of these models, multiple equilibria might exist, and different static hypotheses can be generated. In general, however, these models suggest that (a) participants should benefit from participating, (b) nonparticipants should benefit from not participating, and (c) the institution should provide some welfare benefit to the participants (Barrett 1994; Dutta and Radner 2004). These models usually suggest, moreover, that the greatest gains should accrue to the nonparticipants, because as free-riders they appropriate the value without incurring any of the cost of the program. These expectations have been best explored in connection with the Responsible Care program. Lenox (2006) found that the program's creation generated dramatic financial benefits to most firms in the industry, and that nonparticipating firms benefited considerably more. Barnett and King (2006) found that the devastating chemical accident in Bhopal, India, created a common sensitivity to accidents such that an event at one firm would depress the stock price of another. They found evidence that Responsible Care reduced this tendency, but benefited all firms in the industry, not just the participants.

A theoretical problem for much of the research that uses economic models to explore self-regulatory institutions is that the evidence of environmental and financial consequences often seems to yield contradictory insights. For example, scholars have tended to argue that the Responsible Care program is a means of forestalling government regulation (Rees 1997; King and Lenox 2000). In that case, participants should improve their environmental performance because the program helps them cooperate to prevent regulation. But, as discussed earlier, the opposite seems to be true: the rate at which participants reduced their emissions slowed after joining the program. Financial benefits delivered by such a program might reflect the credulity of stakeholders who ascribe meaning to a program without a rational basis. Alternatively, studies that find adverse selection and moral hazard might have missed important variables of interest to stakeholders (e.g., accident prevention) upon which participants did improve.

Another problem for the literature is that the design of some self-regulatory institutions seems to provide conflicting incentives. Darnall and Carmin (2005) found that variability in the rules and mechanisms employed by self-regulatory institutions confuses the interpretation of participation. The great variation in a programs' objectives, design concepts, and rules leads them to suggest that stakeholders (or researchers) who lump programs together will tend to respond inefficiently to them. Terlaak (2007) observes that some programs actually contain conflicting design objectives, such as providing both useful best-practice guidelines and a means of distinguishing high- and low-performing firms. The problem, she notes, is that the worst firms stand to gain the most from the guidelines, which can lead to adverse selection. Such conflicting objectives, she reflects, can undermine the ability of such programs to identify organizations with superior hidden attributes.

Summary and future directions

Until recently, management research on environmental problems emphasized the search for greater efficiency within firms' hierarchies. This research agenda has begun to change in the light of growing evidence of limits to win/win opportunities and voids in state regulation. Management scholars are increasingly turning their attention to how firms can fill such voids with self-regulatory institutions. In this chapter, we reviewed the emerging management literature on these institutions.

For readers interested in practical solutions to environmental problems, the research presented in this chapter suggests that self-regulation should be taken seriously. Many firms have voted with their feet and joined prominent examples of self-regulatory institutions. Managers in these firms appear to believe that participating in these institutions will help them solve real problems. Initial empirical research suggests that some of these institutions might, indeed, help firms reduce market inefficiencies. Some appear to reduce asymmetries in information, others to facilitate coordinated investment in solutions to common problems. In the aggregate, the research reviewed reveals a world not of inevitable tragedy but of possibility.

But the research also reveals a need for caution in predicting the effect of self-regulatory institutions. These institutions derive their meaning and power from the distributed interpretations and choices of numerous actors. The intentions of the original sponsor might be modified or subverted, and their economic meaning might change over time. Some self-regulatory institutions might be little more than smokescreens deployed to prevent more effective stakeholder or government action. Others might provide incentives for real environmental improvement.

For readers interested in extending management theory, the research reviewed here demonstrates a need for more realistic models of human behavior. Neither undersocialized models of actors with unlimited strategic insight, nor oversocialized models of actors with little choice appear sufficient to explain observed behavior. The pursuit of individual gain plays a central role in the creation of these institutions, and determines how they are understood and used. Yet, the institutions do not appear to be the product of fully rational actors. Some observed behavior appears to be contradictory and inconsistent, outcomes appear to be off equilibrium paths, and the meaning of these institutions becomes both larger and richer than justified by purely economic rationale.

We are not suggesting that there is no longer a need for models of institutions that assume fully rational actors. Such models will continue to provide a valuable benchmark for theoretical and empirical study. We believe, however, that the research discussed in this chapter reveals that the most useful theories might assume that actors have limited ability to anticipate consequences or plan complex strategies, and derive predictions of institutional function from this basis.

We expect that models of self-regulatory institutions based on actors with what Ostrom (1998) terms "thin rationality" will pay more attention

to the history of the institution. The actors observed in our empirical analysis could not predict how institutions would be used, and might even
hold inconsistent goals. Participants could not always estimate costs and
benefits, either in the present or in the future. We look to models based
on actors with limited cognition to help explain observed regularities in
self-regulation. Why, for example, do sponsors often believe that the institutions they help create will play a different role than the one they eventually take? Why did several self-regulatory institutions evolve from more
lenient to more exacting forms?

We also recognize that the institutions reviewed here do not operate in
isolation. As noted in the Introduction to this volume, all of these institutions operate within the context of larger cultures or national regulations. Indeed, some of these voluntary institutions have been initiated
by government regulators more familiar with requiring behaviors than
encouraging them. Many regulators are now seeking to work in partnership with the regulated community in what Delmas refers to in Chapter
8 as "hybrid governance mechanisms," whereby firms are encouraged
to take more responsibility for monitoring their own performance (e.g.,
Short and Toffel 2008) and to perform beyond "compliance" thresholds.
Other governance institutions are fully private, yet perform functions
traditionally done by governmental actors including drafting and enforcing rules that bestow legitimacy. Models that incorporate agents with
limited rationality might help to explain how institutions interact. We
have observed that some self-regulatory institutions are given social or
political authority they do not appear to deserve. We wonder whether
cultural traditions and perceptions might explain why firms are sometimes rewarded for participating in programs that neither improve their
performance nor reveal hidden attributes.

Empirically testing new theories of self-regulation will be a difficult task.[9] Many of the studies documented in this chapter are case
examples that include numerous organizations but explore only a single
self-regulatory institution. We believe that such case research is important
and should continue, but that other research methods should be exploited
as well. Experimental research, in particular, might hold great promise.
Computer systems support the testing of strategic interaction in varying
competitive environments, enabling researchers to adjust regulatory and

---

[9] See Bennear and Coglianese (2006) for a review of empirical methods of program evaluation in the context of environmental self-regulatory institutions, including government
voluntary environmental agreements.

competitive conditions to explore when self-regulation occurs and where it functions best.

Many more questions can be formulated from the literature reviewed in this chapter. For example, to date, few researchers have leveraged the parallels and potential synergies between the literature on self-regulating institutions and research on eco-labeling (e.g., Mattoo and Singh 1994; Caswell 1998). This is particularly surprising, given that many eco-labeling schemes are themselves self-regulating institutions and have been subjected to a growing number of empirical evaluations (e.g., Teisl, Roe, and Hicks 2002; Tejeda-Cruz and Sutherland 2004). We believe that understanding can be advanced by analysis and empirical investigation of related institutional forms and empirical settings. For example, open-source software also includes a type of commons problem. Understanding how these problems are resolved will help clarify both the universal and unique aspects of using self-regulation to solve environmental problems.

Perhaps the most important contribution of the reviewed literature is that it provides the precedents for asking such questions within the field of management. Consideration of self-regulatory institutions is growing rapidly. Many of the scholars now studying self-regulation of standards, knowledge sharing, and open-source software development are drawing on the reviewed literature for inspiration in framing research questions and methods. We hope that the interplay among these studies will change the "state of play" within the management field, and expand our understanding of how firms can create effective institutions for protecting the natural environment.

PART III

The effectiveness of governance for
sustainable development

5

Transnational actors and global environmental governance

VIRGINIA HAUFLER

Introduction

The study of environmental global governance has stimulated increasing interest in the ways in which non-state actors contribute to governance through agenda-setting and rule development, monitoring, and enforcement. The interest spans a range of scholarly fields, including law, economics, political science, and business studies, as demonstrated in various chapters throughout this volume. Our theories of international cooperation and global governance are only just beginning to uncover the complexity of transnational politics beyond the state, even as the demand for governance rises (Rosenau 2000; O'Neill, Balsiger, and VanDeveer 2004). Magali Delmas and Oran Young, in the Introduction to this volume, point out that this increased demand comes at a time when confidence in traditional governing institutions is waning. Given this paradoxical situation, it is not surprising to find people pressing for action by non-state actors to supplement or replace action by governments – or for those non-state actors to step in independently to supply the public goods that traditional governments are unable or unwilling to supply.

Governance is a "social function centered on efforts to steer societies or human groups away from collectively undesirable outcomes (e.g., the tragedy of the commons) and toward socially desirable outcomes (e.g., the maintenance of a benign climate system)" (Young 1999a, Preface). We can view governance as an outcome of strategic bargaining among significant actors over particular issue areas or problems, in a process that is iterated over time, and that occurs within an institutional context (O'Neill, Balsiger, and VanDeveer 2004; Young, Chapter 1, this volume). In order to understand their interactions, we need good models of the actors, their strategies, their preferences, their identities – and their relative power. Existing scholarship provides us with strong models of cooperation among *state* actors, which is the basis for traditional environmental governance at the international level. But once we expand the view of governance to include participation by a range of public and private actors, we have much less understanding of the factors that facilitate or deter collective action among them. The hybrid forms of governance that are increasingly prominent in environmental governance at the global level include a range of actors in a multitude of combinations – from traditional inter-state organizations, to partnerships between myriad public and private actors, to purely private non-state forms of governance (see Auld et al., Chapter 7, this volume).

This chapter reviews different perspectives on the two most significant transnational non-state actors: business and nongovernmental organizations (NGOs). Recent research, particularly in political science, focuses on the preferences and strategies of non-state actors, how their internal organization affects their decision-making, and their relations with other actors.[1] The integration of non-state actors into studies of governance systems requires a more interdisciplinary perspective in which the work of political scientists, sociologists, and legal and business scholars is drawn together in fruitful collaboration. For-profit and nonprofit organizations are typically treated as very different entities, and in many ways they are. But organizationally they face many of the same challenges, are often motivated in similar ways, and select strategies that can lead them to cooperate in international environmental initiatives. Their long-standing contention, standing on opposite sides of environmental issues for decades, has led to both conflict and collaboration, in which each side contributes different functions to global environmental governance, given their different power, capabilities, and identities. Nevertheless, these two actors stand in different relation to the global political system, and their resources are very different. This leads them to play different roles in global environmental governance systems.

The following sections examine first the distinctions between state and non-state actors, public and private authority. The next two sections discuss corporations and then nonprofit actors, examining the ways in which their incentives and organizational structure can lead them to participate in global environmental governance, albeit in sometimes different ways. The two concluding sections address issues of power, role, and

---

[1] This brief overview does not capture the full range of the emerging literature on non-state actors in global governance. It is primarily intended to provide an introduction, from the perspective of a political scientist, particularly for those who are unfamiliar with recent research in this area.

identity and the way in which they influence the character of non-state participation in governance activities.

The actors in global environmental governance

In international relations scholarship, there is a long theoretical tradition of structural analysis, from the structural realism of Waltz to the socio-logical constructivism of Wendt (Waltz 1979; Wendt 1999). While these approaches provide us with an understanding of the context of world pol-itics, my purpose here is to explore the ways in which global environ-mental governance is shaped by the interactions among agents. In this chapter, I take an explicitly actor-centered perspective, focusing on the types of actors, their character, and their strategies.

An actor-centered perspective on world politics could examine a wide array of potential contributors to global environmental governance beyond the state – firms, industry associations, civil society organiza-tions, social movements, epistemic communities, intergovernmental organizations (IGOs), and subcategories of each. The main division we repeatedly see in discussions of new forms of governance is a bright clear line between state and non-state actors. Furthermore, in order to firmly place our discussion in the realm of global – not local – politics, we need to focus attention on actors with international reach. Finally, in order to understand the basic characteristics of these actors, we need to consider whether or not they can be treated theoretically as coherent wholes, or whether we need to take organizational structure into account. We need to answer three questions about the actors under study: (1) Are they pub-lic actors, or are they private? (2) Are they local or transnational in their reach? (3) Can they be treated as unitary actors or not? Each of these ques-tions runs into practical and theoretical problems that create barriers to theory-building and empirical testing. The actors we are interested in do not always fit into our neat categories.

Which non-state actors are public, which are private, and why does it matter? In ordinary discussion, it is clear where the line between public and private actors lies: governments and government agencies are pub-lic actors, and corporations and interest groups are private actors. Closer examination, however, reveals an array of actors that are difficult to define in these simple terms. Intergovernmental organizations, such as the United Nations Environment Programme (UNEP), are creatures of states, and thus are in some sense public; but, at the same time, they are not direct agencies of any particular state and can develop their own bureaucratic interests over time, so they could be viewed instead as autonomous non-state actors (Barnett and Finnemore 2004). Corporations are clearly private for-profit entities – except when they are not, as when they are owned by states and managed as public enterprises. The NGOs that are service organizations, contracting with governments, may become in some sense public actors, as they implement the policies of states (Townsend and Townsend 2004). Most people consider public actors to be authoritative, and accountable through some political process to large numbers of people subject to their authority. But nongovernmental actors may be able to attain some authority and become accountable to a constituency, although the particular lines of accountability may be contested (Cutler, Haufler, and Porter 1999). In general, we need to realize that the distinction between public and private actors is not always clear or useful, but it does provide a rough demarcation between types of actors.

Whether the distinction between public and private actors matters, however, is the subject of some debate (Cutler, Haufler, and Porter 1999; Hall and Biersteker 2002). We can describe both public and private actors similarly by establishing their norms, preferences, roles, and strategies. The traditional perspective on non-state or private actors, however, is that they are not really part of global governance. Only states have authority, and they only have authority over their own domestic affairs. Issues that cross borders can be governed, in this view, only by an exchange of cooperative commitments between states. Private actors can participate at the margins, but they are not central actors in governance. The central contention of recent scholarship, including this volume, challenges this perspective. Private actors do influence the negotiations between public actors but, more importantly, they directly govern in some areas. A treaty determining the allocation of rights and responsibilities among states regarding, for instance, emissions into a particular river is the paradigm for a traditional approach to global governance. The study of private authority allows us to see that an agreement among industry actors regarding rights and responsibilities with respect to carbon emissions is equally a form of governance.

Integrating private non-state actors into our models of global environmental governance introduces enormous complexities at multiple levels. You cannot simply "add actors and stir," as if this is a recipe in a cookbook. For one thing, these actors, unlike states, operate in more than one level or space; they are not territorially defined. Through partnerships, coalitions, and modern communications technology, even the smallest and most local organization can attain global reach today. A multinational corporation can be both local and transnational at the same time; an activist group can be rooted in a particular community while lobbying in international fora. Analyses of governance drawn from international relations scholarship, particularly regime theory, are bounded by a territorial conception of issues and actors, as Conca argues (Conca 2006). Global environmental governance may need to include the governance of local issues, and local efforts to supply governance may have global repercussions. Our mental map of where the different actors "belong" needs to be revised to take account of the increasingly de-territorialized forms that are a central element in globalization (Scholte 2000).

From an analytical perspective, we also face the problem that these actors cannot always be treated as if they are unitary in terms of motivation and policy. They are collective agents, with organizational dynamics that influence how they respond to their environment. In the field of international relations, scholars have begun to erase the artificial line separating domestic from international politics, opening up the "black box" of the state to explore how different aspects of domestic politics influence international outcomes (Rosenau 1997). The model of a "two-level game" in which states bargain with each other and, at the same time, bargain with domestic constituencies in an effort to create a winning set of options has become well accepted (Putnam 1988; Milner 1997; Milner and Keohane 1997). These models typically explore domestic political interests and institutions, and their influence on inter-state bargaining. For instance, individual state and local governments in the United States have negotiated pacts among themselves to address carbon emissions, taking action in a policy area where the federal government has not acted. This has implications for wider efforts to develop regional and global climate policies (VanDeveer and Selin 2009). To understand "the state," in other words, we need to include local and regional politics in our framework. To understand "the firm," or "the NGO," we must disaggregate in similar fashion.

This increasingly sophisticated perspective on the disaggregated state is only beginning to be adopted in the treatment of the other actors in world politics. Barnett and Finnemore (2004) took a step forward in developing an organizational perspective on IGOs, drawing on sociological literature. They argue that IGOs are not simply the outcome of inter-state bargaining. They have interests of their own, drawn from bureaucratic imperatives and internal norms such as rationality (Barnett and Finnemore 2004). Drawing on a principal–agent framework, Nielson and Tierney (2003) explored the ways in which the interests of IGOs may diverge systematically from those of the states that created them, due to the different incentives of the states (principals) and the staff of the IGO (agent) (Nielson and Tierney 2003; Gutner 2005; Hawkins 2006). For instance, within IGOs, different bureaus compete for resources, and individuals strive to pursue their own careers, which can undermine the achievement of the mission of the IGO as set out by the principals.

We need to examine the internal organizational dynamics and incentives of other non-state actors similarly. For instance, the principal–agent framework of analysis originated in the study of industrial organization to explore the differing incentives facing individuals in different positions within the firm (Tirole 1988). More recent research within business studies examines, for instance, the different political motivations and policies of subsidiaries and home offices (Blumentritt and Nigh 2002). We rarely see similarly disaggregated analyses of NGOs, although Cooley and Ron (2002) recently applied a principal–agent analytical approach to the study of humanitarian organizations. What these approaches tell us is that the motivations we ascribe to these organizations are more complex than we often take them to be.

The next two sections take a closer look at recent literature on firms and NGOs in global governance. In recent years, non-state actors have taken on governance tasks on their own or in partnership with others. In a surprising number of cases, particular issues have been addressed through collaboration between the private sector and advocacy organizations, despite long-standing conflicts between them. The emergence of these two sets of actors in the arena of global environmental governance has been particularly significant because it forces us to reconceptualize our understanding of global environmental governance. Some have referred to this in critical terms as the "new corporatism," referencing the cozy and institutionalized relationships among unions leaders, owners, and the state in many European countries. The rise of such alliances and partnerships may or may not be a positive step forward in environmental governance, as discussed in the concluding section.

Corporations and global environmental governance

The nature of the firm has been a subject of intense interest and debate across a range of disciplines and approaches for decades.[2] Here,

---

[2] Anti-corporate sentiment is a common part of the popular discourse, and many people automatically condemn big companies. While this aversion has many different roots, it is part of a larger antipathy to globalization and all its negative effects, which is seen to be benefiting corporate interests disproportionately.

I concentrate primarily on the firm as it relates to issues of global governance. Traditional business scholarship has only recently come to address this more political role for business. In international relations, particularly the subfield of international political economy, the private sector has often been treated as something that has no agency – it is "capital" and "capital flows" that structure the choices of states and other actors. The private sector has at times been analyzed as an instrument of foreign policy, as in the work of realists such as Krasner and Gilpin, or as an instrument of capitalists, as in the work of critical theorists exploring issues of dependency and development (Gilpin 1975; Krasner 1978; Cardoso and Faletto 1979). More recent scholarship explores sectoral- and firm-level interests and how they influence foreign economic policy choice, but without going inside the firm itself to explore the sources of its preferences, interests, and strategic calculations (Milner and Yoffie 1989; Rogowski 1989; Hiscox 2001).

Political scientists, like economists, generally assume that firms are rational actors, responding to narrowly defined profit motivations. Recent research, however, points to the complexity of interests and motivations behind firm-level decisions, and highlights the degree to which "profit" is a very flexible and variable goal (Fort and Schipani 2004). One cannot draw a direct line between "profit" and any one particular market strategy. One of the mostly widely adopted perspectives on the decision by firms to invest abroad is the "eclectic" model developed by Dunning. This incorporates three broad categories of considerations that go into the decision to move from international trade to international investment: organizational, locational, and internalization drivers. While all of these have something to do with profit-seeking, they interact in different ways for different firms (Dunning 1993). More recently, Crystal (2000) argues that the policy preferences of producers cannot be reduced to an analysis of economic returns. Policy preferences are, at least in part, a function of calculations about the costs and benefits of different policies, and the *political* likelihood of obtaining them (Crystal 2000). Furthermore, some scholars argue that both interests *and* ideas are drivers of corporate strategies. Many decisions involve value judgments, and not just expectations of profit (Sell and Prakash 2004).

The definition of the interests of the firm has been complicated in recent years by the extensive transnationalization and disaggregation of the global production process. The boundaries of the firm have become blurred through the widespread adoption of joint ventures, extensive transnational supply chains, and outsourcing. Much of the criticism of the corporation that we see in the popular press focuses on the inability of the company to govern its relationships with multiple suppliers in globally extended supply chains (Gereffi and Korzeniewicz 1994). This goes beyond traditional discussions of the degree to which headquarters or central management can monitor and control lower-level employees, since joint venture partners and subcontractors are not within the hierarchical authoritative control of one single entity. From a governance standpoint, it is becoming more difficult to determine how to govern corporate networks on a global basis. It is difficult to determine where accountability and responsibility lie within networks of production. Dunning refers to this as the rise of "alliance capitalism," in which firms are involved in complex relations of ownership, alliance, and competition, and the boundaries of the firm are no longer coincident with ownership (Dunning 1993). If the boundaries of the firm are determined by the reach of its direct governance, then we can say those boundaries become indeterminate under alliance capitalism. This characteristic of global capitalism is central to many debates about environmental governance today. Within these networks, key firms can set the standards that all other suppliers and partners must follow in order to maintain their place in the network.

This complexity is seen in contemporary debates over corporate governance. Different political systems have established different legal structures defining the relationships and responsibilities of shareholder-owners, management, and employees (Gourevitch and Shinn 2005). Some view the Anglo-American shareholder-dominant model of corporate governance as threatening to the more expansive stakeholder approach that typically characterizes European corporate governance relations. At the same time, even within the USA and the UK, the traditional model of corporate governance is coming under attack. This is in part due to the ethical failings notoriously seen in the collapse of Enron and in other corporate scandals. Some within the business community, both participants and academics, promote a "stakeholder" perspective in which actors outside the firm but affected by it – suppliers, local communities, the environment – have a stake in a firm's decision-making process (Donaldson and Preston 1995). All of this makes it increasingly difficult to argue, as Friedman famously did decades ago, that the interest of the firm is ensuring a return to its owners, i.e., profits (Friedman 1970).[3]

---

[3] Although most people remember the main headline about profits, Friedman was careful to say that the firm must operate within the laws and social mores of society. His central point was that the firm should not itself be making decisions about social goods, and that these choices must be made through a democratic political system.

The activities of firms bring them into contact with a wide range of actors, both through market interactions and increasingly through social and political contacts. Large multinational firms, in particular, are in constant interaction with a wide range of organizations and individuals, engaging in a kind of modern corporate diplomacy on a global scale (Haufler 2003; Hocking 2004). This is where we see the emergence of hybrid forms of global environmental governance, and voluntary action by companies that are responding to public demands for improved environmental performance (Khanna and Brouhle, Chapter 6, this volume; Auld et al., Chapter 7, this volume). The interactions that have produced these activities are often reflected and shaped by the discourse on corporate social responsibility. Corporate social responsibility involves voluntary action by firms that goes beyond complying with existing law, and seeks to adhere to higher standards and global norms. It is typically a response to threats by activists that may harm the corporation's reputation and affect a company's ability to sell its goods and services to consumers or attract investors to buy its shares. The adoption of corporate social responsibility strategies in the environmental field can be an effective political strategy in response to anti-corporate activism and the threat of government regulation (Haufler 2001; Vogel 2005). Voluntary action by corporations on environmental issues may reflect dominant ideas about the mechanisms needed to support further globalization at a time of significant backlash (Newell and Levy 2005).

In response to pressure from transnational campaigns, corporations respond both strategically and based on learning and values (Haufler 2003). Initially, when confronted by demands for a change in behavior – to clean up pollution or reduce carbon emissions – most companies stonewall and actively work against a change in behavior. This is the strategy most prevalent until recently on issues of climate change. But this strategy has, over time, become less and less effective. Many (though not all) companies have learned to be more proactive on environmental issues, gaining goodwill from the wider public consisting of both consumers and citizens. We see this demonstrated in the slow disintegration of the Global Climate Coalition, a business association which opposed early action to prevent climate change, and which lobbied against the Kyoto Protocol (Newell and Levy 2005). The environmental arena is one where companies have had to learn over time that some kinds of environmental action, such as waste reduction, can contribute directly to the bottom line. But the larger issues of environmental governance often do not have such an obvious "payback" for adoption. The incentives for action in these arenas cannot be based on the search for profit, but instead must be built up as a political strategy.

Companies sometimes respond to political pressure not through avoidance and stonewalling, but through forum-shopping strategies. Typically, on any particular issue, they will have a preference for operating in a domestic political arena, where they have more familiarity with and influence on the political process. This can lead to divergence in regulatory systems across multiple jurisdictions, which can increase the costs to global business. Instead, some companies may prefer to support international strategies of harmonization of regulation across national systems. In doing so, however, they seek out the most congenial international forum. When environmental management systems were first proposed, there was some fear among American companies that emerging European standards would become internationalized, which would disadvantage them. They sought instead to ensure that the ISO would be the preferred forum for negotiating what would become ISO 14000 standards (Haufler 1999; Prakash 2000). There is, as yet, relatively little scholarship on forum-shopping by corporations in international environmental governance, but this is an area ripe for more research.[4]

Voluntary self-regulation by companies, often under the label of corporate social responsibility, has provided a stimulus to the emergence of new forms of global environmental governance. Corporate social responsibility policies are a form of self-regulatory behavior, responding to concerns about reputation, the threat of government regulation, the costs of anti-corporate activism, and value commitments. It is, above all, a political response to contemporary pressures. Corporate social responsibility strategies can be undertaken by individual firms or through industry or business associations, and in partnership with NGOs, governments, and IGOs. This strategy involves the private sector directly in governance activities. They participate in establishing or negotiating standards of behavior, implement those standards, monitor and report on compliance, and in some cases undertake enforcement. Examples of self-regulation include everything from the commitment by BP to reduce carbon emissions at all its facilities worldwide, to the global "Equator Principles," in which hundreds of project finance banks voluntarily agree to common social and environmental standards for financing major projects.

---

[4] There is some emerging research on forum-shopping by states, particularly in the trade arena. Analyses of forum-shopping by corporate interests, however, remain rare and are often confined to European studies (Cowles 1998).

Corporate actors partner with NGOs and IGOs in a variety of environmental initiatives in a new governance "space" (Ruggie 2004).[5]

In an ambitious overview of how corporations are regulated internationally, Braithwaite and Drahos (2000) point to the variations that exist across time, sectors, and types of regulation. In general, there is little comprehensive global regulation of international companies that is backed by public authority and strict enforcement mechanisms. Instead, they conclude there is a variety of mixes of regulation and self-regulation, extensive learning of new norms over time, and the dominance of "soft" or voluntary forms of regulation in many issue areas. Any attempt to extend regulation internationally has been contested vociferously by states fearing challenges to their sovereignty and by firms opposing restrictions on their activities. Braithwaite and Drahos also highlight the role played by a number of international organizations in the global governance of business affairs. As Murphy (1994) has argued, international organizations from the beginning have served to further the interests of industrialization and globalization instead of countering or regulating them. However, Braithwaite and Drahos (2000) also point to the success of other actors – citizens, consumers, and activists – in restraining business. Their examination of the varieties of global business regulation lead them to conclude that the multitude of actors and mechanisms at play hamper any ability to model this effectively through a rational choice approach. Indeed, they incorporate Gramscian and constructivist notions about the role of ideas and norms into their assessment of the sources of global governance.

Research and theorizing about the role of the private sector in global governance has advanced significantly in the past ten years. We now know much more about the regulation of business, the emergence of private authority, and the business role in governance than we did in the past. At the same time, much of this research has not been pursued consistently, and no common models have emerged upon which to build a common research program. The most important lesson from this research, I believe, is that we need to move away from approaches that model businesses as purely economic actors pursuing a narrow form of profit. The policies and actions adopted by business – including

---

[5] There is a growing literature on public–private partnerships, with some, such as Reinicke and Ruggie, seeing great potential for them in providing a new form of governance outside the boundaries of territorial states, and others, such as Zammit, raising concerns about their legitimacy, effectiveness, and impact on other authoritative actors (Reinicke 1998; Reinicke, Benner, and Witte 2003; Zammit 2003; Ruggie 2004).

the decision to participate in partnerships and hybrid forms of governance – respond to a complex array of pressures: political, economic, and normative.

Civil society actors in global environmental governance

There is widespread acknowledgment that nonprofit NGOs have flourished in recent years. This has been particularly true in North America and Europe, where the majority are based. Most NGOs are active in local contexts, but there has been an explosion in the number of organizations that stretch across national borders (Anheier and Themudo 2004). Consumers, interest groups, activists, and their coalitions at local, national, and transnational levels have become important voices in different aspects of governance. Increasingly, NGOs – particularly the international ones (INGOs) – have participated in a variety of governance initiatives, particularly in the environmental field (Betsill and Bulkeley 2004). In response, scholars have begun to integrate INGOs into their models of world politics and global governance (Wapner 1996; Boli and Thomas 1997; Finnemore and Sikkink 1998; Keck and Sikkink 1998; O'Neill, Balsiger, and VanDeveer 2004).

The category "NGO" covers a wide range of actors: think tanks, religious organizations, media, activists, humanitarian organizations, etc. The major ones involved in global environmental governance are operational (or service-delivery), advocacy, and scientific NGOs (Princen and Finger 1994).[6] Operational or service-delivery NGOs are those that are directly involved in program or policy implementation. For instance, development or humanitarian NGOs are directly involved in supplying services to needy populations by, for instance, providing the resources for clean water or technical assistance for improved agricultural practices. They may also work on capacity-building within a country.[7] These operational NGOs work directly with governments and IGOs, and often operate under contract to public agencies. One of the most notable shifts in the delivery of foreign and humanitarian aid and technical assistance to developing countries in recent years has been outsourcing

---

[6] This discussion focuses on nongovernmental actors that are truly *nongovernmental*. In many countries, what appear to be NGOs are actually founded, funded, and formed by governments (Naim 2007).

[7] Brown distinguishes between service-delivery and capacity-building NGOs, but both are forms of program implementation and for my purposes are combined here (see Brown and Moore 2001).

by governments to nonprofit organizations as part of the "new public management" that has become popular. The delivery of public services through these private nonprofits may have many benefits, but this shift has not occurred without some controversy. Some observers note that the influence of these organizations goes beyond their immediate project-oriented mission and extends to influencing local politics in unintended ways (Brown, Brown, and Desposato 2007). The competition for contracts from governments and international organizations can often set up perverse incentives, as NGOs compete for attention and resources to the detriment of their mission (Cooley and Ron 2002).

Advocacy NGOs are engaged in policy influence, and do not generally get involved in implementing programs. These are the organizations most commonly referred to in discussions of international NGO influence. They are "groups of persons or of societies, freely created by private initiatives, that pursue an interest in matters that cross national or transcend national borders and are not profit seeking" (Charnovitz 2006). They are the modern agenda-setters, as they identify pressing public concerns and publicize them. They engage in negotiations with other public and private actors in order to shape the rules, norms, and regulations concerning the environment. When we discuss NGOs as organizations with preferences and strategic interests, we often think first of advocacy NGOs. They generally try to establish a more arms-length relationship with states and IGOs than other nonprofit organizations that contract for services. Advocacy NGOs represent a wide range of political interests and values, from extremely radical leftist organizations to those on the far right, despite the overwhelming tendency in the academic literature to concentrate only on the progressive ones. In recent years, more conservative NGOs have begun to participate in international debates and negotiations, gaining accreditation at the United Nations and engaging more directly with their opponents (Bob 2007).

Environmental issue areas are unique in the degree to which science and policy are brought together. The result is the high profile of scientists and scientific organizations in debates over environmental policy. Scientific NGOs present themselves as providing information in a different manner than advocacy organizations do – they produce rational, unbiased information based on scientific empirical investigation.[8] There is a rich

---

[8] All advocacy organizations also provide information, though they clearly do so in order to make a particular point. The value of the information they provide can vary greatly in terms of how biased and substantive it can be. Few analyses have been done of the quality

tradition exploring the intersection of science and policymaking, which I cannot do justice to here. What I am particularly interested in, however, is not science in itself but scientific organizations as organizations that participate in governance. What Litfin describes as "scientific culture" increasingly drives the policymaking process in global environmental affairs (Litfin 1994). Peter Haas, followed by others, has explored the role of scientific organizations in the foundation of "epistemic communities" of scientists and policymakers – groups that share basic understandings about causal processes in an issue area (Haas 1999; Gough and Shackley 2001). The influence of scientific organizations has generated a backlash in some quarters. Backstrand (2003), for instance, discusses the emerging debate over a "civic science," in which various citizen-stakeholders seek to increase participation in the production and use of scientific knowledge beyond the traditional scientific community.

The analysis of the strategies and tactics of advocacy NGOs has generated some of the most exciting work on international cooperation and global governance. NGOs have an array of mechanisms with which to pursue their goals. Broadly speaking, they can pursue individual campaigns to highlight an issue that is of particular concern to their organization; they can pursue coalition-building among civil society actors; and they can seek even broader cooperative arrangements that include working with companies, governments, and IGOs in multi-stakeholder partnerships. These choices about political strategy derive in part from their selection of whom to target or influence. They can also campaign *against* particular actors, exemplified best by anti-corporate campaigns that "name and shame" abuses by high-profile companies. Shell, for instance, will always be the poster child for abuses in Nigeria linked to the government decision to execute Ken Saro-Wiwa and other opponents of the regime. NGOs primarily target public actors, however, in an effort to influence policymaking. Effective campaigning targeted at the international financial institutions has led to increased integration of environmental concerns in decision-making in the World Bank, although with mixed results (Fox 1998; Gutner 2005). International NGOs lobby at multiple levels of government, and increasingly haunt the corridors of international organizations such as the United Nations and the World Bank, particularly regarding environmental issues (Nelson 1997; Raustiala 1997).

of NGO reports on important issues, though see Pegg (2003) for a recent overview of NGO reports on resource conflicts in Africa.

Some of the most important works on NGO strategies examine the creation of transnational activist networks (TANs), such as the now-classic work by Keck and Sikkink (1998). They propose a "boomerang" model in which local political blockages lead local groups to make connections with international NGOs, which then bring pressure to bear on the local government from outside the country. This boomerang model has been further developed and modified, incorporating variations on the boomerang that characterize a range of different issues (Khagram, Riker, and Sikkink 2002). Recent work on environmental issue areas examines the way in which the boomerang can lead to a backlash against Western NGOs. This is the case regarding efforts to protect the Amazon Basin, which have generated heated opposition from governments and local communities seeking to preserve their sovereignty and promote their own policy preferences (Kolk 1998).

The literature on transnational activist networks has been joined by work in comparative politics on transnational social movements. Environmental scholars began to explore the utility of the social movement literature in sociology some time before the latest phase of development in this literature in political science. Princen and Finger (1994), for instance, compared political bargaining and social movement models, and concluded that neither provides a clear picture of NGOs in environmental governance. But there has been a recent elaboration of social movement models using the idea of political opportunity structures, drawn from the field of comparative politics and now applied to transnational activities (McAdam, Tarrow, and Tilly 2001; Tarrow 2002, 2005; Massimiliano et al. 2006). Tarrow has developed an extensive model of social movement activism, and connected it to the political opportunity structure at the domestic and transnational levels. He argues that the institutional make-up of the contemporary world can provide openings for local actors to connect with international actors in ways that promote their strategic interests. They take advantage of these openings through a number of mechanisms: global framing, internalization, diffusion, scale shift, externalization, and coalition-forming (Tarrow 2005). Framing an issue in terms that resonate with global norms and values can provide links to international NGOs while at the same time, through internalization, may appeal to a domestic audience too (Stanbridge 2005).

Other scholars have begun to build upon these ideas to explore more thoroughly the agenda-setting role of NGOs. Most of the agenda-setting literature in political science has been developed for the domestic context, in which the institutional openings for establishing new agenda items are fairly well known. Only recently have attempts been made to model such agenda-setting at the international level. These analyses look at what issues become the subject of negotiation and debate at the international level, and which issues do not. Issues are strategically constructed, as Finnemore and Sikkink (1998) argue, based on techniques of framing and appeals to values and emotions. Agenda-setting models typically examine the character of the problem as one aspect of their adoption; for instance, issues of bodily harm, rights violations, and issues with short causal chains and someone to blame tend to generate mobilization and attention (Keck and Sikkink 1998). Problems are more likely to be adopted into the international agenda when they are congruent with existing moral standards, and when there are political entrepreneurs to champion them. Yet, certain issues do not emerge on to the international agenda, and do not become the subject of international NGO campaigns, despite their meeting these criteria. Carpenter argues that our existing models of agenda-setting do not adequately account for instances when an issue is ignored (Carpenter 2005).

In many cases, the focus is not simply on setting an agenda for policy-makers, but an even broader analysis of the emergence and adoption of new norms. The values at issue in policy debates reflect the underlying norms of different actors and sectors of society. Different NGOs compete for norm influence with other actors (Charnovitz 2006). Finnemore and Sikkink (1998) have proposed a norms life-cycle approach. Norms are promoted by entrepreneurs, who engage in strategic social construction in order to persuade others to adopt the same norms. Once adopted by sufficient numbers of people (or organizations), this stimulates a norms cascade, until that particular norm becomes widely socialized into society.

Some of the most interesting recent work on NGOs explores the self-interested strategies of NGOs, and moves away from treating them as somehow "good." Clifford Bob has furthered our understanding of civil society strategies by exploring the ways in which a campaign based on local issues "markets" itself to the world community (Bob 2005). In his book, he examines insurgents and secessionist movements and their efforts to manipulate NGOs and the media. He argues against the view of NGOs as entirely values-based, and instead reveals their need to engage in hardball politics in order to survive. Just as we can say there is now a "market for virtue" among corporations seeking to gain favor in the commercial market, we can also say there is a parallel market for virtue among NGOs competing for support (Vogel 2005). This raises issues not just of strategy, but of character and preferences. In a somewhat similar vein, Sell and Prakash (2004) argue that NGOs and corporations are similar, and that both types of organization pursue values-based and self-interested strategies. In order to probe more deeply, we may need to consider cognitive factors too in our exploration of NGO (and corporate) behavior.

The internal organization of NGOs has also become a subject of recent scholarly analysis. NGOs display a wide range of organizational forms, from highly bureaucratic transnational organizations to more amorphous forms, at the far end perhaps encompassing mass protests and spontaneous action. Just as a corporation faces internal organizational imperatives that shape its choice of strategies, so too do NGOs, particularly those with a highly bureaucratic structure. Cooley and Ron (2002) argue, in a piece on humanitarian NGOs, that they can be analyzed through a principal–agent model. This model has been applied to both political bureaucracies and commercial ones, but has not been applied to NGOs. They argue that the NGOs they examined suffer from conflicts between their need to pursue a particular mission, maintain fiscal stability, and respond to competition with other NGOs, including contracts for work, donor money, members, media attention, reputation, and value attainment. They conclude, in part, that the attempt to reconcile conflicting material and normative goals can produce a failure in terms of attaining their stated goals (Cooley and Ron 2002). The incentives of the agents of the NGO differ from the principals, in this case, due to the competitive environment in which they operate. This type of analysis of the organizational dynamics of NGOs, particularly of the larger and more bureaucratic ones, could be usefully applied to prominent environmental NGOs..

The study of NGOs has come a long way toward understanding these actors as politically motivated, and not just as moral or values-based organizations. We have a greater understanding today of the wide range of NGO actors, and the fundamental differences between, say, a contractual service organization and an advocacy movement. There are many points at which our analysis of both NGOs and firms looks very similar. And yet we cannot treat them as equivalent. They come to the table with fundamentally different resources and capacities, leading to different functions and roles in environmental governance. These differences are discussed in the next section.

Power and influence in global environmental governance

What is the relative power of firms and NGOs? This question forces us to think of the bargaining power between the two actors when they engage in negotiations that may establish the hybrid forms of governance that have become common in the environmental arena. We can expect that the distinctive qualities of firms and NGOs produce the variation we see in environmental governance forms today. Furthermore, even among firms or among NGOs, we can expect to see variation in the willingness and capacity of actors to contribute resources to the governance of specific environmental issue areas.

Power is, of course, a contested concept, and one that cannot be addressed in detail in this short chapter. We typically view firms as having material power resources that are unavailable to NGOs. They have assets that produce returns on their business operations, and they have access to capital markets to supplement their finances. They have organizational capacity that often outstrips that of most other international actors, combining the expertise and capabilities of a well-trained workforce. In some weak states today, a major foreign corporation – even a controversial one such as Shell in Nigeria – may be viewed as the only truly effective organization in society. Of course, this is only a general statement about corporate resources, and not one that is true of all corporations, no matter how large. Not all companies are profitable, and some cannot take advantage of financial markets. All large organizations can suffer from dysfunction, and a surprising number of firms manage to operate continuously despite flaws that should have eliminated them from the market long ago. The very employees that are a source of strength for some companies can become a liability if they pursue their own personal interests at the expense of the firm (as analyzed via the principal–agent framework), or more directly if they engage in work actions such as strikes and work slowdowns to protest against working conditions or other issues.

Firms also have another type of power that is simply unavailable to NGOs: structural power. As Charles E. Lindblom noted in his analysis of the "privileged position of business" in the USA (in *Politics and Markets: The World's Political-Economic Systems*, published in 1977), the owners of capital can shape policy outcomes even without direct lobbying or other actions, simply through their decisions about where and when to invest their resources. On a global scale, it is the modern multinational corporation that decides where in the world to establish new plants and thus stimulate economic activity. Because the multinationals have this structural power, governments may find themselves competing to attract foreign investors, and may be willing to make compromises on environmental issues in order to provide incentives. There is an ongoing debate today, not yet resolved, over whether we are witnessing a "race to the bottom" among government regulatory agencies, which would undermine the prospects for international cooperation (Vogel 1995).

One final corporate resource is both a source of power and of weakness: it is, after all, the corporations that are most directly involved in producing environmental externalities. Chemical companies pollute the land and water; agribusiness strips the soil of nutrients; power generation companies belch carbon dioxide into the air; and on and on. It is the behavior of corporations that must be changed if we are to have any ability to promote sustainable development policies in the future. Corporations are central organs in the modern production system that causes environmental harm. Their choices have direct influence on environmental outcomes. When thousands of companies adopt ISO14001 Environmental Management Systems standards, they can have a significant impact on environmental outcomes (Prakash and Potoski 2006).[9] When it comes to environmental governance, it is generally the firms that are the targets of NGO activism and government policymaking – and they are often perceived as being more susceptible to pressure than governments are (Spar and La Mure 2003). But it is also firms that have the expertise and information that could potentially resolve some of the problems we face. This gives them a certain degree of authority in setting international standards or designing and implementing environmental programs (Cutler, Haufler, and Porter 1999). In the eyes of some people, it is natural and inevitable that firms are both the "governors" and the "governed" in environmental issue areas.

The influence of NGOs on world politics, and environmental governance in particular, is undeniable – though often not measurable. Finger and Princen (1994) went so far as to argue that NGOs are now the key actors in environmental policy. The resources that NGOs bring to politics and environmental governance include information and expertise, the ability to raise the costs for other actors through their activism, and most of all their perceived legitimacy. They may not have much in the way of material resources, but their reputation is one of their most valued assets.

Although it may seem like a very weak resource, the research and information that NGOs provide to policymakers and the public have a significant impact on how an issue is framed and whether action is taken to address it. Nonprofit organizations conduct much of the

---

[9] ISO 14001 does not actually establish standards for environmental outcomes, and is instead a management standard. However, the widespread adoption of these standards indicates the degree to which firms take seriously the need to include environmental considerations in their decision-making.

research into environmental science, both within traditional educational establishments, and through think tanks and other organizations. Their work is viewed as more impartial than research done in the private sector, and therefore is often taken more seriously. NGOs are often a source of new and innovative policy ideas, or they may promote innovations developed by others that may later be taken up by governments and IGOs. For instance, carbon trading is a creative innovation in how governments approach the need to reduce carbon emissions; it was taken up by influential NGOs, and eventually by firms that saw it as an effective way to combine profit-making with sustainable production.

One of the critical points of leverage for NGOs is their ability to change the costs and benefits of action and inaction for other actors. In a positive vein, NGOs may facilitate the ability of states or IGOs to design and implement desired policies. For instance, Raustiala (1997) argues that NGOs can provide the following benefits to states in international environmental negotiations: policy research, monitoring compliance, serving notice when delegations are deviating from their charge, providing information to policymakers and the public about negotiations, helping state policymakers signal to constituents about the negotiations, and facilitating domestic ratification of an agreement due to their domestic influence (Raustiala 1997, pp. 727–31). Activist NGOs can also significantly raise the costs to businesses of "business-as-usual" through boycotts, shareholder activism, litigation, and protests. They have become increasingly expert in pursuing a range of campaign strategies against companies. Many of these efforts have been successful in provoking changes in corporate behavior. Some NGOs and firms have partnered in specific governance initiatives, ranging from the program between the Worldwide Fund for Nature (WWF) and McDonald's to switch to more sustainable packaging for food, to broader initiatives such as the Forest Stewardship Council.

NGOs are generally viewed as values-based organizations, which gives them a degree of legitimacy that corporations cannot hope to match. Charnovitz argues that the voluntary nature of most NGOs brings them moral authority, while others argue that their status and influence come primarily from formal or informal delegation by states (Cooley and Ron 2002; Charnovitz 2006). Some observers view NGOs as representatives of an emerging global society that brings to the forefront the voices of those who are unheard (Clark 1995; Boli and Thomas 1997; Charnovitz 2006). Still others, such as Braithwaite (2006), view NGOs as partners of government in enhancing the regulatory capacity of developing countries in ways that bypass the regulatory state, promoting a "regulatory society" model instead, in which NGOs and civil society help achieve the objectives of regulation in weakly governed states. However, their legitimacy can at times be tenuous. As noted by Cooley and Ron in their analysis of humanitarian aid organizations, the need to obtain financial resources can cause them to compromise their values in the competition for funding (Cooley and Ron 2002). In recent years, their rising influence has brought increasing criticism and demands for accountability (Brown and Moore 2001).[10] Streeten (1997) has argued that NGOs are not even very good at what they claim to be good at – they are not participatory, often depend on government support, and do not reach the disadvantaged people they often claim to represent. Others view them as unrepresentative and undemocratic (Anderson 2000). Nevertheless, in general, we can say that one of the main resources of NGOs is their legitimacy and moral authority.

The material and structural power of business organizations would seem to put them in a dominant position vis-à-vis NGOs. They have the resources to ignore the demands of activists, and have been the driving force behind globalization and the extension of capitalism internationally. Nevertheless, we can see the influence of NGOs in the very existence of hybrid forms of global governance, as discussed elsewhere in this volume. Corporations have adopted environmental policies and standards that they probably would have rejected a few decades ago. Both for-profit and nonprofit organizations participate in partnerships to address environmental issues. More significantly, the discourse of sustainable development – and not just environmental protection – has come to dominate policy discussions, as noted in the Introduction to this volume. Sustainable development entails a much broader set of interconnected issues that cannot be addressed by any one actor on its own.

The significance of non-state actors in global environmental governance

Global environmental governance today goes well beyond traditional inter-state agreements, treaties, and organizations. One of the most striking changes that we see is the degree to which non-state actors participate

---

[10] Brown and Moore (2001) argue that who NGOs are accountable to, and for what, varies depending on the character of the organization; e.g., service-delivery organizations are accountable to donors and regulators.

in every stage of the development of new governance initiatives. From a functionalist standpoint, we can say that NGOs are prominent in agenda-setting, norm development, and monitoring of compliance; while the private sector is more likely to be involved in rule generation and implementation. These hybrid forms include everything from major global initiatives such as the World Commission on Dams, to many variations of partnerships among different actors from the global to the local levels (Tully 2004). In Chapter 7 of this volume, Auld et al. bring our attention to the emergence of non-state market-driven initiatives as a distinctive form of global environmental governance. King and Toffel (Chapter 4, this volume) point to the importance of understanding self-regulatory programs undertaken by the private sector as a form of governance. Clearly, global environmental governance is not undertaken only by governments and IGOs, but by the efforts of a variety of non-state actors forming new networks of governance activities.

Different approaches to the rise of non-state actors take very different positions on the evolution and significance of their growing influence in world politics. They can be categorized as approaches that take a top-down approach, those that look at them from the bottom up, and an emerging organizational approach. The top-down approach derives from traditional international relations perspectives that view the state as the central force in global affairs. From this perspective, the rise of non-state actors is due to the permissive environment constructed by state actors. Some argue that non-state actors do not pose any fundamental challenge to states, while others argue that states derive benefits from the participation of non-state actors. Raustiala argues that it is states that stand at the juncture of domestic and international politics, and it is states that have the power to achieve the goals desired by NGOs. He detects a pattern in environmental negotiations in which states have played with only a subset of environmental NGOs and have established the terms of their participation (Raustiala 1997). We could say the same about the relationship between states and firms: it is states that establish the framework within which corporations operate domestically and internationally. In this perspective, non-state actors provide benefits to states that make them valuable partners in hybrid forms of global environmental governance. Some have looked upon them as a form of international corporatism, or a means for corporations to undermine the legitimacy of international organizations (Gereffi, Garcia-Johnson, and Sasser 2001; Zammit 2003). Others argue instead that they are an innovative means of addressing gaps in governance, and may even enhance state capacity. In fact, in Chapter 2 of this volume, Lyon emphasizes "governance failures" as a counterpart to "market failures." Nevertheless, alternative forms of governance suffer from a lack of genuine legitimacy and participation (Raustiala 1997; Ruggie 2004; Stern and Seligmann 2004).

A different perspective, prominent in sociological analyses of NGOs, looks at them as an expression of civil society that balances against both state and firm in setting the direction of the world polity. NGOs can form coalitions, networks, or larger social movements that influence the direction of policy either directly or through fundamentally altering our conceptions of appropriate action. In Chapter 3 of this volume, Lemos and Agrawal highlight the degree to which the interactions of various global actors are complex and embedded in civil society; in order to understand contemporary governance, we must integrate our understanding of all relevant actors instead of the common practice of emphasizing one or the other. Both business and NGOs are involved in adopting and spreading particular norms. Recently, there has been a spate of analyses of ideas diffusion, but most of this has examined purely economic ideas and has not been applied to environmental issues (Simmons, Dobbin, and Garret 2006). Although Boli and Thomas (1997) portray some business ideas as central to an emerging global society, these ideas are highly contested. Environmental values are held in opposition to business ideas, although there is an increasing attempt to find some way to make them more compatible, such as through the entire concept of sustainable development. O'Neill, Balsiger, and VanDeveer (2004) propose an "agency diffusion hypothesis," arguing that agency in world affairs is shifting away from states to the international polity. This is combined with a "transformative cooperation hypothesis," that through cooperation, domestic and international agents and structures may be changed in fundamental ways.

Finally, one important strand that has recently developed is to analyze both firms and NGOs within the framework of organizational theory. In other words, both actors can be analyzed with similar tools, since they engage in similar behaviors and may be driven by comparable motivations. While these actors are distinctive in many ways, they both must answer to organizational imperatives that may operate in a similar fashion.[11] The organizational approach does not make any large claims

---

[11] Interestingly, business scholars have begun to consider ways to integrate the study of NGOs into models of global governance (see, e.g., Teegen, Doh, and Vachani 2004).

about non-state actors and world politics, but it does highlight the need for us to disaggregate firms and NGOs, and look inside to see how their internal dynamics drive their choices of both strategies and norms.

The research surveyed here points to a number of areas where we need to continue to work on developing models and gathering empirical data. For the private sector, we need to continue the development of a more complex model of "rational" business behavior (Fort and Schipani 2004). Profit alone is not the main motivator of business activity at the global level, but is influenced by contention and contact with other actors. We still lack a common model based on an interdisciplinary understanding of corporate motivation. Coupled with this is a need to further research the political implications of the networked transnational enterprise of today, where responsibility and accountability for actions at the farthest reaches of the supply chain are indeterminate. Finally, we need to comprehend better the changing character and identity of the corporation itself. "Identity" goes beyond brand-name reputation to consider the ways in which corporations are embedded within society at national and global levels.

Despite the explosion of research on NGOs in recent years, there are still many gaps in our knowledge. We are only at the early stages of understanding the internal organizational dynamics of these groups. Furthermore, we need to have a better understanding of the inter-organizational dynamics of coalition-building and contestation among different advocacy groups. This has become more important as we see the emergence on the international stage of groups with a message that counters the norms of the groups that dominate Western media coverage.[12] In addition, given the emergence of multi-stakeholder partnerships among business, international organizations, and NGOs, there is still a dearth of theoretical analyses that go beyond the mere recounting of examples. We have no systematic understanding of the range and character of these new forms of governance, their functions and effectiveness.

The study of global environmental governance requires us to adopt an interdisciplinary and multi-method approach to explore and understand the transformations taking place today. At this stage, it is probably counter-productive to argue in favor of establishing a single common

---

[12] Clifford Bob's most recent research explores the international debate over the small-arms trade, focusing attention on the emergence of the National Rifle Association and pro-gun ownership groups in international fora, countering the overwhelmingly liberal bias in the study of NGOs (Bob 2007).

model or framework. The transformations in governance are not just tied to the changing role of the state, but to the accompanying changes in the roles and institutional structures of other political actors too. Just because there is no central governor does not imply that there is no governance, but the type of governance and who is involved in it is shifting terrain. Each issue may be governed by a variety of different mechanisms involving different groups at different times. The idea of governance as a process and not as an endpoint is central to the evolution of governance activity at the global level. This process involves heated debate over central values, including sovereignty, democracy, and accountability (Grant and Keohane 2005).

6

The effectiveness of voluntary environmental initiatives

MADHU KHANNA AND KEITH BROUHLE

Introduction

Voluntary environmental initiatives (VEIs) by firms are increasingly being relied upon to address major environmental problems such as climate change, toxic release reduction, waste reduction, and forest management, as well as to improve compliance with existing environmental regulations in the USA. These mechanisms for encouraging private governance have emerged as the capacity of governments to establish mandatory regulations to provide environmental protection has become increasingly constrained (Young, Chapter 1, this volume). We refer to VEIs as including voluntary programs established by regulatory agencies, codes of conduct designed by trade associations and third parties, standards for certification of environmental management systems set by the International Standards Organization (ISO), as well as self-regulation by firms who set internal standards, goals, and policies for environmental performance improvements. These VEIs aim to encourage firms to voluntarily reduce pollution, increase energy efficiency, adopt environmental management practices, and make other efforts to improve their environmental performance beyond the requirements established by existing regulations. More than 150 such initiatives have been sponsored by government, industry, and independent third parties in the last two decades (Carmin, Darnall, and Mil-Homens 2003). Voluntary programs established by the US Environmental Protection Agency (US EPA) alone have increased from twenty-eight in 1996 to fifty-four in 1999 and to eighty-seven in 2005 (US EPA 2005).

From the point of view of government agencies, environmental self-governance is more appealing than enacting mandatory regulations, because it reduces the administrative burden on regulatory agencies and avoids the delays inherent in enacting legislation, while encouraging a collaborative relationship between firms and regulators. Both regulators and industry organizations recognize that VEIs have the potential to allow for more cost-effective pollution control as compared with the traditional command-and-control regulations that are prescriptive and media-specific, because they provide firms with the flexibility to tailor their pollution control strategies to meet the needs of their operations. Additionally, VEIs enable firms to signal their commitment to environmental responsibility and mitigate public concerns about their environmental impacts while possibly pre-empting stringent environmental regulations. VEIs have therefore been enthusiastically promoted by regulatory agencies and industry organizations, and most VEIs have attracted a large number of participants. VEIs differ in their private benefits, such as the reputation value they offer firms, and the studies reviewed in this chapter explore the incentives for self-interested firms to participate in VEIs.

Participation in voluntary initiatives by a firm does not guarantee actual improvements in its environmental performance. Firms may avoid making any costly changes in environmental behavior and simply join a VEI to benefit from its reputational value. To overcome this incentive to shirk, a VEI can set goals or performance standards for participants and establish mechanisms to monitor and enforce the achievement of those goals by participants. VEIs differ considerably in the type of standards set – numerical or qualitative, performance-based or practice-based – and how compliance with those goals and standards is enforced. VEIs typically do not require public accountability and oversight by third parties or actual improvements in environmental performance, making it possible for firms to participate only symbolically to improve their public image, engage in free-riding behavior, and shirk their environmental responsibilities (Barber 1998; Gunningham, Kagan, and Thornton 2003; Macdonald 2007). We review the empirical evidence on the effectiveness of these initiatives in achieving improvements in environmental performance and the extent to which VEIs fulfill their promise of achieving social objectives and serving the public interest rather than simply the interests of firms.

Evaluating the effectiveness of VEIs in improving environmental performance of firms is a challenging task, primarily due to a lack of quantifiable data on performance measures impacted by these VEIs. Additionally, since the program participation decision is unlikely to be made randomly by firms, studies analyzing the impact of VEIs must include not only program participants but also nonparticipants in order to avoid sample selection bias, which arises when performance is evaluated for only a restricted, nonrandom sample. Program evaluation involves isolating the causal impact of a VEI on performance, and this requires controlling the unobserved factors, such as management support, that could influence both participation in a VEI and its environmental outcome. Since the participation decision is made endogenously (jointly) by a firm together with its performance decisions, disregarding that in empirical analysis results in a biased estimate of the VEI's impact. Program evaluation also involves controlling for other observable factors such as existing or anticipated regulatory pressures that could create incentives to improve environmental performance even in the absence of the program.

The purpose of this chapter is to look broadly at evidence on the effectiveness obtained from a wide range of studies on diverse VEIs in order to identify possible patterns of outcomes that can be linked to the attributes of the VEIs themselves. VEIs differ in the incentives they provide for participation, such as public recognition, and in the extent to which they require improvements in environmental performance. We identify the attributes of the VEIs that have implications for environmental outcomes examined here, and make inferences about the impact of the design of VEIs on their effectiveness.

A number of studies have focused only on analyzing the incentives for firms to participate in VEIs (see reviews by Khanna 2001; Lyon and Maxwell 2002; Khanna and Ramirez 2004). Among other factors, these studies emphasize the importance of regulatory pressures in motivating self-regulation by firms. VEIs are viewed by firms as a strategy to preempt tougher regulations, to influence future regulations, and to reduce the stringency with which existing regulations are enforced (Lyon, Chapter 2, this volume). Using a new institutional economics perspective, King and Toffel (Chapter 4, this volume) review the role of cognitive, normative, or coercive pressures in motivating firms to participate in VEIs. We review here some of the empirical evidence available on incentives for participation and their implications for performance outcomes. The empirical studies included in this review are those that (1) have used either secondary or survey-based data on performance and its determinants to analyze the effectiveness of VEIs quantitatively, (2) include both participants and nonparticipants in their sample, and (3) control for the possible endogeneity of the participation decision. We classify these VEIs into four broad categories: public voluntary programs, industry association programs, third-party initiatives, and internal self-regulation by firms. We identify differences in the attributes of existing VEIs across these categories and then draw more general inferences for the design of

VEIs that effectively motivate not only participation but also performance improvements.

The remainder of this chapter is organized as follows. In the next section we discuss the different types of VEIs and their characteristics as well as the different incentives they provide to firms for participation and their differing requirements for performance improvement. The following section discusses the methodological issues in evaluating the effectiveness of VEIs. The fourth section presents the findings of these studies with regard to motivations for participation, and this is followed by a discussion of the implications of VEI design for their effectiveness. The final section presents some concluding comments.

Voluntary environmental initiatives: key attributes

The environmental performance goals of the VEIs reviewed in this chapter, together with the findings of the studies analyzing the outcomes of these VEIs, are summarized in Table 6.1. Key attributes of these VEIs are summarized in Table 6.2.

Public voluntary programs

The public voluntary programs included in this review are the 33/50 program; the Accelerated Reduction and Elimination of Toxics (ARET) program for reducing releases of toxic chemicals; the Strategic Goals program, which addresses toxic chemicals from the metal finishing industry; the Climate Challenge program for reducing greenhouse gas emissions by electric utilities; and the Climate Wise program, which seeks to reduce greenhouse gas emissions from the manufacturing sector.

In this chapter, we examine the following studies that investigated the effectiveness of these programs. The effectiveness of the 33/50 program in reducing releases of some or all of seventeen toxic chemicals was studied by Khanna and Damon (1999), Gamper-Rabindran (2006), Vidovic and Khanna (2007), Innes and Sam (2008), and Sam, Khanna, and Innes (2009). The ARET program was evaluated by Antweiler and Harrison (2007). The impact of the Strategic Goals program on toxic releases was examined by Brouhle, Griffiths, and Wolverton (2009). The performance of the Climate Challenge program in reducing carbon dioxide emissions was studied by Welch, Mazur, and Bretschneider (2000) and Delmas and Montes-Sancho (2007), while that of the Climate Wise program in reducing fuel use was analyzed by Morgenstern, Pizer, and Shih (2007).

Table 6.1. *Summary of voluntary environmental initiatives and studies reviewed*

Voluntary program	Environmental goals	Study	Sample studied	Environmental outcome studied	Effectiveness of program on environmental outcome
Public voluntary programs					
33/50	33% reduction in releases of 17 toxic chemicals by 1993 and 50% reduction by 1995.	Khanna and Damon (1999)	123 firms in chemical industry for period 1991–3.	Aggregate releases of 17 toxic chemicals.	Statistically significant (−)28% (for 1991–3) relative to 1990 levels.
		Innes and Sam (2008)	319 firms from SICs 20–39 invited to participate in the program in 1991 with three or more years of complete data (1988–95).	Aggregate releases of 17 toxic chemicals; frequency of inspections under Clean Air Act.	Statistically significant negative impact from participation over 1992–5.
		Vidovic and Khanna (2007)	365 firms from SICs 20–39 (1991–5).	Aggregate releases of 17 toxic chemicals.	Statistically insignificant. 1% of estimated decline in 33/50 releases.
		Gamper-Rabindran (2006)	Facilities from SICs 26 (n=216), 28 (n=791), 33 (n=488), 34 (n=1043), 36 (n=358) and 37 (n=364) for the period 1991–6.	Aggregate releases and health-indexed releases of 15 toxic chemicals.	Statistically significant (−)51% and (−)95% in fabricated metal and paper sectors. Statistically significant (+)170% in chemical sector and (+)97% primary metals sector. Insignificant effect on other sectors.

	Sam, Khanna, and Innes (2009)	107 S&P 500 firms from SICs 20–39.	Adoption of Total Quality Environmental Management (TQEM) practices and aggregate and health indexed releases of 15 and 17 toxic chemicals.	Statistically significant 55% increase in probability of adoption of TQEM and statistically significant reduction in emissions due to 33/50 program (both due to direct and indirect TQEM adoption effect).
Climate Challenge	Reduction in utility's greenhouse gas emissions to 1990 levels by 2000; or a specified amount below the 1990 levels by 2000; Reduction in emissions per kilowatt-hour generated or sold to a specified level; Adoption of specific measures to reduce greenhouse gas emissions.			
	Welch, Mazur, and Bretschneider (2000)	40 largest electric utilities east of the Rockies between 1995 and 1997.	Change in emissions of CO_2, SO_2 and NO_x.	No statistical difference in the change of emissions of participants and non-participants. Also, some evidence that those utilities that pledged greater levels of reductions in emissions achieved fewer emissions reductions.
	Delmas and Montes-Sancho (2007)	133 investor-owned electric utilities between 1995 and 2000.	Change in CO_2 emissions per Kwh.	Early participants reduced emissions more than nonparticipants. However, when late participants are taken into account, changes in emissions between participants and nonparticipants are not different.

Table 6.1. *cont.*

Voluntary program	Environmental goals	Study	Sample studied	Environmental outcome studied	Effectiveness of program on environmental outcome
Climate Wise	Reductions in greenhouse gas emissions; encourage "lean and clean" manufacturing; innovative technology adoption.	Morgenstern, Pizer, and Shih (2007)	1,024 participating facilities (roughly 150 firms) and 65,008 nonparticipating facilities from Longitudinal Research Database between 1994 and 2000.	Cost of fuel; Total value of shipments; Electricity purchased.	In the first year after participating, firms achieve a statistically insignificant 3% reduction in fuel use and a statistically significant 5% increase in electricity purchased. However, after year 2, there is no difference between fuel use and purchased electricity of participants and nonparticipants.
Strategic Goals	50% reduction in water usage, 25% reduction in energy use, 90% reduction in organic TRI releases, 50% reduction in metals released to water and air (as reported to TRI), 50% reduction	Brouhle, Griffiths, and Wolverton (2009)	199 facilities in the metal finishing industry between 1995 and 2003.	Aggregate releases and health-indexed releases of toxic chemicals.	No evidence that emissions from participating facilities are different than nonparticipating facilities.

150

		in land disposal of hazardous sludge, 98% metals utilization, and reduction in human exposure to toxic materials in the facility and surrounding community.			

Industry association programs

Responsible Care	King and Lenox (2000)	Promote continuous improvement in environmental, health, and safety performance of firms.	3,606 facilities (approximately 1,500 firms) in the chemical industry (SIC 28) between 1987 and 1996.	Health-indexed releases of toxic chemicals.	Rate of improvement in environmental performance of participants was lower than nonparticipants.
Sustainable Slopes	Rivera and de Leon (2004)	Promote "beyond-compliance" principles that cover 21 general areas of environmental management, including expansion management, natural resource	109 western USA ski resorts in 2001.	Environmental scorecard grades produced by the third-party Ski Areas Citizens Coalition.	Participants receive lower environmental score-card grades relative to nonparticipants.

151

Table 6.1. *cont.*

Voluntary program	Environmental goals	Study	Sample studied	Environmental outcome studied	Effectiveness of program on environmental outcome
	conservation, pollution management, and wildlife and habitat management.	Rivera, de Leon, and Koerber (2006)	110 western USA ski resorts between 2001 and 2005.	Environmental scorecard grades produced by the third-party Ski Areas Citizens Coalition.	No significant difference between overall environmental scorecard grades of participants and nonparticipants. Participants score higher than nonparticipants in the area of "natural resource management."
Third-party initiatives					
ISO 9000	Possible complementarities between lean production methods and elimination of wastes or pollution.	King and Lenox (2001)	17,499 manufacturing facilities between 1991 and 1996.	Health-indexed releases of toxic chemicals.	Certified firms generate less waste and have lower emissions than non-certified firms.
ISO 14001	To improve firms' environmental and regulatory performance through the adoption	Potoski and Prakash (2005a)	3,709 facilities regulated as "major sources" under the US	Compliance with air regulations regarding	Certified firms spend less time out of compliance (approximately 7% or about 25 days per year) than non-certified firms.

and use of environmental management systems.	Clean Air Act between 2000 and 2001.	emissions levels and procedural requirements of operating permit.	
Potoski and Prakash (2005b)	3,052 facilities regulated as "major sources" under the US Clean Air Act between 1995 and 2001.	Health-indexed releases of toxic chemicals.	Certified firms achieve greater reductions in emissions (approximately 3% more) than non-certified firms.
Arimura, Hibiki, and Katayama (2008)	792 Japanese manufacturing facilities in 2003.	Self-reported performance measures of natural resource use (fuel and water), solid waste generation, and wastewater effluent.	Certified firms achieve lower environmental impacts regarding the use of natural resources, solid waste generation and wastewater effluent.

Table 6.1. *cont.*

Voluntary program	Environmental goals	Study	Sample studied	Environmental outcome studied	Effectiveness of program on environmental outcome
Firm-structured management practices					
Environmental management system	Integrate environmental and operational decisions.	Anton, Deltas, and Khanna (2004)	167 firms belonging to S&P 500.	Intensity of toxic releases, on-site releases, off-site transfers, and hazardous air pollutants.	Negative impact on intensity of toxic releases, on-site releases and off-site transfers for firms with high pollution intensity in past. Negative but statistically insignificant impact on intensity of hazardous air pollutants.
ISO 14001-type environmental management practices	Improvement in compliance with Mexican environmental regulations.	Dasgupta, Hettige, and Wheeler (2000)	236 firms from food, chemicals, non-metallic minerals, and metals sectors in Mexico.	Compliance with Mexican environmental regulations.	Increased likelihood of compliance.

The 33/50 program was established by the US EPA in 1991 to voluntarily induce firms to reduce their releases of seventeen toxic chemicals by 33 percent by 1993 and by 50 percent by 1995. The baseline level and goals for 33/50 releases were set with reference to the level of firms' emissions in 1988. A total of 1,294 firms (17 percent of those eligible) agreed to participate in the program. Among these, the firms that joined the program in 1991 and 1992 accounted for 61 percent of the total 33/50 releases in 1988. Similar to the 33/50 program, the ARET program targeted the release of toxic chemicals. Introduced by the Canadian government in 1994, this program aimed to reduce emissions of thirty "toxic, persistent, and bio-accumulative" chemicals by 90 percent as well as to reduce eighty-seven other chemicals by 50 percent by the year 2000 relative to a self-selected baseline level in any of the six years prior to the start of the program. The Strategic Goals program also targeted the release of toxic chemicals but focused on the metal finishing industry. The program was launched in 1998. It established several goals, such as reducing toxic emissions, lowering water and energy consumption, and reducing human exposure to toxic materials in the surrounding community by 2002. Performance achievements were measured relative to a 1992 baseline. Over the course of the program, 550 firms participated. The Climate Challenge program, started in 1994, was targeted toward electric utilities and gave participants the flexibility to choose from a number of actions such as reducing greenhouse gases to the utility's 1990 baseline level or to some specified level below that by the year 2000, reducing emissions per kilowatt-hour generated, or developing projects to invest in renewable energy and sequestration (US DOE 2002). At the end of the program in 2000, there were 124 utilities participating in the program, representing 60 percent of the year 1990 electric utility carbon emissions. The Climate Wise program was established in 1993 by the US EPA to encourage voluntary reductions in greenhouse gas emissions in the industrial sector through the adoption of energy efficiency, renewable energy, and pollution prevention technologies. At its peak, more than 600 firms, covering several thousand facilities nationwide, had enrolled in the program.

In the case of each of the five programs described above, it was believed that participants would identify win/win opportunities for emissions reduction that would be in their self-interest. Therefore, the programs emphasized pollution prevention or waste reduction as the preferred (but not required) method for pollution reduction, and thereby sought to demonstrate the potential for economic benefits through leaner and cleaner methods of production. To assist firms in identifying

Table 6.2. *Key attributes of voluntary environmental initiatives*

Type of VEI	VEI	Features of VEI			
		General characteristics		Regulatory environment	
		Numerical goals at program level	Adoption of certain practices or principles	Potential threat of regulation	Technical or information assistance
Public voluntary	1. **33/50**	Yes	No	Yes	Yes
	2. **Climate Challenge**	No	Practices	Weak and distant	Yes
	3. **Climate Wise**	No	Practices	Weak and distant	Yes
	4. **Strategic Goals**	Yes	No	Yes	Yes
Industry associations	5. **Responsible Care**	No	Principles	Possible	Yes
	6. **Sustainable Slopes**	No	Principles	Possible but weak	No
Third-party initiatives	7. **ISO 9000**	No	Practices	No	No
	8. **ISO 14001**	No	Practices	No	No
Firm-structured initiatives	9. **Environmental management system**	No	Practices	No	No

those opportunities that would lead to cost-effective emissions control, technical assistance via public workshops and information exchanges was common. The programs also expected firms to benefit from the favorable publicity that they would receive for reducing their emissions. After the release of the Toxic Release Inventory (TRI) in the USA in 1989 and the National Pollutant Release Inventory (NPRI) in Canada in 1992, the large polluters were subject to adverse publicity in the media (see, for example, New York Times 1991). The 33/50 program, the ARET program, and the Strategic Goals program provided these firms with a way of having their progress toward toxic pollution reduction recognized through a formal government-sponsored program that would attract broad

Table 6.2. *cont.*

VEI		Features of VEI				
		Market incentive		*Monitoring and enforcement by program sponsors*		
	Regulatory relief	External publicity for participation	Public disclosure of emissions by third party	Self-reporting of emissions / practices	Third-party auditing	Sanctions
1.	Potential	Yes	Yes	Mandatory to TRI	No	No
2.	Possible	Yes	No	Mandatory to 1605(b) registry and to US DOE	No	No
3.	Possible	Yes	No	Voluntary to 1605(b) registry but mandatory progress reports to the EPA	No	No
4.	Potential	Yes	Yes	Mandatory to TRI	No	No
5.	Potential	Yes	No	Optional	Yes[a]	No
6.	Potential	Yes	No	Optional	No	No
7.	Potential	Yes	No	Optional	Yes	No
8.	Potential	Yes	No	Optional	Yes	No
9.	Potential	No	No	Optional	No	No

[a] Third-party auditing for the Responsible Care program was adopted in 2002.

public attention. The early 1990s was also a time when climate change issues were at the forefront following the adoption of the United Nations Framework Convention on Climate Change in 1992. All of these public voluntary programs publicized participation by firms through their annual progress update reports, and through press releases, awards, and public events staged in order to recognize special efforts made by firms.

The Climate Challenge program gave utilities the flexibility to undertake one of the following actions: reducing greenhouse gas emissions to 1990 levels or a specified amount below the 1990 levels by 2000; reducing emissions per kilowatt-hour generated or sold to a specified level; or adopting specific measures to reduce greenhouse gas emissions. Utilities were required to provide a progress report to the US Department of Energy (US DOE). The Climate Wise program required the firm to develop a baseline estimate of its emissions of greenhouse gases for the year it joined the program, or any prior year since 1990, and provide a progress report to the US EPA. While the 33/50 program, the ARET program, and the Strategic Goals program specified numerical goals for the program, none of them required participating firms to make firm-specific numerical commitments for reducing emissions, although the 33/50 program and the ARET program did encourage firms to do so. None of the programs penalized or sanctioned firms (through adverse publicity or expulsion from the program) if they did not reduce their emissions. Thus, the programs sought to impose few costs on firms while providing firms with a great deal of flexibility in the extent of their participation and methods of pollution control. All five programs allowed firms to receive credit for any emissions reductions they may have achieved prior to the start of the program.

There were also some key differences between the programs. The US EPA stated that the 33/50 program was enforcement-neutral; participants would not receive preferential treatment of any kind in the form of relaxed regulatory oversight or enforcement of other US EPA regulations, nor would nonparticipants be subjected to special scrutiny. There was an implicit threat of regulation if voluntary actions were not fruitful in reducing releases of these chemicals. There were already some imminent regulations for some types of 33/50 releases. Air emissions of these seventeen toxic pollutants (which were included in the 189 air pollutants classified as hazardous air pollutants) had already been targeted for quantity limits under the provisions of the 1990 Clean Air Act. The US EPA was expected to set maximum available control technology (MACT) standards for these air pollutants by the year 2000. These MACT standards were to be based on emissions levels already being achieved by the best-performing similar facilities. By participating in the 33/50 program and reducing releases, firms could establish themselves as environmental leaders in the industry and shape the MACT standards to be set by the US EPA. They could also use the reductions achieved under the 33/50 program to qualify for the early reduction incentive provided by the Clean Air Act Amendments (GAO 1994; US EPA 2000). Additionally, two of the organic substances targeted by the 33/50 program were ozone-depleting chemicals – carbon tetrachloride and 1,1,1-trichloroethane (TCA) – that were targeted for phasing out by January 1, 1996 by the Montreal Protocol.

The ARET program also overlapped with different regulatory environments in Canada. In particular, one-quarter of the emissions in the base year of the ARET program also faced regulation under the Canadian Environmental Protection Act (CEPA). Furthermore, another 11 percent of ARET substances were undergoing review for potential regulation under CEPA when the ARET program was launched. In this light, firms may have had a greater incentive to participate in ARET and reduce emissions of these chemicals than they would have had otherwise (Harrison 2002; Antweiler and Harrison 2007). Similar to the 33/50 program and the ARET program, the Strategic Goals program was launched in the face of existing and possibly escalating regulations, and the program did not promise any explicit regulatory relief.[1] For the metal finishing industry, the key regulatory threat during this time was the Metal Products and Machinery Act, which was proposed in 1995.[2] This regulation sought to impose strict new effluence guidelines and pre-treatment standards for wastewater discharges from metal products and machinery facilities.

In contrast, the climate change voluntary programs offered possible regulatory relief; the programs offered the possibility that firms undertaking voluntary reductions would be rewarded with transferable credits to meet commitments under a future climate policy regime. A voluntary reporting program was established under Section 1605(b) of the US Energy Policy Act of 1992 to provide a mechanism for participants to quantify and report greenhouse gas reductions achieved through voluntary actions.[3] While there was a threat that market-based mandatory

---

[1] While the 33/50 program, the ARET program, and the Strategic Goals program did not offer explicit regulatory relief, it is possible that some participants in these programs believed that participation would offer the *potential* for regulatory relief either in the form of pre-empting future regulations or increased stringency of enforcement of existing regulations at some point in the future. Innes and Sam (2008) found empirical evidence of this in the case of the 33/50 program.

[2] The regulation is officially known as the Effluent Limitations Guidelines and New Source Performance Standard for the Metal Products and Machinery Point Source Category. The regulation was initially proposed in 1995, only to be resubmitted in 2001 and finally passed in 2003. Interestingly, the final form of the regulation exempted the metal finishing industry. Nonetheless, the threat of the regulation was present during the time that the Strategic Goals program was being studied.

[3] The Section 1605(b) program permits participants to decide which greenhouse gases to report, and allows for a range of reporting options, including reporting of total emissions or emissions reductions, or reporting of just a single activity undertaken to reduce part of their emissions (see www.policy.energy.gov/documents/Formatted1605bGeneralGuidelinesfinal.pdf).

regulations, such as transferable emissions permits, would be imposed in the future if current approaches were unsuccessful in achieving goals and if sound science justified further action to mitigate climate change, the threat was not definitive.

Moreover, unlike the climate change programs, information about the 33/50 releases, ARET releases, or toxic releases of the Strategic Goals program was publicly available for all firms (participants and nonparticipants) because they were mandated to report their releases of all toxic chemicals to the TRI in the USA and to the NPRI in Canada. In the case of the climate change programs, participants in Climate Wise (Climate Challenge) were encouraged but not required (required) to report their annual progress to the US DOE through the 1605(b) registry program. However, this registry was not publicly available and emissions (and reductions) reported were not facility-wide but project-specific. Firms participating in the climate change programs could voluntarily report information regarding their emissions, but they were not required to do so by a mandatory reporting system such as the TRI. Firms in the climate change programs, then, were not subject to the same public pressures as those participating in the 33/50 program, the ARET program, and the Strategic Goals program. Thus, the climate change programs differed from the 33/50 program, the ARET program, and the Strategic Goals program in the extent to which firms might have perceived the potential for forestalling tougher regulations and gaining stakeholder goodwill in the near term through participation.

Industry association programs

Two industry association programs whose effectiveness has been examined empirically include the Responsible Care program and the Sustainable Slopes program. The Responsible Care initiative was implemented by the chemical industry in the USA in 1988, partly in response to the Union Carbide accident in Bhopal and subsequent concern about possible future regulation. It is a set of guiding principles and codes of management practices to ensure that facilities operate in an environmentally responsible manner, protect and promote the health and safety of employees and communities, and prevent pollution. Responsible Care participants are allowed to use a registered trademark to promote public recognition. Participation is a condition for membership in the American Chemistry Council (formerly the Chemical Manufacturers Association). Prior to 2002, firms had discretion in the level of implementation of these practices, the level of resources committed, and the specific activities they undertook. They were required to self-report annually on implementation progress and, although the association encouraged third-party verification to confirm that adequate systems were in place, it had limited control over members' implementation of the codes, due to anti-trust rules (Maitland 1985). While it could revoke membership for noncompliance with the codes, in practice it relied on offering technical assistance and peer pressure to induce firms to implement the management codes. Its approach therefore resembled a "velvet glove, but no iron fist" (Reisch 1998). In 2002, the Responsible Care program was substantially modified to include an integrated management system, mandatory third-party certification, and required performance reporting to the trade association that would be publicly disclosed.[4]

The Sustainable Slopes program was established by the National Ski Areas Association in the year 2000 in response to criticism from environmental groups about ski resorts' impacts on air and water quality, wildlife, and sprawl. It promotes "beyond-compliance" principles that cover twenty-one general areas of environmental management. Participant ski areas are expected to implement annual self-assessment of their environmental performance, but no specific environmental performance standards have been established and there is no third-party oversight of participants. Program guidelines are non-binding, and if resorts do not follow them or do not report annually there are no consequences; they can continue to use the program logo for marketing and advertising. The number of ski resorts participating in the program has been increasing, and there were 178 participants, representing 36 percent of US ski areas, in 2005. However, the number of participants submitting the self-assessment survey of environmental performance declined from 52 percent in 2002 to 30 percent in 2005.

We review the findings on the effectiveness of Responsible Care (prior to its modification in 2002) reported by King and Lenox (2000) and on the Sustainable Slopes program obtained by Rivera and de Leon (2004) and Rivera, de Leon, and Koerber (2006). The former study examines the impact of the Responsible Care program on toxic releases, while the latter two studies examine the effect of the Sustainable Slopes program on an environmental rating or score given by a third party.

---

[4] See www.americanchemistry.com/s_responsiblecare/sec_members.asp?CID=1300&DID=4843.

Third-party initiatives

The International Standards Organization (ISO) established the ISO 9000 and the ISO 14001 standards to develop generic standards for quality management and for environmental management systems, respectively. ISO 9000 was established in 1987, while the ISO 14000 series of standards was launched in 1996. ISO 9000 is a quality assurance standard; compliance with it indicates the consistent use of standardized procedures to produce the product as specified and a greater likelihood of defect-free products. ISO 9000 standards comprise twenty quality system elements that include assessment of management involvement, leadership, trained work force, internal audits, continuous improvement, and proper use of statistical process controls (Anderson, Daly, and Johnson 1999). Third-party audits are needed to attest to a facility's compliance with the standard; certificates are issued for three-year periods, with biannual surveillance audits to assess compliance.

Unlike ISO 9000, which ensures product uniformity, ISO 14001 certifies that the management of a facility is environmentally sound. It requires a facility to establish an environmental management system (EMS), to undertake environmental auditing, performance evaluation, and life-cycle assessment, and to commit to continual improvement in their environmental management. Firms have to form an environmental policy, develop plans to implement an EMS, involve top management in reviewing and monitoring it, and take corrective action as needed. ISO 14001 is a process-based EMS standard and not a performance-based or technology-based standard. To join ISO 14001, facilities have to subject their EMS to third-party audits to verify that they meet the ISO standard. Following certification, they need to conduct annual re-certification audits to monitor their EMS. These audits require firms to document details of all environmental aspects of their operations, even if they are not required to maintain compliance with existing regulations.

Performance improvements for either of the ISO standards do not establish commonly acceptable quality or environmental performance indicators that could be used to track progress. Firms are only required to establish goals and measure and track quality or environmental performance, and managers have flexibility in setting their goals. For example, while some firms seeking ISO 14001 certification may specify goals to reduce pollution at the source, others may specify training workers who are handling hazardous waste (Kuhre 1995). By 1996 there were 6,838 facilities with ISO 9000 certification in the USA (Anderson, Daly, and

Johnson 1999). There were 3,553 facilities with ISO 14001 certification in the USA in 2003 (Darnall and Edwards 2006). Studies analyzing the environmental performance of ISO-certified facilities include those by King and Lenox (2001), who investigated the effect of ISO 9000 certification on the toxic releases of facilities, and Potoski and Prakash (2005a, 2005b) and Arimura, Hibiki, and Katayama (2008), who studied the impact of ISO 14001 certification on compliance with environmental regulations in the USA and in Japan, respectively. Johnstone et al. (2004) examined the effects of a certified EMS on the adoption of environmental actions to reduce environmental impacts.

Firm-structured management practices

Many firms are also adopting a non-certified EMS to systematically consider their impact on the environment and internalize those impacts in their operational decisions. These EMSs represent internally driven efforts at policymaking, assessment, planning, and implementation by adopting an interrelated set of management practices. The adoption of an EMS involves securing an organization-wide pledge to be environmentally responsible by establishing environmental policies and objectives, conducting environmental audits to identify opportunities for pollution reduction, and setting protocols to improve environmental management (Darnall and Edwards 2006). Anton, Deltas, and Khanna (2004) examined the impact of adopting a more comprehensive EMS on the toxic release intensity of firms, while Dasgupta, Hettige, and Wheeler (2000) examined the effect of the adoption of ISO 14001-type environmental management procedures on self-reported compliance with Mexican environmental regulations.

Measures of effectiveness of voluntary environmental initiatives

A seemingly objective and easily observable measure of the extent of environmental self-governance is the number of firms participating in such initiatives. A larger number of participants, particularly if they are also the firms with the largest environmental impacts, indicates that more firms are willing to commit to efforts to be environmentally responsible. However, participation in a VEI, while necessary, is not a sufficient condition for environmental performance to improve beyond levels that would have been achieved in the absence of the VEI. Defining participation may, however, not be as straightforward as it seems. Most studies that seek to analyze participation decisions or the effectiveness of participation rely on discrete measures of participation in a VEI. This does not capture differences in the extent to which these firms are making efforts to change their organizational behavior. Furthermore, environmental management practices that indicate efforts at self-regulation offer firms considerable flexibility not only in the extent to which they implement various practices but also in the number and mix of practices adopted. Studies of the motivations for adopting such practices have used the count of practices as a measure of the comprehensiveness of their environmental management system (Dasgupta, Hettige, and Wheeler 2000; Khanna and Anton 2002; Anton, Deltas, and Khanna 2004).

Measuring the impact of participation on an environmental outcome involves determining the change in that outcome that would not have occurred in the absence of the program. A before-and-after estimate of environmental performance of participants does not allow us to isolate the effect of program participation on environmental performance. This is because there could have been many other changes that were unrelated to program participation that could have occurred over the same time period and affected environmental performance as well. Instead, a with-and-without analysis is required to determine the causal effect of an initiative on environmental performance. This would be straightforward if the researcher could observe a firm's performance both as a participant and as a nonparticipant; the causal effect of the program would then be the simple difference between the two levels of performance. The challenge in evaluating the causal effects of environmental governance is to use the observed data, namely the environmental outcome for participants and the outcome for nonparticipants, in order to make an inference about the unobservable theoretical performance of participants in the absence of participation.

If firms are assumed to be randomly assigned to participate, or not, in a program/initiative, then there would be no systematic differences among the participants and nonparticipants based on any firm characteristics, and any difference in environmental outcome between the two groups could be attributed to program participation. In reality, however, a firm chooses whether or not to voluntarily engage in self-governance and its incentive to do so could, for example, depend on various characteristics, such as size, type of product produced, and the magnitude of the pollution problem it is dealing with. Some of these characteristics might explain both program participation and its environmental outcome. To the extent that the factors that affect both program participation and its outcome are observable (from the perspective of the researcher), then regression analysis can be used to obtain the causal effects of participation on outcome conditional on these observable (control) variables. This isolates the effect of participation by holding all the control variables constant. Alternatively, the researcher could create a matching sample where each participant is matched with a nonparticipant that is otherwise very similar. When there are many variables that need to be matched between participants and nonparticipants, one could use the propensity score matching method developed by Rosenbaum and Rubin (1983). A propensity score is simply the probability of participating, conditional on the control variables. Each observation for a participating firm is then matched with that of a nonparticipating firm with the closest probability of participating, to create a matched control group sample. The average difference between the changes in environmental performance of the participating firms and the changes in the performance of their matching nonparticipating firms is then estimated to be the impact of an environmental initiative.

These techniques, however, assume that the factors that influence both the participation decision and the environmental outcome are observable. Quite often, this may not be the case. For example, a manager's green preferences could increase the likelihood of a firm participating in a program and of it improving its environmental performance. If this is an unobserved variable that can be used to systematically explain participation and performance, then the propensity score method, as well as simple regression techniques to estimate program impact (by including program participation as an explanatory variable), would be biased because they would be unable to separate out the "manager effect" from the program effect on performance.

In such cases, researchers have relied on two other techniques to evaluate the effectiveness of environmental self-governance. The first is a fixed effect or a difference-in-differences estimator. The program effect is then estimated as the difference in average outcome for the participants before and after participation minus the difference in average outcome in the nonparticipants over the same time period. A comparison of the difference between the two differences is the program effect. This strategy ensures that any variables that remain constant over time (but are unobserved) that are correlated with the participation decision and the outcome variable will not bias the estimated effect. This technique thus requires repeated observations of firms. The key assumption of this approach is that the average change in the outcome is presumed to be the same for both the nonparticipants and, counterfactually, for participants *if they had not participated.* In other words, it assumes that the unobserved factors either do not change over time, or if they do, then they affect both the participants and the nonparticipants in similar ways.

In the event that it is not correct to assume that the unobservable variables that affect participation and outcomes have remained the same over time, then the appropriate technique is the instrumental variables method. This can be applied if a variable or an "instrument" can be defined and measured that is correlated with participation but uncorrelated with the unobservable factors affecting the outcome variable. Instrumental variable models are typically formulated as two-regression-equation models. The first equation is based on the notion that participation is a choice determined by comparing the expected benefits of participating and not participating, which specifies the relationship between the participation/nonparticipation decision factors. This model yields a predicted probability of participation for each firm (similar to a propensity score) which can be used as an instrumental variable in the second equation, which relates the environmental outcome to the participation decision and other explanatory variables that capture heterogeneity between firms. Alternatively, instead of using the predicted probability as an instrument, one could use the explanatory variables hypothesized to influence the likelihood of participation directly as instruments in the second equation. Identification of the effect of the participation variable on the environmental outcome requires that there is at least one explanatory variable that influences participation that is not included in the outcome equation.

To examine the effectiveness of environmental self-governance, we need reliable measures of environmental performance. The availability of publicly available data has limited the empirical studies reviewed here to a few measures of performance. These include toxic releases and pollution prevention techniques adopted to reduce toxic releases from the Toxics Release Inventory (TRI), carbon dioxide emissions and fuel use from the Federal Energy Regulatory Commission, and compliance outcomes with various environmental regulations, such as the Clean Air Act from the US EPA's Integrated Data for Enforcement Analysis System (IDEAS) database. While the TRI data suffer from the limitation of being entirely self-reported and covering only facilities that emit emissions above a reporting threshold, they do provide a panel dataset at a detailed facility and chemical level. Finally, data on other factors that influence environmental outcomes, such as production levels, innovativeness, and proxies for regulatory and market-based pressures faced by firms that create incentives for them to improve environmental performance also need to be included as control variables.

Motivations for participation in voluntary environmental initiatives

Environmental self-governance by firms challenges the view of the profit-maximizing firm as a passive organization that takes environmental regulations as given, is unable to appropriate the benefits of private abatement efforts or exclude others from benefiting from them, and focuses only on the cost of compliance; it therefore chooses to do the minimum needed to stay in compliance. There is a growing literature in economics that rationalizes "beyond-compliance" activities (that is, activities or performance not mandated by law) by profit-maximizing firms as being in the self-interest of the firm because it affects their markets and their relationship with the government. An environmentally responsible firm can influence market shares for its products, obtain higher prices for its products, and lower the costs of labor and capital (Khanna 2001). Even without any potential benefits via the market, engaging in environmentally responsible activities may still be profitable if these activities allow firms to delay, block, or alter forthcoming environmental regulatory threats (Harrison 1998; Macdonald 2007; Lyon, Chapter 2, this volume). Other explanations for beyond-compliance behavior are advanced by institutionalists, who believe that firms are affected by other social institutions besides markets and governments, and that they take into account the preferences of multiple stakeholders and not simply those of shareholders (Prakash 2000; King and Toffel, Chapter 4, this volume). The desire for external legitimacy, a reputation as a good environmental citizen, and the view that it is the "right thing to do" could also motivate firms to undertake beyond-compliance activities whose impacts on profitability may not be quantifiable using established methods. The impacts of such activities on conventionally measured profitability could, however, impose an upper limit on many beyond-compliance environmental activities of firms that might appeal to communities and environmental groups (Gunningham, Kagan, and Thornton 2003). The costs and benefits of undertaking these initiatives can be expected to vary across firms with different characteristics. They also vary across different VEIs, due to differences in the extent to which these initiatives may generate benefits and in the costs of participation. The next section presents empirical evidence from existing studies on the incentives for firms to participate in VEIs, and discusses the inferences that can be drawn about the impact of program features on participation decisions.

Participation in public voluntary programs

The studies reviewed here examine participation as a discrete choice, with the 0/1 participation decision as a dependent variable. In general, public voluntary programs generate incentives for participation to firms by providing public recognition to participants through US EPA newsletters and awards, by providing technical assistance on methods for pollution control, and through keeping the costs of participation low by not requiring external auditing and not imposing sanctions on firms that do not improve environmental performance (Table 6.2). While none of these programs explicitly offer regulatory relief from existing regulations or the potential to pre-empt mandatory regulations, they were established under the threat of regulation if voluntary actions did not succeed. In some cases, such as the 33/50 program and the ARET program, some of the toxic pollutants targeted by the program either were being phased out under other regulations or were already targeted for future regulation. In other cases, such as the climate change programs, the threat of regulation was weak and distant.

The importance of public recognition as a motivator for participation in public voluntary programs has been examined most directly by studies focusing on the 33/50 program.[5] The desire for public recognition is expected to be higher among firms that primarily produce finished goods and hence are in closer contact with consumers, or among firms in industries with higher advertising expenditure per unit sale and which are therefore more visible to consumers (Arora and Cason 1996; Khanna and Damon 1999; Vidovic and Khanna 2007). Such firms were found to be more likely to participate in the 33/50 program. The likelihood of participation was also found to be higher among firms that possibly had a stronger desire for public recognition because they were facing adverse publicity from previous boycotts (Innes and Sam 2008), published annual environmental reports (Videras and Alberini 2000), or were publicly owned (Gamper-Rabindran 2006).

---

[5] These include Arora and Cason (1995, 1996), Videras and Alberini (2000), Khanna and Damon (1999), Gamper-Rabindran (2006), and Innes and Sam (2008).

Studies on the 33/50 program, the ARET program, and the climate change programs show that larger firms in terms of size or amount of pollution, and therefore more visible (Arora and Cason 1996; Khanna and Damon 1999; Gamper-Rabindran 2006; Antweiler and Harrison 2007; Delmas and Montes-Sancho 2007; Morgenstern, Pizer, and Shih 2007; Innes and Sam 2008), and those belonging to trade associations and possibly facing peer pressure to improve environmental performance, were more likely to participate in these public voluntary programs (Khanna and Damon 1999; Antweiler and Harrison 2007; Delmas and Montes-Sancho 2007; Morgenstern, Pizer, and Shih 2007). The finding that firms producing larger volumes of 33/50 releases or other releases were more likely to participate in voluntary programs could imply that such firms had greater incentives to signal that they were making good-faith efforts to improve their environmental performance.

The public voluntary programs considered here did not explicitly impose costs of participation or enforce environmental performance improvements, and none of the studies directly examined the impact of this on participation decisions. However, one might expect that these costs would be implicitly lower for firms that had already achieved large reductions between the baseline year used for program performance measurement and the start of the program. For example, in the case of the 33/50 program, emissions reductions would be measured relative to those in 1988, although the program was not established until 1991. Most studies, however, did not find that the percentage reduction in emissions achieved prior to the start of the program influenced participation in either the 33/50 program or the Strategic Goals program (Arora and Cason 1995; Khanna and Damon 1999; Brouhle, Griffiths, and Wolverton 2009; Innes and Sam 2008; Sam, Khanna, and Innes 2009). An exception is the study of Vidovic and Khanna (2007), which found that firms who had achieved greater absolute reductions in emissions were more likely to participate in the 33/50 program. Studies also show that firms with a high ratio of 33/50 releases to all TRI releases have a statistically significantly lower likelihood of participating in the 33/50 program; this suggests that such firms may have anticipated higher costs or technical difficulties in finding alternative substitutes for these chemicals and of reducing their emissions (Khanna and Damon 1999; Gamper-Rabindran 2006; Vidovic and Khanna 2007).

There is fairly consistent evidence across the various public voluntary programs examined here that regulatory pressures were important in motivating participation. Regulatory pressures have been proxied by the stringency of enforcement of existing regulations and the threat of liabilities for Superfund sites (Khanna and Damon 1999; Videras and Alberini 2000; Vidovic and Khanna 2007). Innes and Sam (2008) and Sam, Khanna, and Innes (2009) also found that firms with higher rates of inspections in the past were more likely to have participated in the program, though Gamper-Rabindran (2006) found this to be the case for firms in the chemical industry only. Additionally, Khanna and Damon (1999) and Gamper-Rabindran (2006) found that firms in the chemical industry that had a high ratio of hazardous air pollutants to total toxic releases, and therefore faced a stronger threat of high costs of compliance with anticipated regulations, were more likely to participate in the 33/50 program. Firms whose emission stream was more affected by proposed legislation restricting emissions of several metals, and those located in counties that were out of attainment of air regulations, and hence potentially subject to stricter regulations, were more likely to join the Strategic Goals program. Utilities that incurred more regulatory expenses and were located in states with a higher legislative voting record in favor of environmental issues were found to be more likely to participate, to be among the early joiners, and to be more likely to develop ambitious goals and targets in the Climate Challenge program (Welch, Mazur, and Bretschneider 2000; Delmas and Montes-Sancho 2007).

Participation in industry association programs

Rivera and de Leon (2004) examined the incentives for participation in the Sustainable Slopes program in the first year of the program's existence (2001), while Rivera, de Leon, and Koerber (2006) examined incentives for participation between 2001 and 2005. King and Lenox (2000) examined the motivations for participation in the Responsible Care program.[6] These studies, like those above, estimated discrete choice econometric models to examine the factors influencing the likelihood of participation in a program. The studies found that the factors influencing participation are relatively stable over time. All three studies found that larger, more visible firms or ski areas, and those subject to higher levels of government oversight and other pressures for environmental improvement were more likely to participate. King and Lenox (2000) also found that "dirtier"

---

[6] Participation in the Responsible Care program is a condition of membership of the Chemical Manufacturers Association. Therefore, the participating decision of firms should be viewed in the context of the joint benefits and costs of both the Responsible Care program and membership of the Chemical Manufacturers Association.

firms, firms that had higher emissions relative to their competitors in their sector, and firms in "dirtier" sectors were more likely to participate in the Responsible Care program. Dirty firms or firms in dirty sectors may have more opportunities to address pollution and hence may have lower marginal costs of abatement. These firms may also have the most to gain from an improvement in their environmental performance.

Participation in third-party initiatives

The motivations for obtaining ISO 14001 certification were investigated, using discrete choice models, by King and Lenox (2001) and Potoski and Prakash (2005a, 2005b) for US firms, and by Arimura, Hibiki, and Katayama (2008) for Japanese firms. Johnstone et al. (2004) analyzed the incentives for European firms to adopt a certified environmental management system such as ISO 14001 or the Environmental Management and Audit System (EMAS). The likelihood of participation is higher among firms that have previously adopted ISO 9000 (King and Lenox 2001), possibly because of lower learning costs, and among larger firms. The latter could be due to economies of scale as well as the greater availability of human and financial resources. The costs of making the necessary internal changes in environmental management practices needed to obtain certification may also have been lower for firms that were always in compliance with environmental regulations. Potoski and Prakash (2005b) found that such firms were more likely to obtain certification. All three studies found that regulatory pressures are important in motivating participation. Potoski and Prakash (2005a, 2005b) found that frequently inspected firms and those that are either always in compliance or most frequently out of compliance were more likely to obtain ISO 14001 certification. Such firms could be seeking certification to signal to regulators their efforts at becoming, or remaining, environmentally responsible. Arimura, Hibiki, and Katayama (2008) found that firms facing a performance standard are more likely to seek certification, particularly if offered assistance by regulatory authorities. They also found that Japanese facilities with international links either in terms of ownership structure or sales markets are more likely to seek ISO 14001 certification. Johnstone et al. (2004) found that firms with an environmental management department and a larger firm size are more likely to have an environmental management system. None of these studies directly examined the incentives to obtain certification to credibly signal environmental responsibility to customers and to differentiate their products.

Participation in firm-structured initiatives

Anton, Deltas, and Khanna (2004) and Dasgupta, Hettige, and Wheeler (2000) examined the motivations for adopting a more comprehensive environmental management system using a count of practices adopted (such as having an environmental policy, total quality environmental management, environmental reporting, and self-auditing) and an adoption score scaled 0–100 to index the completeness of plants' EMS (such as having procedures to prioritize objectives, review, plan, implement, and measure performance), respectively. These studies show the importance of inspections, regulatory policies, and the threat of liabilities for Superfund sites in motivating the adoption of environmental management practices. Anton, Deltas, and Khanna (2004) also found that firms producing final goods, particularly if they are small polluters, are more likely to adopt a more comprehensive EMS. Dasgupta, Hettige, and Wheeler (2000) also note that more comprehensive EMS adoption is positively related to larger, multidivisional firms, and firms with higher levels of worker education.

The studies reviewed above suggest that several factors that motivate participation in VEIs are common across different types of programs. In particular, it appears that regulatory pressures, costs of participation, firm size, and external benefits of participation are important determinants of participation across most VEIs. Firms facing a stronger threat of enforcement of current regulations or higher costs of anticipated regulations or environmental liabilities are more likely to participate in a VEI. Larger (dirtier) firms are found to be more likely to join VEIs, suggesting the importance of the availability of internal resources to participate in VEIs and the larger potential gain to reputations by demonstrating good-faith efforts to improve environmental performance. While the findings on regulatory environment and firm size are consistent across different types of VEIs, other influences are more clearly highlighted within a given type of VEI. Public recognition, for example, was found to play a key role in several public voluntary programs, especially the 33/50 program.

Effectiveness of voluntary environmental initiatives

Early voluntary environmental initiatives such as the 33/50 program and the ARET program are often touted as success stories by government regulators. The US EPA, for example, points out that the 33/50's goal of a reduction in emissions by 50 percent was achieved one year prior to the target date. Similarly, the ARET program's goal of a 50 percent reduction in eighty-seven substances was met three years prior to its target date. While commendable, it is clear that not all of these emissions reductions can be credited to the voluntary programs. In both cases, overall emissions in the industry as a whole were falling during the time period in question.[7] In addition, the lenient guidelines that allowed firms to baseline their emissions prior to the start of the program (three years in the case of the 33/50 program and up to six years in the case of the ARET program) allowed the programs to take more credit for emissions reductions than they deserved. For the ARET program, roughly half of the reductions attributed to the program were achieved before the program was even announced.

While emissions reductions may have been overstated, it is still possible that the voluntary environmental initiative encouraged participants to reduce pollution more than nonparticipants. Several studies have examined this issue in regard to the 33/50 program and have found that the impact of the program varied across industry sectors and samples. Khanna and Damon (1999) found that program participation led to a statistically significant decline in the 33/50 releases of a sample of publicly traded firms from the chemical industry over the period 1988–93. They estimated that the program led to an expected reduction of 28 percent in 33/50 releases over the period 1991–3, relative to the pre-program level of releases in 1990. The study also found that program participation had a significant negative impact on emissions to all major media to which they were discharged: air, land, water, and disposal facilities. This suggests that the design of the program, which was not media-specific, encouraged integrated environmental management and reduction in total emissions and did not create incentives for cross-media substitution. The study found that program participation had a negative impact on releases of other TRI chemicals but it was less significant than on 33/50 releases, suggesting that program participation had scope effects that led to a reduction in releases of other chemicals as well.[8]

---

[7] Several papers suggest that stricter regulatory environments in the USA and Canada led to lower emissions during this time. As discussed earlier in the chapter, several substances targeted in the 33/50 program faced new regulations under the provisions of the 1990 Clean Air Act. With regard to the ARET program, new federal and provincial regulations appear to have encouraged large emissions reductions, especially in the pulp and paper industry (Antweiler and Harrison 2007).

[8] They also found that large and increasing potential liabilities under the Superfund Act and costs of compliance with the proposed NESHAP standards had statistically

Gamper-Rabindran (2006) analyzed the change in releases due to the 33/50 program over the period 1990–6 using data for all facilities eligible to participate in the 33/50 program that are covered by the Clean Air Act reporting requirements. Only fifteen of the seventeen program chemicals were included in the analysis, excluding the two ozone-depleting chemicals whose phase-out was mandated by the Clean Air Act. Industry-specific analysis showed that the impact of the program varied across sectors: the program led to a statistically significant reduction in releases in the paper and fabricated metals sector only, while it led to significant increases in releases in the chemicals and primary metals sector. The effects of the program on releases from the electric, transport, rubber, and stone sectors were statistically insignificant. Releases in the fabricated metals sector fell by 50 percent of participants' pre-program emissions, while in the paper industry the corresponding decrease was by 95 percent. The program led to a 170 percent increase in releases from the chemical industry and a 95 percent increase in releases from the primary metals industry. The effects of the program on toxicity-weighted releases were found to be similar. Additionally, the program was found to have led to an increase in toxicity-weighted off-site transfers to recycling in all industries except the primary metals, chemical, and transport industries over the 1991–5 period.[9]

Innes and Sam (2008) examined the effect of the 33/50 program on releases and on the frequency of inspections of firms from seven different two-digit SIC codes that were invited to participate in the 33/50 program in 1991. Using data for 1989–95, they examined the impact of the program on 33/50 releases from 1992 onwards.[10] They found that program participation did lower 33/50 releases starting in 1992 and that

significant deterrent effects on the level of 33/50 releases generated by a firm. The level of 33/50 releases was found to be positively affected by the volume of sales and negatively by the sales per unit assets ratio, a measure of the idle capacity in a firm. Firms with newer assets, or those with a high rate of asset replacement, have lower 33/50 releases.

[9] This study found that program participants reduced their toxicity-weighted 33/50 releases in politically active counties (i.e., those with high voter participation rates). The paper does not provide details of the direct effects of other explanatory variables capturing consumer, investor, regulatory, and community pressure on the change in 33/50 releases.

[10] Instead of defining participation as a 0/1 dummy variable (equal to 1 for a participant and 0 otherwise) for 1991 only and examining the effect of participation in 1991 on releases thereafter, they determined the incremental effect of each year's participation on 33/50 releases by constructing four participation variables. Each of these is defined as a 0/1 variable for a firm for each of the remaining years of the program.

this effect persisted until 1995.[11] In contrast to these studies, Vidovic and Khanna (2007) found a statistically insignificant effect of the program on 33/50 releases, using a sample of firms drawn from nineteen different SIC codes for the period 1991–5. They also found that firms that had reduced their emissions the most just prior to the start of the program (between 1988 and 1990) had higher 33/50 emissions than they would have had otherwise during the program years, suggesting that firms exhibited free-riding behavior on their previous reductions. This led these authors to conclude that the 33/50 program was largely ineffective. More recently, Sam, Khanna, and Innes (2009) find that the 33/50 program led to the adoption of Total Quality Environmental Management (TQEM) Systems. They also find that TQEM had a significant negative effect on 33/50 pollutant releases and that 33/50 participation produced additional direct benefits in pollution reduction both during and after the program years.

The impact of the ARET program on toxic releases was examined by Antweiler and Harrison (2007). They estimated the impact of program participation on emissions separately for seventeen different chemicals. They were unable to find differences in the emissions behavior of program participants and nonparticipants for ten of the seventeen chemicals. For five chemicals, they found that program participants reduced emissions more than nonparticipants, although they caution that in some cases other factors were also in play (in particular, a strong regulatory threat).[12] They did not explicitly control for regulatory pressures that could have also affected emissions. For two chemicals, they found that program participants performed worse than nonparticipants. In addition to examining the changes in emissions across individual chemicals, Antweiler and Harrison (2007) also examined how each facility's overall emissions (weighted by toxicity scores) changed over time. They found that participants in ARET reduced emissions more slowly than nonparticipants. As

---

[11] Additionally, they found that firms that were in more concentrated industries and had higher R&D expenditure were more likely to have lower 33/50 releases, possibly in order to set high environmental standards and gain a competitive advantage by raising the costs of abatement for rival firms. They found evidence that firms may have reduced 33/50 releases to pre-empt a demand for more stringent regulations by environmental interest groups and to deter boycotts in states with a large presence of environmental interest groups. They also analyzed the effects of program participation on the frequency with which firms are inspected and found that it led to a significant decline (by 17 percent relative to sample average) in inspection rates from 1993 to 1995.

[12] For example, tetrachlorethylene and dichloromethane were both deemed toxic chemicals in 1993 and were subject to extensive stakeholder negotiations during the 1990s.

a result, they conclude that the ARET program was largely ineffectual in encouraging firms to engage in emissions reductions.[13]

Brouhle, Griffiths, and Wolverton (2009) examined the effectiveness of the Strategic Goals program on aggregate and toxicity-weighted emissions of TRI releases. Similar to studies of the 33/50 program, the ARET program, and the Responsible Care program, they note that industry emissions were falling during the time the voluntary program was in existence. However, they failed to find significant differences in emission reductions over the entire life of the program between participants and nonparticipants in the program.[14]

Morgenstern, Pizer, and Shih (2007) adopted a difference-in-differences approach to measure the effectiveness of the Climate Wise program. They considered the difference in the change in the cost of fuels (which they used as a proxy for emissions) for participants and nonparticipants who were matched through the propensity score technique. They failed to find a significant impact of the program on the cost of fuels (i.e., emissions) between participants and nonparticipants. Although participants experienced a 3 percent reduction in the cost of fuels in the immediate year after joining, this result is not statistically significant and disappeared after the initial year.

The effectiveness of the Climate Challenge program was examined by Welch, Mazur, and Bretschneider (2000) and Delmas and Montes-Sancho (2007). Welch, Mazur, and Bretschneider (2000) found no support for the idea that the program participants reduced their emissions of carbon dioxide more than nonparticipants. This general conclusion is shared by Delmas and Montes-Sancho (2007). While neither study found that the program impacts on the emission patterns of participants, the studies did find differences in emissions within subgroups of their samples. Welch, Mazur, and Bretschneider (2000) note that participants who pledge larger reductions in emissions actually achieve *fewer* emissions reductions. Delmas and Montes-Sancho (2007) separated participants into those that joined early and later in the program and found that early participants reduced emissions more than nonparticipants. It appears, then, that late participants have higher than average emissions and effectively free-ride off the voluntary agreement.[15]

---

[13] Antweiler and Harrison (2007) found that more pollution-intensive facilities and larger facilities reduced their emissions faster.

[14] Emissions reductions were more likely by firms facing a stronger regulatory threat through more frequent inspections and those with larger emissions to begin with.

[15] A number of other factors are also found to influence the change in carbon dioxide emissions experienced by firms in the Climate Challenge program. Welch, Mazur, and

Effectiveness of industry association programs

The Sustainable Slopes program focuses on the environmental perform-ance of ski operators. In the service sector, the environmental output measure is not as clearly defined as it is for many programs that focus on manufacturing firms. Rivera and de Leon (2004) and Rivera, de Leon, and Koerber (2006) used environmental scorecard grades produced by the Ski Area Citizens Coalition as a measure of performance. Ski opera-tors are assigned a numerical score (1–100) and corresponding letter grade (A to F) based on their performance in four main environmental management areas: ski area expansion management, natural resource use and conservation, pollution management, and wildlife and habi-tat management. Controlling for other factors that influence whether a ski operator would join the Sustainable Slopes program, Rivera and de Leon (2004) found a *negative* relationship between participation in the program and environmental performance in the initial year. Since the study only utilized environmental scorecard grades in the year that the Sustainable Slopes program began in 2001, the results suggest that the program attracted "dirtier" firms. Rivera and de Leon (2004) note the lack of sanctions and monitoring of the Sustainable Slopes program and thus hypothesize that "dirtier" firms may free-ride off the agreement by signing up to participate but then fail to undertake real environ-mental improvements. Rivera, de Leon, and Koerber (2006) tested this hypothesis by examining the impact of the program on ski operators' overall environmental scorecard grades over a longer period (2001–5) and continued to find a statistically insignificant impact of the program. Looking at specific areas of environmental performance, they also failed to find a significant relationship between program participation and performance in the areas of expansion management, pollution manage-ment, and wildlife and habitat management. Only in the case of natural resource management did they find a positive impact of participation in the Sustainable Slopes program.[16]

Bretschneider (2000) found that newer plants are more likely to decrease their emissions rate over time. To the extent that newer plants have more environmental technology, this result is consistent with the finding of Delmas and Montes-Sancho (2007) that plants with more environmental technology have lower emissions. Unsurprisingly, facilities that reduced their total electricity generated had lower emissions (Welch, Mazur, and Bretschneider 2000), as did facilities that reduced the percentage of their generation that came from fossil fuels (Delmas and Montes-Sancho 2007).

[16] Other factors that impact on the overall environmental performance of ski operators include federal government oversight, ownership structure, size, and state environmen-tal pressure. Rivera and de Leon (2004) found that public ownership was correlated with

The effectiveness of the Responsible Care program was examined by King and Lenox (2000). During the time period studied, they note that overall emissions by the chemical industry were falling. Looking at industry emissions behavior before and after the program, they found that the rate of improvement in reducing emissions increased following the program. While the program appears to have improved the environmental performance of the industry as a whole, they found no evidence that the program had a positive effect on its members. In particular, they did not find that participants in the Responsible Care program improved their environmental performance relative to nonparticipants. In fact, they provide some evidence that members of Responsible Care actually improve their performance more *slowly* than non-members. To explain these contradictory results, they suggest that the Responsible Care program may have attracted greater attention to the chemical industry and empowered environmental activists to apply more pressure on nonparticipants, inducing them to improve their environmental performance.[17]

Evidence from third-party initiatives

ISO certification, both ISO 9000 and ISO 14001, has generally been found to be effective in encouraging participants to achieve improved environmental performance relative to nonparticipants. While ISO 9000 is not directly focused on environmental processes, King and Lenox (2001) hypothesize that the emphasis of ISO 9000 on quality assurances or "lean" production methods may impact on environmental performance through several avenues. Pollution may be reduced as an inadvertent by-product of the adoption of lean production practices, or pollution may be reduced due to specific practices that firms will take once they recognize the value of their waste stream and the lower costs of implementing pollution reduction measures; things that they learn once lean production methods are implemented. Examining facilities that qualified for ISO

---

lower environmental performance, while the level of state environmental pressure was correlated with higher environmental performance. Rivera, de Leon, and Koerber (2006) found that federal government oversight and facility size have a negative impact on the environmental performance of ski operators.

[17] They also found that "dirtier" firms improve their environmental performance more, as do larger firms. They suggest that "dirtier" and larger firms may have more opportunities to engage in environmental improvements and may have a lower cost in doing so due to the "low-hanging fruit" argument or economies of scale in pollution reduction.

9000 certification, King and Lenox (2001) found that these facilities generated less waste at the source and had lower emissions than non-certified facilities, which led them to conclude that "lean is green."

ISO 14001 focuses efforts on the adoption of environmental management systems. Potoski and Prakash (2005a, 2005b) examined the impact of this certification on firms' compliance with air regulations as well as emission levels of toxic chemicals. Potoski and Prakash (2005b) hypothesize that different features of ISO 14001 have the potential to reduce violations of environmental regulations. Third-party audits, for example, may reduce deliberate violations of environmental regulations, while the adoption of EMS standards may help educate firms about environmental regulations and hence reduce the noncompliance that stems from ignorance of these types of regulations. In their study, they found evidence that ISO 14001 facilities spend less time out of compliance with air regulations than non-certified firms.[18] Potoski and Prakash (2005a) investigated the role of ISO 14001 on firms' emissions of toxic chemicals. They again found a positive impact of ISO 14001, with ISO 14001-certified firms experiencing larger reductions in emissions than non-certified firms.[19] They attribute the positive impact of ISO 14001 in terms of compliance status and emissions behavior to the increased focus on environmental issues that results from the adoption of an EMS, and third-party auditing, which limits shirking behavior on the part of firms. Since other VEIs, such as Responsible Care, which were found to be ineffective, also encourage EMS adoption but do not have third-party auditing, they place special emphasis on the role that third-party auditing can play in reducing the incentives of firms to shirk on their responsibilities.

Arimura, Hibiki, and Katayama (2008) examined the impact of ISO 14001 on environmental performance in three areas: natural resource use (of fuel and water), waste generation, and wastewater effluent. In regard to all three measures, they found that ISO 14001-certified firms performed better than non-certified firms (based on self-reported data on environmental performance). They also note that firms that published or released reports documenting their activities and accomplishments related to ISO 14001 performed significantly better in all three measures relative to firms that did not release such reports. Johnstone et al. (2004)

---

[18] Other important factors that relate to better compliance include increased regulatory flexibility at the state level, greater number of voluntary initiatives sponsored by a state, and more stringent state-level air quality regulations.

[19] As with many other studies of VEIs, Potoski and Prakash (2005a) also found that dirtier facilities are able to achieve greater reductions in emissions.

found that the presence of a certified EMS increases the likelihood of a firm undertaking measures to reduce the generation of wastewater, air pollution and accidents, but does not have a statistically significant impact on solid waste generation or energy use.

Evidence from firm-structured initiatives

Anton, Deltas, and Khanna (2004) examined the effects of the adoption of a comprehensive EMS on toxic release intensity (toxic releases per unit sales) of a sample of S&P 500 firms over the period 1994–6. They found that the adoption of a more comprehensive EMS has a significant negative impact on the intensity of toxic releases, and that this impact is greater on firms that have inferior past environmental records. They also found that adopting an EMS has a negative effect on the intensity of on-site releases and off-site transfers, though not on hazardous air pollutants per unit sales. These findings suggest that the adoption of an EMS is targeted broadly to reduce waste and encourage pollution prevention and not toward reducing specific types of pollutants. None of the market-based or regulatory pressures considered by them were found to have had a significant direct impact on the pollution intensity of firms. Rather, the effect of these pressures appears to be indirect and operates through inducing the adoption of a more comprehensive EMS.

Dasgupta, Hettige, and Wheeler (2000) examined the effects of different environmental practices on self-reported compliance with environmental regulations by firms in Mexico. In particular, they looked at the role of four different environmental practices: adoption of ISO-type management procedures, expanded use of personnel for environmental inspection and control, assignment of environmental responsibilities to general managers rather than specialized environmental managers, and general environmental training for all employees rather than training focused on environmental specialists. They found that the adoption of ISO-type management procedures, assignment of environmental responsibility to general managers, and general environmental training for all employees result in improved compliance with environmental regulations. Surprisingly, they failed to find a significant effect of the number of personnel for environmental monitoring and enforcement. Several other factors, such as regulation, worker education, multi-plant status, and plant size positively impact on compliance behavior, although this effect is mostly indirect via the greater adoption of environmental management practices.

Conclusions

The review presented in this chapter indicates that evidence on the effectiveness of VEIs is mixed. Public voluntary programs were found to be largely ineffective, with the notable exception of the 33/50 program for some samples and sectors. Similarly, industry association programs such as Responsible Care and Sustainable Slopes did not appear to enhance the environmental performance of firms. In contrast, the third-party ISO program has encouraged participants to improve their environmental performance relative to nonparticipants.

Prakash and Potoski (2006) suggest that participation in VEIs can be viewed as gaining membership of a "green club." These clubs differ in the credibility of their enforcement mechanisms and the stringency of their environmental expectations of their members. By requiring third-party auditing to maintain membership in the club and by providing an excludable benefit in the form of an enhanced environmental reputation bestowed by the club, ISO 14001 limited the incentive for firms to shirk and increased the incentive to maintain the reputation of the club so that it continued to serve as a credible signal of superior environmental performance to external stakeholders. In contrast, Responsible Care, while also a green club, lacked strong enforcement mechanisms (prior to 2002) and, although it set stringent codes of conduct for member firms, it did not require the implementation of those codes.

The green club view of VEIs, however, does not explain the empirical evidence that unilateral actions by firms, such as the adoption of an EMS, also led to improved performance outcomes. The adoption of an EMS does not provide the same benefits of membership of a green club as ISO 14001 and Responsible Care. Instead, one explanation for this finding is that firms adopt these EMSs primarily to obtain internal efficiency gains. Improvement in external image is an indirect outcome of adoption. To the extent that internal efficiency gains and waste reduction are driving adoption, firms benefit from them only if they achieve those improved outcomes. In other words, incentives for shirking and free-riding may be less pervasive here because firms are adopting EMSs, and possibly improving their environmental outcomes, simply for reasons of private gain.

It is important to note that none of the VEIs reviewed here had mechanisms to sanction firms that participated but did not make environmental performance improvements. Some of the VEIs did not even require firms to set baselines for environmental performance or specific targets for improvement. The absence of sanctions by regulators and industry associations creates a void that can be filled, at least to some extent, by public sanctions by stakeholders. The latter are only possible if existing information asymmetries can be reduced by requiring public disclosure of firm-specific information on program-related performance. The 33/50 program, the ARET program, and the Strategic Goals program did set numerical targets and baselines at the overall program level and were accompanied by public disclosure of emissions via the TRI or the NPRI, unlike the climate change programs and the industry and third-party initiatives. The lack of mandatory reporting of greenhouse gas emissions by participants and nonparticipants in climate change programs provided greater opportunities for free-riding. However, even public sanctions may not be enough to induce performance improvements in the absence of credible mechanisms for monitoring and enforcement, and a strong threat of regulation if voluntary actions are not effective.

This review of the effectiveness of VEIs focused on a limited set of environmental performance measures which are appropriate for VEIs with narrowly defined goals, such as the 33/50 program or the climate change programs. Future research efforts examining the broader impacts of VEIs such as Responsible Care and ISO 14001 on worker and community safety, reductions in environmental spills and accidents, and changes in product composition and mix could provide a fuller picture about the role of VEIs in the portfolio of approaches to achieve environmental protection.

7

The emergence of non-state market-driven (NSMD) global environmental governance: a cross-sectoral assessment

GRAEME AULD, CRISTINA BALBOA, STEVEN BERNSTEIN, AND BENJAMIN CASHORE

Introduction

The failure of states and intergovernmental processes to address some of the most important environmental problems facing the planet – explanations of which can often be traced back to "tragedy of the commons" or "collective action" dilemmas (see Delmas and Young in their Introduction to this volume) – has resulted in the proliferation of alternative nongovernmental approaches. Often grouped under the broad rubric of "corporate social responsibility" (CSR) these efforts comprise an array of initiatives including self-regulation (see King and Toffel, Chapter 4, this volume), voluntary environmental agreements (Khanna and Brouhle, Chapter 6, this volume), and public–private partnerships.[1]

Just how these innovations might become enduring and effective features of global environmental governance is arguably one of the most critical questions facing scholars and practitioners in the global era. This chapter focuses on one of the most unique nongovernmental institutional innovations that has attracted the attention of both practitioners and scholars: certification systems that attempt to reward environmentally responsible business practices through positive recognition and market incentives. That they do not appeal to the state for rule-making authority, but instead derive authority from evaluations of stakeholders who choose whether to demand such products, has led Cashore (2002) and Cashore, Auld, and Newsom (2004) to refer to them as "non-state market-driven" (NSMD). With certification institutions, firms are often coerced

---

[1] See Gunningham, Kagan, and Thornton (2003), Howlett (2000), Rosenau, P. (2000), Ruggie (2004), Webb (2002), Hay, Stavins, and Victor (2005), and Vogel (2005).

and cajoled by problem-focused environmental groups or, in some cases, mission-driven but incapacitated governmental officials or agencies.

Despite increasing practitioner and scholarly interest in NSMD certification institutions, it is curious that, with the exception of Bartley's work on sweatshop labor practices (Bartley 2003, 2007), few analyses have compared their emergence and institutionalization across sectors or problem areas.[2] Such a gap is problematic, however, since without such analyses we are unable to understand where certification might result from sector-specific functional needs, or whether the role of ideas and norms is important in promoting diffusion across sectors. Moreover, without such analyses, it will be difficult to generalize about the conditions that facilitate and debilitate these non-state efforts. This chapter represents an initial effort to fill the gap in comparative work and, in so doing, to advocate a problem-focused research protocol.

We argue that any research project aimed at addressing effectiveness must undertake three tasks.

1. It must engage in sophisticated conceptualization and theory development about how such institutions might evolve. That is, drawing on Delmas and Young's review in the Introduction, scholars must address how these innovations withstand the "tragedy of the commons" or "collective action dilemma" tests in ways that traditional governmental and intergovernmental processes clearly have not.

2. Scholars must elaborate exactly what environmental problem they expect to solve with the fully formed and durable institutional innovation. That is, given the gravity, severity, and deterioration of environmental problems around the world, it is inadequate to simply reveal that an environmental institution gained support, if a fully formed and functioning institution could never be expected to reverse, in any meaningful way, the decline of an environmental problem.

3. The methods chosen for understanding effectiveness must be consistent with the strategies undertaken to achieve the first two tasks. We argue – in contrast to those who are concerned that superior large-N correlational data are not available – that the best strategy to use in order to understand effectiveness is problem-focused "historical process tracing" (Hall 2003), followed by an attempt to theorize about what processes or pathways might be taken in the future.

---

[2] We are limiting our empirical cases in this chapter, given the focus of this volume, to those addressing global environmental challenges.

While statistical significance tests of large-N data are certainly important, we have chosen our approach for two reasons.

1. Advances in historical process tracing (Buthe 2002) reveal the critical role that a careful examination of complex processes and sequencing has for understanding institutional evolution – an understanding that large-N studies are not suited to provide.
2. The question guiding all new environmental governance regimes ought to be focused, we argue, on whether the institution provides direct or indirect pathways to environmental problem-solving.

Therefore the effectiveness test must be placed in the context of environmental problem-solving, which requires attention to causal complexity that this historical process tracing approach is well suited to handle. Of course large-N statistical techniques are also critical to understanding effectiveness but should be seen as sitting alongside, rather than being superior to, historical process tracing. Whatever approach they take, scholars must carefully justify their method and discuss why, and how, it sheds light on environmental problem-solving. As a result, a critical distinction, given the rapid deterioration of the environmental health of the biosphere, is that "better than it would otherwise have been" definitions of effectiveness, or those that assess an outcome in relation to its "collective optimal" solution, must give way to definitions of effectiveness that involve a reversal of the deterioration. If this distinction is not made, we might end up determining as successful, policy innovations that never had any hope of ameliorating environmental deterioration.

For these reasons we begin by noting that, since NSMD certification systems are in their emergent early stages, reflecting highly dynamic and often fluctuating support across and within environmental, social, and economic communities, a number of questions arise:

- In what direction are these systems headed?
- Will they become "models" of appropriate behavior but relegated to small and/or niche markets?
- Will they gain widespread support but have standards so weak that they have little influence on complex problems?
- Do they represent simply a "fad" that will eventually disappear, perhaps being overcome by reinvigorated state-based efforts?
- Or are they headed on the path toward status as full-fledged governance systems with legitimate authority to create policy within an adaptive, reflexive, and inclusive governing process?

In order to address these questions, we proceed inductively through the following procedure. First we develop an analytical classification framework/template with which to present what we know about the emergence of NSMD certification systems in different sectors. We then apply the framework empirically to issues of forest degradation, coffee production (both of which address marginalized producers and environmental impacts), and the destructive practices of the ornamental fish trade. Rather than abstracting out particular variables for each case, we present brief case studies for each issue and then discuss some of the similarities and differences in the conclusions.

The chapter is organized as follows. Following this introduction, the second section reviews the rationale for NSMD certification governance. We then develop a classification framework, drawing on Bernstein and Cashore (2007), Bartley (2003, 2007), Cashore, Auld, and Newsom (2004), and Cashore (2002), which focuses our attention on the emergence of NSMD systems and institutionalization within, and across, problem arenas. This section reviews the template designed for an initial exploration of the nature of the problem in question, and the historical and current state of NSMD governance. Here, we are interested, specifically, in taking a first cut at understanding the competition and fragmentation that tend to occur in a sector when an NSMD system arrives (or, in some cases, occurs through the actions of those fearing, or anticipating, the arrival of an NSMD system); and the corresponding countervailing patterns of coordination and integration that can occur. We pay particular attention to understanding the evaluations and endorsements of relevant NSMD organizations. In the following section, we empirically review our three cases. We have chosen to probe in detail these three NSMD certification systems because they all address the global environmental challenges that this volume seeks to highlight, and because they represent three distinct product chains. Forestry harvesting is practiced in developing, developed, and emerging economies; coffee is a commodity produced largely in developing countries but destined, by and large, for consumers in developed nations; while the ornamental fish trade occurs along a global supply chain but represents a niche market. Taking advantage of this variation, the final section assesses the implications of our empirical findings for theory-building on the emergence of NSMD systems. We reflect on whether differences across cases are the result of their structural features (i.e., particular features of the sector's supply chain), problem-specific factors (i.e., whether the product is ingested by humans), or whether differences might diminish over time (i.e., some are in earlier stages of development than others), or whether there are other explanations for the patterns of divergence across cases.

The rise of non-state market-driven (NSMD) global governance

Beginning in the early 1990s, a number of NGOs, frustrated with their efforts to influence governmental or intergovernmental processes, began to develop their own sets of socially and environmentally responsible business practices. They developed systems to reward firms that accepted these standards, often by creating a social or environmental "label." The intention was to provide companies with an economic "carrot" by providing recognition in the marketplace for their responsible business practices, with a corresponding promise of market access and/or a price premium.[3]

Buoyed in part by a strong interest in the forest sector,[4] NSMD certification programs are now proliferating to address some of the most critically important problems facing the planet, including fisheries depletion, food production, mining, construction, rural and community poverty, inhumane working conditions, human rights abuses, and sustainable tourism (see Appendix to this chapter). Their potential impact is far from trivial – if completely successful, current efforts alone would govern 20 percent of products traded globally.[5] Cashore (2002), Cashore, Auld, and Newsom (2004), and Bernstein and Cashore (2007) discern five key features that, taken together, render NSMD systems distinct from other forms of public and private authority (see Table 7.1).

The most critical feature is that governments do not create or require adherence to the rules. That is, the sovereign authority that governments

---

[3] While often referred to as "certification systems" (Gereffi, Garcia-Johnson, and Sasser 2001), this term conflates other forms of authority with NSMD governance. For similar reasons we do not address all of the initiatives identified by scholarly work on political consumerism (Micheletti, Føllesdal, and Stolle 2003).

[4] The majority of industrial or commercial forest lands in the United States, Canada, and Western and Eastern Europe are under some type of third-party certification system. Major retailers in Europe and the United States have announced a preference for certified forest products. Concerted efforts are under way to expand support for certification in developing countries (Cashore et al. 2006a).

[5] This figure was derived from the World Trade Organization (WTO 2003). We divided the total amount of products traded under sectors represented in the Appendix by the total amount of all products traded globally.

Table 7.1 *Key features of NSMD governance*

Role of the state	The state does not use its sovereign authority to directly require adherence to rules
Institutionalized governance mechanism	Procedures in place designed to create adaptation, inclusion, and learning over time across a wide range of stakeholders
The social domain	Development of prescriptive rules governing environmental and social problems, to which firms must adhere
Role of the market	Support emanates from producers and consumers along the supply chain, who evaluate the costs and benefits of joining
Enforcement	Compliance must be verified

Source: Adapted from Cashore (2002), Cashore, Auld, and Newsom (2004), and Bernstein and Cashore (2007).

possess to develop rules, and to which society more or less adheres, does not apply. No one can be incarcerated or fined for failing to comply.

A second feature of NSMD governance is that its institutions constitute governing arenas in which adaptation, inclusion, and learning occur over time and across a wide range of stakeholders. The originators of the NSMD approach justify this on the grounds that it is more democratic, open, and transparent than the domestic public policy networks and intergovernmental efforts that it seeks to replace.

A third key feature is that these systems govern the "social domain" (Ruggie 2003, 2004), requiring profit-maximizing firms to undertake costly reforms that they otherwise would not pursue. That is, they pursue prescriptive "hard law," albeit in the private sphere (Meidinger 2000). This distinguishes NSMD systems from other arenas of private authority, such as business coordination with regard to technological processes (the original reason for the creation of the International Organization for Standardization), which can be explained by profit-seeking behavior through which the reduction of business costs is the ultimate objective. This also distinguishes NSMD systems from voluntary environmental management system (EMS) approaches in which firms are certified for developing internal procedures, but which develop no prescriptions about "on the ground" behavior (Clapp 1998; Delmas 2002, 2005). EMS systems in general, and ISO in particular, which give firms complete discretion in deciding what they want to do to ameliorate environmental or social problems, are important phenomena but very different from NSMD institutions, which develop prescriptive rules to which firms must adhere.

The fourth key feature is that authority is granted through the market's supply chain. To increase economic incentives, environmental organizations may act through boycotts and other direct-action initiatives to convince large retailers to adopt purchasing policies favoring NSMD certification schemes.

The fifth key feature is the existence of verification procedures designed to ensure that the regulated entity actually meets the stated standards. Verification is important because it provides the validation necessary for a certification program to achieve legitimacy, as certified products are then demanded and consumed along the market's supply chain. This distinguishes NSMD systems from many forms of corporate social responsibility initiatives that require limited, or no, outside monitoring (Gunningham, Grabosky, and Sinclair 1998). The market's supply chain is the institutional arena in which evaluation of support occurs; it contains verification procedures to ensure regulatory compliance.

At the heart of the struggle to build NSMD governance is the effort to address the negative consequences of neoliberal globalization, which frees mobile multinational firms from inconvenient national regulation and discourages countries that are desperate for foreign investment and trade from setting social or environmental standards (Braithwaite and Drahos 2000). NSMD systems aim to reverse global neoliberalism's impact on policy and regulatory development by targeting multinational companies with market incentives (price premiums, market access, "social licenses" to operate) or disincentives (boycott campaigns, shaming), which, in turn, should put pressure along the market's supply chain to encourage compliance with the governing system's rules and procedures. The logic is not simply rooted in material incentives, however, since the ultimate goal of such systems is to establish governing mechanisms with sufficient legitimacy to be recognized as authoritative in the sector or policy domain in question.

Like activist critics of economic globalization, NSMD supporters view neoliberalism as a culprit in states' failures to address serious ecological and social problems. However, instead of rejecting the market, NSMD systems attempt to harness arenas of private authority to achieve their aims. These efforts can be likened to what Ruggie (2004) has called "taking embedded liberalism global"; that is, finding a way to socially embed globalizing markets. While a variety of mechanisms are emerging to fill this governance gap, NSMD systems are arguably the most promising because they create governing authority directly in the global marketplace. Thus, they must be classified according not only to their use of markets, but also to whether they contain purposeful social steering efforts.

Toward an analytical classification framework

In this section, we follow the following template, designed to facilitate comparative empirical work:

1. What is the problem for which certification was created?
2. What appear to be the key background features important for understanding its emergence?
3. When did certification emerge as an alternative?
4. Drawing on Bernstein and Cashore's (2007) classification of the historical development of NSMD systems (Figure 3) we assess what kind of support existed in Phase I (initiation) and in Phase II (efforts to obtain widespread support), and toward what kind of future these initiatives appear to be headed.

We envision five different scenarios to which NSMD certification efforts might head:[6]

Scenario One: Fully fledged political legitimacy

Under this scenario, the full range of stakeholders within a sector recognize their membership in a political community that grants an NSMD system the authority to govern.

Scenario Two: NSMD exists as a strong, but niche or small-market-focused system

Under this scenario, NSMD is important for norm generation but is unable to address widespread, globally important problems.

Scenario Three: NSMD institutionalizes as a weak system

Under this scenario, NSMD certification gains widespread support, but it is institutionalized as a weak form of authority, unable or unwilling to address the enduring social and environmental problems for which it was originally created.

Scenario Four: Hybrid

This scenario involves a combination of government and private authority in which governmental arenas and NSMD combine to produce new forms of authority. This would occur when governments required that some, but not all, parts of the supply chain adhere to the rules.

Scenario Five: "Bringing the state back in"

Under this scenario, the combination of increased public awareness and competition among systems has put pressure on governments to move in

---

[6] The authors thank Kelly Levin, Doctoral Candidate, Yale FES, for her insights into the development of the range of scenarios, especially concerning potential hybrid results, which was integral to shaping our analytical classification framework.

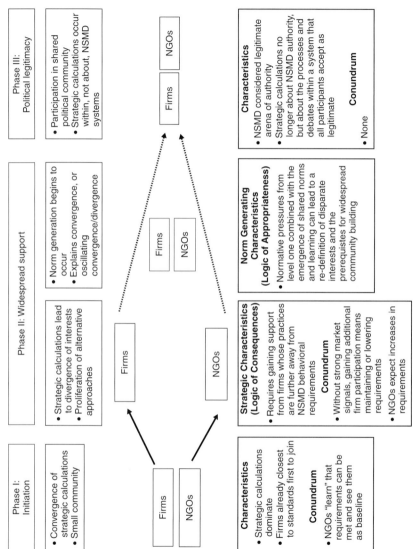

The three phases of NSMD governance (Bernstein and Cashore 2007)

Figure 3

and regulate the problem. Under this scenario, certification has played an important role in facilitating learning across different stakeholders, but is ultimately viewed as being unable to progress further, and government moves in with a newly invigorated sense of mission.

Applying the classification framework to the case studies

Global forest deterioration

The problem

A host of scientific evidence and research has revealed significant and widespread deterioration of the world's forests.[7] Scientific data collected on biodiversity, species decline, deforestation, and global climate change reveal a troubling picture: forest-dependent species continue to be lost – part of what some refer to as the sixth major mass extinction in the earth's history (Leakey and Lewin 1995; Pimm and Brooks 2000). Nearly 100 million hectares of tropical forest were lost in Africa and Latin America between 1990 and 2000 (UNEP 2002). Conservation biologists studying protected areas have found that the existing efforts to preserve 12 percent of the world's forests from industrial extraction will not be enough to address declining biodiversity, and that not only preservation but rehabilitation of degraded lands is required (Sinclair et al. 1995).

Background factors

An array of governmental, intergovernmental, and nongovernmental efforts to address global environmental deterioration were attempted in the years leading up to the emergence of forest certification. These included the creation of the International Tropical Timber Organization (ITTO) to improve forest management practices in the tropics (Gale 1998), efforts to sign a global forest convention at the 1992 Rio Summit (UNCED) (Humphreys 1996; Bernstein and Cashore 2004), and tropical timber boycott campaigns.

The failure of the ITTO to make a dent in the rate of deforestation, the inability of the world's governments to agree on a binding global forest convention, and the perverse incentives that tropical timber boycotts gave forest owners to convert "unproductive" forest land to other uses (Cashore, Auld, and Newsom, 2004) created considerable frustration

---

[7] This section draws on Cashore, Auld, and Newsom (2004) and Cashore et al. (2006a, 2006b).

on the part of those environmental groups who had devoted most of the 1980s to these efforts.

A variety of meetings about the problem gradually focused on the idea of eco-labeling (Cashore et al. 2006a), and eventually forest certification. Efforts included the Rainforest Alliance's SmartWood program formed in 1989 to certify timber from well-managed forests, Friends of the Earth-UK's "Good Wood" scheme, formed in 1987 (Bartley 2003), and Hubert Kwisthout's "Ecological Trading Company," which was incorporated to source sustainable timber directly (Viana et al. 1996, p. 144).

Phase I: The NSMD certification solution

The combination of these efforts resulted in a wide coalition spearheaded by the World Wide Fund for Nature (WWF) and allies who decided to avoid what they deemed to be futile efforts to achieve a meaningful and binding global forest convention and instead decided to develop and promote a market-based approach.[8] In 1990, the WWF, together with a variety of NGOs, European retailers, and US foundations, held a meeting in California to explore the possibility of developing an independent global certification organization. Three years later, they held a founding meeting in Toronto for a global "forest certification" system, known as the Forest Stewardship Council (FSC). Their approach was based on a relatively simple idea: develop a set of environmental and socially responsible rules governing sustainable forest management, and recognize companies who adhere to such practices by providing them with a market advantage – which would come in the form of a "boycott shield," an important but difficult to measure reputation as being responsible stewards, and – it was hoped – a label that could be used to market eco-friendly forest products to concerned customers. It was a relatively simple solution that would have an enormous impact and complex implications.

To accomplish its objectives, the FSC created nine "principles" (later expanded to ten) and more detailed "criteria," which are performance-based, broad in scope, and address tenure and resource-use rights, community relations, workers' rights, environmental impact, management plans, monitoring and conservation of old-growth forests, and plantation management (see Moffat 1998, p. 44; Forest Stewardship Council 1999). The FSC program also mandated the creation of national or regional

---

[8] This section draws on, in addition to the references cited in the text, Cashore et al. (2006b).

working groups to develop specific standards for their regions based on the broad principles and criteria.[9]

Perhaps more important than the rules themselves is the FSC "tripartite" conception of governance in which a three-chamber format of environmental, social, and economic actors – every chamber with equal voting rights – has emerged.[10] Each chamber is internally divided equally between North and South representation (Domask 2003). Two ideas were behind this institutional design. The first was to eliminate business dominance in policymaking processes, in the belief that this would encourage the development of relatively stringent standards and facilitate on-the-ground implementation. The second was to ensure that the North could not dominate at the expense of the South – a strong criticism of the failed efforts to achieve a binding global forest convention at the Rio Earth Summit (Meidinger 1997, 2000; Lipschutz and Fogel 2002; Domask 2003).

Initial support

When forest certification first emerged, the vast majority of industrial forest companies around the world fended off such pressures, asserting, as they had during the initial efforts to increase domestic and international policy processes, that there was no need for such an effort and that, if anything, forestry problems occurred elsewhere. Forestry-focused governmental agencies in Europe and North America reflected and supported this approach and, with their industrial forest companies, pointed to tropical forest degradation as the real culprit, while they already practiced responsible forestry. However, after select forest companies and forest owners began to express interest in the FSC, and as retail giants such as Britain's B&Q (later followed by Home Depot) came to support the

---

[9] The FSC decided to allow national and regional standard-setting to adapt the FSC principles and criteria in order to incorporate regional stakeholder concerns and to "ensure the consistency and integrity of standards" in every country or region. In large federated countries such as the USA and Canada, this led to the development of subnational standards, with eleven such processes established in the USA and nine in Canada. The Canadian regional processes are unique among countries in that they include a fourth chamber in the decision-making structure, known as the Indigenous People's Chamber.

[10] Originally, there were two chambers: an environmental and social chamber with 75 percent of the votes and an economic chamber with 25 percent of the votes. However, the balance has since been changed to three chambers each carrying equal weight in FSC policy decisions. In addition to the division along interest-group lines, the FSC has also distributed votes evenly between Northern and Southern members in order to ensure more globally equitable decisions.

FSC, a growing number of industrial forest companies, including those in Canada, began to express interest in the idea of forest certification. Poland was quick to have most of its forest lands FSC certified, followed by Sweden, with all of its industrial companies supporting the FSC; an option, however, that Swedish private forest owners – who constituted 50 percent of the commercial land base – rejected (Cashore, Auld, and Newsom 2004).

Phase II: Assessing patterns of divergence and convergence

As support for the FSC began to grow, the idea of forest certification came to be embraced by most of the industrial forest sector in Europe and North America, although mostly through the establishment of FSC competitors, who gave forest owners and/or industrial companies the dominant role in the certification policy process (Rametsteiner 1999; Vlosky 2000; Sasser 2002). In the USA, the American Forest and Paper Association (AF&PA) created the Sustainable Forestry Initiative (SFI) certification program. In Canada, the Canadian Standards Association (CSA) program was initiated by the Canadian Sustainable Forestry Certification Coalition, a group of twenty-three industry associations from across Canada (Lapointe 1998). And in Europe, following the Swedish and Finnish experiences with FSC-style forest certification, an "umbrella" Pan European Forest Certification (PEFC) system (renamed the Program for the Endorsement of Forest Certification in 2003) was created in 1999 by European landowner associations that felt especially excluded from the FSC processes.

In general, FSC competitor programs originally emphasized organizational procedures and discretionary, flexible performance guidelines and requirements (Hansen and Juslin 1999, p. 19). For instance, the SFI originally focused on performance requirements, such as following existing voluntary "best management practices" (BMPs), legal obligations, and regeneration requirements. The SFI later developed a comprehensive approach through which companies could choose to be audited by outside parties for compliance with the SFI standard, and developed a "Sustainable Forestry Board," independent of the AF&PA, with which to develop ongoing standards. And, similar to the SFI, the CSA's focus began as "a systems-based approach to sustainable forest management" (Hansen and Juslin 1999, p. 20), where individual companies were required to establish internal "environmental management systems" (Moffat 1998, p. 39). The CSA allows firms to follow the criteria and indicators developed by the Canadian Council of Forest Ministers, which are themselves consistent with the International Organization for Standardization (ISO) 14001 Environmental Management System standard and include elements that correspond to the Montreal process for developing criteria and indicators for sustainable forest management. The PEFC, which strongly supports national sovereignty, is now emerging as the global competitor, and is itself a mutual recognition program of national initiatives. It draws on criteria identified at the Helsinki and Lisbon Forest Ministers Conferences in 1993 and 1998, respectively (PEFC International 2001). However, national initiatives are not bound to address the agreed upon criteria and indicators (Ozinga 2001), as the PEFC leaves the development of certification rules and procedures to the national initiatives. A PEFC Secretariat and Council, which tends to be dominated by landowners and industry representatives, determines the acceptance of national initiatives into the PEFC recognition scheme (Hansen and Juslin 1999).[11]

At this juncture, then, there is strong support for the idea of forest certification in the developed North, but strong disagreement about which program is most appropriate; and emergent, but thus far limited, support in the global South (Cashore et al. 2006a). The top regions globally in terms of area certified under all schemes – North America and Western Europe – encompass most of the developed North, including the USA, Canada, Sweden, the UK, and Germany. Of the almost 60 million hectares of FSC-certified forests in 2005, over 31 million ha (53 percent) was in developed countries and slightly over 9 million ha (15 percent) was in developing countries. For the PEFC, the ratio is even starker. As of 2005,

---

[11] The PEFC Council's membership comprises twenty-five national governing bodies, nineteen of which are European. Authority to endorse these schemes rests with the PEFC Council, and twenty-eight of these have been endorsed as of May 2009. The US SFI, Tree Farm, and the Canadian CSA became members of the Council in 2000, while the CSA achieved the additional step of formal endorsement by the PEFC in July 2005. The PEFC provides for single, group, and regional forest certification. Regular audits are conducted of forest owners participating in group certification. Under regional forest certification, an applicant's region must be certified by a third party as meeting the requirements of the national standard. Landowners within a defined geographical area that has been granted regional certification status can apply to be recognized participants in the PEFC system only after committing to implement the national performance standards. Once the regional certification is complete and the landowner demonstrates his/her individual commitment to participating in the program (that is, he or she is committed to complying with national criteria), forest owners can apply to the PEFC Council, or the relevant PEFC national governing body acting on behalf of the PEFC Council, to obtain permission to use the PEFC logo. The PEFC offers a chain of custody certificate, based on "physical separation" of the certified product from non-certified products, or based on a "percent-in, percent-out" type of approach.

PEFC had about 193 million ha of certified forests,[12] but only just over 7 million ha (3.6 percent) was in developing countries (Brazil, Chile, and Malaysia) (Cashore et al. 2006a). Almost all the remainder was in high-income, developed countries, except for two countries in Eastern Europe (the Czech Republic and Latvia). There is some irony here. Forest certification was supported by some in order to promote good forest management in tropical developing countries, but has been adopted by developed-country operators seeking a market advantage from their comparatively lower cost of compliance.

The future?

There are two central questions facing the future of forest certification: "Will those supporting competing schemes agree to redirect efforts toward institutionalizing meaningful behavioral change in a way that does not put supporters at a competitive disadvantage?" and, related to this, "Could certification become entrenched in global supply chains so that those operating under weak or unenforced government policies might also be subject to similar restrictions as their competitors?" There are signs that shared understandings and norms indicating that certification as an institution is an appropriate way to regulate in an increasingly globalized economy might be part of a broader Phase III institutionalization process. However, to achieve such support will take a reinvigorated effort on the part of all stakeholders to engage in meaningful and deliberate debate about what constitutes forestry practices that will make a difference in addressing global environmental deterioration of the world's forests. This effort will have to transform rhetoric into meaningful commitments that have real and serious timetables for implementation.

If Phase III does not occur, we envision other potential scenarios, owing to certification's undisputed role as an initiator of new ideas and understandings across diverse groups. First, it might become a hybrid system in which some governments require their license-holders to adhere to certification, with the market's supply chain providing additional recognition, but from which demand would not be a prerequisite for support. Second, we suspect that if certification does not show signs of speeding up toward Phase III fairly soon, it is entirely possible that existing efforts could pave

---

[12] This figure includes PEFC-endorsed schemes as well as applicant and harmonized schemes such as SFI, ATFS, Cerflor, and MTCC. Indonesia's LEI is excluded because, at the time of writing, it had not applied to nor been recognized by PEFC.

the way for reinvigorated, and urgent, governmental and intergovernmental efforts (as described in Scenario Five).

Coffee

The problem

Two problems have emerged which have influenced and promoted certification in coffee. First, serious environmental problems have resulted from industrial coffee production. Although these are often country-specific, they are also typically connected with the increased intensity of coffee production.[13] They involve the negative human health and environmental effects of chemical fertilizers, herbicides, and pesticides (Rice and Ward 1996). Intensive coffee production is also responsible for significant forest clearing (Dicum and Luttinger 1999). Recent research in Indonesia found a strong positive correlation between rising prices for *Coffea canephora* (Robusta) and rates of deforestation in and around the Bukit Barisan Selatan National Park in the Lampung province of Sumatra (Kinnaird et al. 2003). In Latin America, on the other hand, forest clearing comes with the threat of coffee leaf rust (*Hemileia vastatrix*), which is notorious for destroying coffee crops in Sri Lanka and India. With the arrival of leaf rust in the Americas in around 1976, funding from governments and the United States Agency for International Development (USAID) helped Latin American coffee growers replace shade-grown coffee – where coffee was grown under the cover of overstory trees – with newer coffee varieties that could grow in full sunlight and thus hopefully hold in check the spread of the leaf rust (Rice and Ward 1996). In subsequent years, this would transform the character of coffee production in many Latin American countries;[14] unfortunately it would also have significant negative affects on Neotropical bird populations reliant on forests for their habitat.[15]

Second, coffee price volatility dramatically affects poor and marginalized coffee growers; a process made worse by the collapse of support

[13] Dicum and Luttinger (1999) note the adverse affects of "technified systems," which involve conversion to "sun coffee" as well as high inputs of chemical fertilizers and pesticides.

[14] Rice and McLean (1999) reported that these efforts resulted in the conversion of over 1.1 million ha of Latin American shade-grown coffee into sun coffee plantations.

[15] In Colombia, for instance, Rice and Ward (1996) explain how by the mid-1990s over 68 percent of the coffee-plantation acreage was technified (755,000 ha out of a total of 1,104,000 ha). In the 1970s, nearly all coffee was grown under traditional shade systems.

for the International Coffee Agreement in the late 1980s. Historical volatility stems from a combination of supply shocks, the nature of coffee consumption and production, and the ongoing efficiency and quality improvements in production processes.[16] Because of their disproportionally high investment in the coffee crop, small farmers are especially risk-prone (Lewin, Giovannucci, and Varangis 2004). Unlike exporters or roasters, who can stockpile coffee or seek alternative sources of supply when coffee crops fail in a particular country, farmers can be entirely reliant on their coffee crop for revenue. As many as 20 million families are reliant on coffee production and often find themselves selling their crops for less than their costs (Lewin, Giovannucci, and Varangis 2004).[17] For similar reasons, countries where coffee is a principal export also suffer disproportionately from price volatility.[18]

Background factors

Coffee grows best in countries that straddle the equator, as is apparent in the profile of the countries that dominate production. The modern coffee industry includes approximately seventy producing countries located mainly in Africa, Southeast Asia, and Central and South America. Brazil has long been the dominant producer. Between 1961 and 2003, its production accounted for an average of 28 percent of the annual global total. In the same time period, other significant producers have included Colombia, the Ivory Coast, Angola, Ethiopia, Uganda, Mexico, and Indonesia, with Vietnam emerging late in the 1990s as a significant new player.[19]

---

[16] Lewin, Giovannucci, and Varangis (2004) explain the connection of price cycles to weather-induced supply shocks and the "low, short-run inelasticity of both demand and supply" (p. 3). Inelastic demand means that consumption is insensitive to price changes: a percentage change in price leads to a smaller percentage change in quantity consumed. Conversely, this means small changes in quantity supplied can dramatically affect price. Thus, if supply contracts quickly, due to a drought or frost, prices will rise. This, in turn, greatly encourages increased production (either through replanting or the entry of new producers) with new production technologies that act to depress prices because of the inelastic demand. Even without another shock, a cycle of high and low prices can persist for a number of years as producers come into and out of the market.

[17] In Latin America, rural labor employment in coffee production is reported to range from a low of 17 percent in El Salvador to a high of 42 percent in Nicaragua (Lewin, Giovannucci, and Varangis 2004).

[18] For 2000, Gresser and Tickell (2002) reported that 79 percent of Burundi's total export value came from coffee. Ethiopia, Uganda, Rwanda, and Honduras are also highly reliant on coffee exports. All these countries suffer when prices decline dramatically.

[19] See http://faostat.fao.org/site/535/default.aspx.

Brazil is also the world's largest exporter of green coffee, accounting for an average of 24 percent of world exports (in metric tons) between 1961 and 2003. The major producers just listed are also significant exporters; however, re-export figures have been continually growing. By 2003, Germany, Belgium, France, Spain, and Italy accounted for 12.7 percent of the total quantity of green coffee exported.[20]

The institutional context of coffee production changed dramatically when the International Coffee Agreement (ICA) collapsed in 1989. This, along with a growing consolidation of the roasting sector (in 1998, Philip Morris and Nestlé between them held a 49 percent share of the roasting and instant coffee market), has shifted the balance of power away from producing countries (Ponte 2004). Indeed, before the fall of the ICA, around 20 percent of the total income generated from a coffee product went to producing countries, while 55 percent stayed in the consuming country. From after the fall in 1989 to 1994, only 13 percent of the income went to producers, with 78 percent captured by the consuming countries (Ponte 2004).

In recent years, per capita consumption in importing countries has ranged from a high in the Scandinavian countries of around 10 kg/year to a low of around 2 kg/year in Ireland (Lewin, Giovannucci, and Varangis 2004). However, relative to the growth in supply, annual growth in consumption has not kept pace; a point that is relevant when we discuss the fall of the International Coffee Agreement in 1989.

Many attempts, from local to global, have been made to address the problem of fluctuating coffee prices. For nearly a hundred years, countries have sought to regulate market prices and to smooth price cycles through means such as destroying excess production. In 1931, for instance, the price of coffee fell by nearly two-thirds. Excess stocks were huge. Brazil, the world's largest producer, held 26 million bags, which was 1 million more than the estimated world consumption at the time (Lewin, Giovannucci, and Varangis 2004). To limit the price fall, Brazil destroyed 7 million bags in 1931, and between 1931 and 1939 the country reportedly destroyed close to 80 million bags (Dicum and Luttinger 1999). Brazil's efforts, although successful, were a boon for other countries seeking to enter the coffee market. As prices rose, they were able to sell their coffee without restriction.[21]

---

[20] See http://faostat.fao.org/site/535/default.aspx.

[21] Colombia benefited especially; Dicum and Luttinger (1999) explain how Colombian coffee producers were free-riders on Brazil's self-imposed restraint. They note that "As

Not surprisingly, the price cycles have encouraged many attempts at cooperative resolution. In 1936 Brazil and Colombia – the world's two largest coffee producers – sought agreement on price differentials between their principal coffee products. However, this simply opened the market to other countries that were able to exploit the rise in world prices (Dicum and Luttinger 1999). Although many other initiatives were enacted in the coming years, it would take the onset of the Cold War and the consolidation of the roasting sector in the USA to enable the signing of the International Coffee Agreement in 1962.[22] Unlike its predecessors, the ICA involved both producer and consumer countries (Lewin, Giovannucci, and Varangis 2004). "Under the ICA regime," Ponte (2004) explains, "a target price (or a price band) for coffee was set, and export quotas were allocated to each producer. When the indicator price calculated by the International Coffee Organization (ICO) rose over the set price, quotas were relaxed; when it fell below the set price, quotas were tightened. If an extremely high rise in coffee prices took place (as in 1975–1977), quotas were abandoned until prices fell down within the band."

The ICA served as a reasonably stable international agreement for nearly thirty years (Gresser and Tickell 2002; Ponte 2004). Its strength partly stemmed from the inclusion of both producer and consumer countries, and yet the agreement did not include all consuming countries. This proved to be an important flaw. Certain producers, mainly in those countries that were not well served by the quota system, sometimes sold coffee at lower prices to non-member importers (Financial Times 1985). Guatemala, Costa Rica, and Indonesia were the principal culprits, exporting excess coffee to non-member countries – mainly Communist countries – for prices 60 percent lower than coffee sold under the ICA (Gowers 1985). Not surprisingly, this undermined the strength of the ICA and gave member producer and consumer countries cause to rethink its value. Further, the agreement was flawed in that it only controlled export

Colombian production continued to grow, this became more than just annoying to Brazilians; they had to withhold more and more coffee in order to maintain prices, only to see their work partially undone by unconstrained Colombian exports" (Dicum and Luttinger 1999, p. 77).

[22] Dicum and Luttinger (1999) explain how the Cold War encouraged the USA to subsidize and stabilize coffee prices in order to ward off any communist incursions in Latin America. US coffee roasters, represented by the National Coffee Association (NCA), accepted higher, stable prices because they helped protect market share from substitute products such as tea and soft drinks. Although the free-market price lows benefited roasters, when prices topped out, roasters saw their customers switch to these alternative beverages.

quotas; it did not regulate production or bean quality. Since quotas were renegotiated annually, countries with small quotas had an incentive to increase production in the hope of negotiating a larger quota share in the next round. Finally, this focus on production volumes meant that countries had little incentive to improve quality.

These flaws underpinned the agreement's demise, which came about in July 1989 when the USA pressed for a resolution to the practice of selling to non-member countries at low prices and for an increase in the supply of high-quality Arabica coffee (Financial Times 1989; World Commodity Report 1989). Brazil, on the other hand, refused to budge on the issue of its market share, and the ICO was unable to create an effective mechanism to regulate exports to non-member countries. The consequences were predictable. Prices plummeted. Weeks after the failed talks, prices slipped to 78 cents per pound, almost half the target range of 120–140 cents per pound specified under the ICA (Financial Times 1989). Although prices peaked in 1995 and 1997 due to crop-ruining frosts in Brazil, the overall price trend after 1989 was lower than the average prices experienced under the ICA regime (Gresser and Tickell 2002). Indeed, by 2002, prices had reached their lowest point in thirty years (or a hundred years when adjusted for inflation) (Lewin, Giovannucci, and Varangis 2004).

Thus, private governance emerged as international agreements on price stability were in decline. They operated, in part, to fill the void produced by the exit of government.

Phase I: The NSMD certification solution

Owing to the two different problems that coffee certification sought to resolve, programs developed in two largely separate streams: one focused on social and the other focused on environmental impacts. Curiously, and unlike the forestry case examined above, thus far the social and environmental streams have been housed in different systems, rather than being united under one umbrella. More recently, however, both the streams have sought to include more of what the other offers; that is, their respective standards have increasingly addressed both social and environmental factors concurrently.

Socially responsible stream

Fair trade coffee   Alternative trade organizations (ATOs) were an important player in the eventual establishment of fair trade labeling programs. "World shops" – such as Ten Thousand Villages – have been around since at least the 1950s in Europe and the USA (Kochen 2003).[23] In 1973, the Dutch Fair Trade Organization began selling "fairly traded" coffee from a Guatemalan cooperative. Although distribution via world shops expanded, throughout the late 1970s the market for fair trade coffee remained small (Giovannucci and Koekoek 2003). By the end of the 1980s, fair trade advocates saw a need for a new tool, one to "exert pressure on commercial companies to change their procurement practices" (Bird and Hughes 1997). They needed a system that would allow them to verify that products sold by non-fair trade committed shops were in fact fair trade products. As Bird and Hughes (1997) explained: "There was a fear that manufacturers would capitalize on the marketing advantage (provided by the fair trade proposition) without altering their trading methods, encouraging damaging consumer skepticism."

This interest in a new approach led to experimentation with a new model – a fair trade labeling program for coffee. By most accounts the first of these – the Max Havelaar label – took shape in 1988 as the brainchild of a priest who was working with Mexican coffee farmers and who had connections with a Dutch church-based nonprofit organization (Kochen 2003). The label (and the Max Havelaar Foundation) came into existence as a coffee-branding effort aimed at stimulating fair trade by promoting coffee grown by smaller farmers and cooperatives. It would facilitate distribution beyond the network of world shops but would also ensure that fair trade claims were credible. Under the program, companies wanting to use the label would buy coffee from farmers for three times the world price and would guarantee producers a credit of 60 percent of harvest value before the harvest had begun (Carpio 1993).[24]

Experimentation continued. Three years after the Max Havelaar launch, Oxfam, Twin Trading, Equal Exchange, and Traidcraft set up Cafédirect as a company that would buy coffee from fair trade producers for more than the world price. [25] Although not a governance program, Cafédirect exemplified one of the many market-based efforts used at the time as a means to help struggling coffee farmers. It joined Equal Exchange – a US-based fair trade company set up in 1986 – as another model of how to promote coffee grown by smaller farmers and cooperatives.[26]

---

[23] These are "specialist shops for fair trade products. They sell fair trade products to consumers, but they also organize information and educational fair trade promotional activities for the public" (Krier 2005). Initially these shops sold mainly craft products (Kochen 2003).

[24] See http://www.maxhavelaar.ch/en/.   [25] See http://www.cafedirect.co.uk/.

[26] See http://www.equalexchange.coop/.

While this was happening, the Dutch Max Havelaar model was spreading to other European countries (Giovannucci and Koekoek 2003). In 1991, Belgium set up a Max Havelaar Foundation office. In the UK in the same year, CAFOD, Christian Aid, New Consumer, Oxfam, Traidcraft, and the World Development Movement copied the Max Havelaar model, creating the UK Fairtrade Foundation.[27] One year later, Switzerland added its own Max Havelaar office to the list.[28] By 1994, France, Luxembourg, and Denmark were also a part of the network (Bird and Hughes 1997). All remained committed to the same ends as their Dutch predecessor.

The creation of the Max Havelaar Foundation and its expansion throughout Europe occurred concurrently with a general increase in the formal coordination of the fair trade community. In 1987, the European Fair Trade Association was established as a representative of fair trade importers. Two years later, the International Federation for Alternative Trade (now the International Fair Trade Association) formed as a global network of organizations committed to improving the livelihoods of the poor through trade (Kochen 2003).

A culminating point for these coordination efforts came in 1997 with the creation of the Fairtrade Labelling Organization (FLO) (Raynolds 2000). FLO was created as the global fair trade standards-setting and certification organization. Comprising national fair trade labeling organizations, such as the Max Havelaar and the UK Fairtrade Foundation, FLO was established to create a consistent standard and label for fair trade products and to ensure consistency in the certification of fair trade producers (Krier 2005). Private governance, as an NSMD system, had arrived in the coffee sector.

Environmental stream

Organic coffee   In a parallel development to the Alternative Trade movement, organic agriculture gained support as early as the 1940s in Europe and North America.[29] Based on the ideas of Rudolph Steiner and Sir Albert Howard (Raynolds 2000; Reed 2001; Dankers and Liu 2003),[30] the proponents of organic food production saw it as a clear and

---

[27] See http://www.fairtrade.org.uk/about_us.htm.

[28] See http://www.maxhavelaar.ch/en/.

[29] For instance, the Soil Association – an early advocate of organic husbandry in the UK – was established in 1946 (Reed 2001).

[30] Guthman (2004) describes how Sir Albert Howard's writings on composting and the negative effects of chemical inputs on soil fertility served as important justification for the work of the organic movement in the UK.

environmentally appropriate alternative to modern agriculture. Other arguments for organic production included alternative, back-to-the-land lifestyle ideas and health benefits (Guthman 2004), an argument that gained significant credence after the publication of Rachel Carson's *Silent Spring* in 1962 (Dankers and Liu 2003). However, early on, the issue of certification was not at the fore. Organic farmers were writing the standards as they practiced, learning from experience. "On-site inspections," Dankers and Liu (2003) point out, "did not commence until the mid-1970s." Certification services were first developed to serve members of organic farming associations;[31] only later, as the number of consumers grew, did independent certification gain ground, reportedly as a means of avoiding conflicts of interest (Dankers and Liu 2003).

Organizationally, the organic movement began formalizing its structures when representatives from a handful of countries met to create the International Federation of Organic Agriculture Movements (IFOAM) in 1972 (Langman 1999; Bourgeois 2002). The founders included organic movement organizations from the USA, France, the UK, Sweden, and South Africa, all of whom shared the same belief that they would benefit from information exchange on both the principles and the practices of organic agriculture (Langman 1999).

The idea of certifying the application of organic practices to coffee production reportedly began some thirty-five years ago, when Finca Irlanda (an organic coffee plantation in Chiapas, Mexico), in collaboration with Demeter Bund (a German biodynamic agriculture association), developed the first organic-certified coffee (Giovannucci and Koekoek 2003). Harmonization of standards for coffee certification then occurred after the formation of IFOAM: in 1976 it released guidelines for coffee production in a revised version of its "basic standards of organic agriculture and food processing" (International Coffee Organization 1997).

Notably, it took very little time for governments to provide legislation controlling organic claims. In the state of Oregon, organic regulations were introduced in 1974; California had regulations by 1976. France was the first European country to adopt organic regulations, which it did in 1985. The EU then followed with Regulation 2092/91, covering organic foods, adopted in 1991 (Dankers and Liu 2003). In spite of these state incursions, the organic practices remained voluntary. The state merely stepped in to ensure the credibility of the claims, not to mandate that all producers practice organically.

---

[31] According to IFOAM, this began as early as the 1940s (International Federation of Organic Agriculture Movements 2006).

Shade-grown coffee Compared with fair trade and organic coffee initiatives, efforts to use the market to promote shade-grown coffee emerged rather late. A team of researchers from the Smithsonian Migratory Bird Center (SMBC)[32] first became interested in coffee plantations after calculating that populations of bird species that wintered in Caribbean and Latin American countries were declining by 1 percent per year (Miller 1994). Coffee grown in the shade of overstory trees was found to provide one of the only remaining habitats available for these birds (Giovannucci and Koekoek 2003, p. 52).[33] With the ever-present pressure to convert the remaining shade-grown coffee to higher-yielding sun coffee plantations, the SMBC scientists felt that they needed to act.

In September 1996, these scientists initiated discussions on shade-grown coffee and its importance for conservation, by bringing together environmentalists, farmers, and gourmet companies (Silver 1998). They hosted the First Sustainable Coffee Congress in Washington DC and began to lobby for a certification program that went beyond organic and fair trade requirements (Rice and Ward 1996).[34] In the aftermath of the event, the SMBC commenced work on a standard to define acceptable shade-grown systems. By 1997 it had released a set of criteria for labeling coffee as shade-grown (Rice and McLean 1999). Late in the same year, Café Audubon, a company supported by the National Audubon Society, had a line of its organic coffee third-party certified by Quality Assurance International against the SMBC's shade criteria (Rice and McLean 1999).

Rainforest Alliance sustainable coffee Like the shade-grown initiative spearheaded by the SMBC, other programs entered the coffee sector following the growing acceptance of fair trade and organic certification. The first of these began in 1995 as a collaboration between the Rainforest Alliance and Fundación Interamericana de Investigación Tropical (FIIT), a Guatemalan-based NGO (Rice and McLean 1999). The program was designed to promote sustainable agriculture by setting a reasonable

---

[32] The US Congress established the Smithsonian Migratory Bird Center in 1990 to help conserve populations of Neotropical migrant birds (Luxner 1996).

[33] Research by Smithsonian scientists found that shaded coffee plantations supported 180 species of birds; many more than traditional agricultural lands and very close to the numbers found in intact tropical forests (Rice and Ward 1996).

[34] For instance, in a report collaboratively written by the SMBC and the Natural Resource Defense Council, Rice and Ward (1996) pinpointed a need to "develop and apply a broader range of environmental criteria than may be covered by existing certification regimes."

standard to reach a broad set of farmers (Mas and Dietsch 2004). In fact, according to Rice and McLean (1999), "The Rainforest Alliance's Eco-OK program was the first coffee certification program to include shade trees in the criteria as part of overall land stewardship and watershed protection. Eco-OK criteria also include specific social standards addressing worker safety and living conditions." In this way, Eco-OK represented one of the first attempts at creating an overarching or comprehensive coffee standard (Ponte 2004). A Guatemalan farm was issued the first certification under the program in 1996. With the help of Coffee America (a US-based trading company), the Central America Coffee Company (a broker), and European Roasterie Inc. (a US-based roaster), 3,000 pounds of Eco-OK coffee was able to reach the US market (Shalaway 1996).

A few years later, the Dutch retailer Ahold launched another broad sustainability program. Starting as a set of sourcing guidelines, Utz Kapeh (meaning "good coffee" in a Mayan language) has been managed by an independent foundation since 2001 (Utz Kapeh 2005). The program's code is built from the Euro-Retailer Produce Working Group's 1997 initiative EurepGAP – an effort by twenty-two European retailers to promote good agricultural practices by their suppliers (Dankers and Liu 2003; EurepGAP 2006). By all accounts, the program does not intend to set a high bar for its certification (Giovannucci and Koekoek 2003; Ponte 2004), instead it hopes to influence a large number of producers, just a little bit. Indeed, this intention is clear in its 2004 annual report, which states that

> Every certification program encounters tradeoffs between these four points – stricter certification leads to higher "proof" and "impact" in production, and higher acceptance by civil society, but costlier compliance and hence lower supply and demand; a "lighter" certification program will have a lower claim of proof and impact, but higher supply and demand.

While past initiatives that have come from civil society and producer origins have not achieved high levels of market penetration, Utz Kapeh's ambition is to find the right balance in this equation to create a truly mainstream initiative (Utz Kapeh 2005). The program's first certification occurred in 2002 (Ponte 2004); since then it has become an important player, as will be seen in the next section.

Initial support

More research is needed to trace the early development of the programs listed above. Secondary sources note that organic and fair trade products have been the most successful in finding a niche in the marketplace. As of 2003 there were 166 organizations registered with FLO. In total, they represented over 500,000 individual producers in twenty-four countries (Giovannucci and Koekoek 2003).

Phase II: Assessing patterns of divergence and convergence

The introduction of a label allowed fair trade to expand considerably beyond the scope of its supportive world shops. Between the creation of the Max Havelaar label and the launch of FLO, market share rose as high as 3 percent in the Netherlands, for instance (Giovannucci and Koekoek 2003). More recently, studies have put numbers on the size of certified coffee markets. According to Giovannuci (2001), in 2000 a reasonable estimate for the North American market for organic certified coffee was $122 million, representing less than 1 percent of the $20.7 billion world coffee market. Shade-grown coffee performed poorly, with a value of approximately $15 million, or less than 0.1 percent of the world market. In Europe, there are data on the market for fair trade and organic coffee for 1999 through 2002, with estimates for 2003 and 2004. These indicate growing volumes certified, but still small totals relative to the entire coffee market (Giovannucci and Koekoek 2003).

The future?

Thus far the incursion of the state into organic and sustainable coffee certification has only been through setting standards and guidelines. The programs remain voluntary and therefore their authority still relies on pressure through the marketplace. Due to the number of initiatives out there, some form of coordination is certainly being discussed. Indeed efforts have been made to develop a single unifying sustainability standard, but little has come of this yet. The most successful coordination seems to occur between organic and bird-friendly certification, which now happens concurrently as a requirement of the SMBC program. Much more research is needed here to understand how the various programs are interacting and the forms of futures that might be possible.

Destructive impacts of the tropical ornamental fish trade

The problem

Since the 1950s, the trade in live reef fish for food and aquarium use has grown throughout Southeast Asia (Baquero 1999). While considerably smaller than other natural resource trades, the live reef fish trade has a disproportionate impact on coral reef ecosystems (Barber and Pratt 1997; Rubec et al. 2001). Since its inception, it has struggled with problems caused by the use of destructive fishing techniques, especially the use of sodium cyanide and other chemicals, which are squirted on to the reef to stun the fish and make them easier to capture (Erdmann, Pet-Soede, and Cabanban 2002). Sodium cyanide has been documented as a coral-destroying substance, not to mention an extremely dangerous substance for fishermen to handle (Barber and Pratt 1997).

Background factors

While some claim that these destructive practices have been happening since the 1960s (Baquero 1999; Best 2002), it was not until the 1980s that the international community started to take notice (Bunting 2001). Initially documented by the International Marinelife Alliance, a then-small nonprofit organization, it was not long before larger international nonprofits such as the WWF and the Nature Conservancy took notice. These nonprofit organizations brought the trade in tropical fish to the forefront of debate both in the conservation community and the industry (Barber and Pratt 1997; Bunting 2001). In 1986, US ornamental fish importers created the Pet Industry Cyanide Fact Mission (Barber and Pratt 1997; Baquero 1999).

The trade in ornamental fish is valued at approximately $200 million globally – a small amount compared with forest or seafood products (Barber and Pratt 1997; Shuman, Hodgson, and Ambrose 2004). However, the effects of cyanide fishing on the reef are devastating, killing the coral and often killing the fish that are caught. Since the 1960s, over a million kilograms of sodium cyanide has been administered to coral reefs in the Philippines alone (Barber and Pratt 1997). As of the mid-1990s, the majority of the trade was concentrated in two countries: Indonesia and the Philippines (Barber and Pratt 1997; Rubec et al. 2001). These two countries claim some of the world's most diverse and extensive reef ecosystems. They are also two countries where the use of cyanide has been heavily documented (Barber and Pratt 1997).

The ornamental fish trade is unusual on several levels. First, the product is a live animal. The product will not sell if it is dead, giving each actor in the chain of custody an incentive to keep the product alive. Cyanide use is not the only problem within the ornamental fish trade. Variance in the handling of the animal from reef to consumer can greatly impact on its mortality and, therefore, increase the number of fish taken off the reef. Second, not only are the source countries fairly concentrated, so too are the consumer countries. The USA consumes the majority of the trade (Erdmann, Pet-Soede, and Cabanban 2002) – anywhere from 48 to 60 percent of the fish – with European countries consuming the rest; creating a directed and strategic opportunity to address the trade (Balboa 2001). Lastly, these animals are pets – each product has sentimental value. Those who work in the industry often start as hobbyists. This is not just an industry of "products," it is an industry of enthusiasts, which makes the industry take more notice of the habitats from which their pets come.

Since the highly publicized documentation of destructive fishing methods for this trade, several efforts have begun to address the problem at differing scales and locations within the chain of custody (Barber and Pratt 1997; Rubec et al. 2001; Holthus 2002). The Philippine government has outlawed the use of cyanide in the industry (Philippine Headline News Online 1998). Nonprofit organizations began to train fisherfolk to use the less destructive net-barrier methods of fishing rather than cyanide (Baquero 1999; Erdmann, Pet-Soede, and Cabanban 2002). The US Pet Industry donated nets to this effort in the hope of cleaning up the trade (Various 2001–6). These efforts, however, were technical and lacked the social and economic incentives to participate (Baquero 1999).

To raise and address the social and economic drivers of destructive fishing, the Federation of Fish Collectors in the Philippines (PMP) was formed in the late 1990s (Baquero 1999). While fishers often wanted to use less destructive fishing methods, there was significant pressure to continue. The middlemen to whom they sold their fish were often also the providers of cyanide – and at times would not purchase fish if the fisher had not purchased cyanide from them. Fishers also recognized that there were costs to net-fishing that would not be recovered, given the pricing structure of the industry. Fishers were not in a position to name their price (Barber and Pratt 1997). Through the PMP, fishers became their own middlemen. They created their own holding facilities and could demand a higher price by cutting out one link in the chain of custody (Baquero 1999). This more integrated approach was not, however, a large enough effort to make a significant change in the industry.

Phase I: The NSMD certification solution

In 1997, the WWF's Bruce Bunting gathered a group of conservation NGOs and industry leaders to think of potential systemic solutions to the problems of the ornamental fish industry (Bunting 2001). After much deliberation, the Marine Aquarium Council (MAC) was created in 1998. After the Executive Director had performed a stakeholder consultation process, he developed and circulated draft standards. These draft standards were reviewed in several multi-stakeholder sessions over the course of the next two years. In November 2001, the final working version of the standards was approved by the MAC Board of Directors (Marine Aquarium Council 2002). Also in November 2001, the label was announced and the race to certification began (Holthus 2002). At the announcement of the label, MAC had commitments from thirty-three companies in nine countries, including seventeen wholesale importers – an effort equaling one-third of the US importing capacity (Bunting 2001) (approximately one-sixth of the entire world trade; Balboa 2001).

The standards apply to both the product and the supplier at each stage in the chain of custody. There are three basic areas of standards thus far in the process: ecosystem and fishery management (EFM); collection, fishing, and holding (CFH); and handling, husbandry and transport (HHT). EFM addresses the management of the reef resource and total allowable catch of each area (Marine Aquarium Council 2001b). Total allowable catch is determined through monitoring and evaluation by an organization called ReefCheck, with the input of fishers. CFH addresses how the fish (or other organisms) are caught and transported to a handling facility (primarily focused on the fishers) (Marine Aquarium Council 2001a). HHT focuses on each link of the chain of custody thereafter (Marine Aquarium Council 2001c). There are efforts under way to create standards for aquaculture products (Marine Aquarium Council 2001a, 2001b, 2001c).

Efforts at improving the marine ornamental trade have been made by many stakeholders in the trade. After many piecemeal efforts to change various parts of the industry, stakeholders were looking for a more holistic approach to making the trade more sustainable. Efforts to create the Marine Aquarium Council were spearheaded by the WWF (Bunting 2001).

Initial support

In this phase, industry joined MAC for different reasons in different locations within the chain of custody. MAC documents indicate that fishers join in the hope of obtaining a higher price for their goods and of ensuring the resource is available in the future. Importers join in order to guarantee quality for the product they receive and to differentiate themselves from other importers. Other sources indicate that actors join to avoid heavy government regulation (on the importer/exporter side) or a complete ban of the industry (on the fish collectors' side).

Certain kinds of support were immediate. As stated above, at the launch of the label, companies comprising almost half the importers to the United States signed up to be certified (Bunting 2001). While there was debate about what the standards should be, these discussions were housed within the MAC (Marine Aquarium Council 2002). Fish collectors were eager to join, for fear that if they did not join their livelihood would be in jeopardy.

There are currently no published data on how much of the trade is captured by the MAC system. The type of industry structure varies with each link in the chain of custody. Fisher collector operations are small, with each individual fisher needing to be certified. The majority of fish, however, come from the Philippines, Indonesia, and Fiji (Erdmann, Pet-Soede, and Cabanban 2002), making the training of large numbers of fishers possible. The USA is the largest importer of ornamental fish, consuming approximately half of the trade, which arrives through only a few ports in the USA (Balboa 2001). There are a few vertically integrated companies. Walt Smith International, based out of Fiji, catches fish and farms live rock, and exports the product to Los Angeles to its importing facility there (Cristina Balboa, personal communication).

In reality, only the larger importers initially signed up for certification. While the standards have been agreed upon, there is still considerable debate concerning them (Various 2001–6), with members struggling over just how flexible the process and standards can be. There seems to be a divide between businessmen and scientists.

Phase II: Assessing patterns of divergence and convergence

There are few data available on efforts to increase support through the marketplace. MAC is at a critical juncture. The first wave of certified companies are starting to speak out about the realities of certification – questioning its time and financial burden, but also its effectiveness (Various 2001–6). Proponents of certification will have to address these concerns soon if they want to broaden their support, or even keep support at the current level. Not only industry leaders are being vocal of their concerns; one high-profile company decided not to reapply for certification and published its reasons for not applying. These conversations seem to be damaging to the institutionalization of MAC.

Since there was such an impressive initial commitment to MAC, one could state that MAC is now in the support-building stage. The converging/diverging dance is very apparent in present-day MAC discussions (Various 2001–6). Current data only illustrate the industry side of the conversation, which calls both for a MAC with more teeth (and a cyanide detection test that works) and fewer costs and obligations for the certified businesses (Various 2001–6).

Data indicating NGO strategic efforts on boycotting and shaming of non-members are not currently available, however, it seems that members of the industry are taking over this role on their own. From the data available, it seems possible that competing schemes may emerge soon. What is unique to the MAC story is that the competing schemes that may emerge will come from the industry and will attempt to raise the bar of conservation standards (Various 2001–6).

One ongoing disagreement regards the legitimacy of the test that the International Marinelife Alliance created to check for cyanide in fish (International Marinelife Alliance 1999). There is doubt within the MAC community regarding whether or not it works. There are those who believe it works, those who want MAC to invest in finding another method, and those who think that cyanide is not the most important issue for the industry to address. There is a fear that if there is no cyanide testing, then there will be no real monitoring or enforcement of the rule against cyanide use (Various 2001–6). Despite all these calls for reform, there has only recently been a demand for a competing certification scheme (Various 2001–6). There is no documentation indicating that this request has made any progress.

The future?

With only five years since the certification of the marine aquarium fish industry began, MAC still seems to be in its infancy. There have been some very concrete and very vocal criticisms of MAC to date. Whether or not these criticisms will take root is an open question. The important phenomenon regarding MAC's institutionalization is that governments and funding agencies seem to see MAC as the legitimate forum for addressing issues within the ornamental fish trade.

Nonprofit organizations see MAC as a part of the solution, but not the only one. The trade itself has mixed opinions regarding MAC's legitimacy. There are too few data, and it is too early in Phase II to predict what outcome MAC will have. Of the scenarios listed above, government regulation seems the least likely. While the USA has discussed regulating the industry, the source countries lack the capacity to regulate it in any meaningful way. Serious discussion must take place about reform and potential alternative certification schemes before any clear picture of the second phase emerges.

Conclusions

This preliminary review of the emergence of certification systems across a range of sectors raises a series of important questions.

1. Are the noted differences simply a matter of time? The forest and coffee certification systems seem to reveal increasing support for the policy instrument, although with significant differences in preferences over which system is most relevant and/or appropriate. Could other sectors institutionalize in the same direction?

2. What are the supply chain features that appear to shape support for, and interest in, forest certification? The Fair Trade Coffee program, by rewarding marginalized producers, for example, raises no questions about why producers would become involved. However, in the forestry and Marine Aquarium Council cases, cost-imposing burdens are placed on producers. If the market does not compensate for these costs, they appear to result in watered down or limited standards, or limited support. Does it also matter whether humans ingest the product? That is, does this give a potentially more durable future to organic coffee and other programs such as the Marine Stewardship Council (see Appendix), which also carry with them a real or perceived human health benefit?

3. How is the process of the diffusion of the certification idea/prototype working? Although the apparel sweatshop labor practices certification model is beyond the scope of this chapter, we note that the forestry certification case appeared to emerge simultaneously, with little awareness between them (Bartley 2007). However, NSMD systems emerging since this time appear to be acutely aware of other systems. Indeed, efforts to learn about causal impacts appear to be facilitated by the Rainforest Alliance and the WWF. These organizations have spearheaded many of these efforts, informed strategic interests of other groups who want to avoid mistakes, and have adopted and promoted mechanisms that seem to hold promise.

4. What is the role of the state in all of these systems? While the absence of state authority is a key feature, it is clear that the role of the state is important. The state is a key source of existing global rules and norms with which NSMD systems must be consistent (Bernstein and Cashore 2007). In addition, the role of governments as actors is often critical in shaping support. For example, international development agencies in many countries have provided resources and support for burgeoning systems in cases where sympathetic officials saw the potential of

NSMD governance to accomplish goals that they had been unable to achieve through regulatory processes. Similarly, intergovernmental institutions such as the International Tropical Timber Organization and the World Bank have provided intellectual and financial resources in cases where officials have seen their mandates compatible with the NSMD model. Governmental agencies have also facilitated dialog and deliberations over NSMD rule development. Finally, governments may facilitate and support NSMD systems by virtue of their position in the supply chain – either as producers (in the case of government-owned corporations) or as purchasers (through their procurement policies).

5. What is the best unit of analysis with which to address NSMD certification? Is it by each sector? By the commodity? By the nature of the problem? Each choice could carry with it different causal understandings. For instance, whether coffee certification is the key instrument or whether we separate it into the biodiversity impacts, on the one hand, and community livelihoods, on the other, will yield different treatments of the dependent variable.

6. Following on from the previous question, what are the key levels and drivers of support by firms, NGOs, governments, and other actors?

7. What "meanings" attached to the systems have changed over time? For instance, some have argued that the FSC has shifted from a tool for differentiating truly green operations into a global policy tool – and in the process, "certification" has become more important than the problem it was created to address.

Paying attention to these questions would be a first step toward thinking about the emergence of shared understandings surrounding NSMD governance.

APPENDIX

Examples of NSMD governance systems

	Origin	Initiators	Policy problem	Market	Regulatory target	Tracking process?
Fair Labor Association (FLA)	2001[a]	Industry, Clinton administration, consumer and labor rights organizations	Labor conditions, workers rights	Apparel, shoes	Producers, i.e., sweatshops	Yes
Forest Stewardship Council (FSC)	1993	Environmental groups, handful of socially concerned forest management companies	Global forest deterioration	Forest products	Industrial forest companies and forest owners	Yes
Fair Trade Labelling Organization (FLO)	1997[b]	European NGO and consumer groups	Poor and marginalized producers in the developing world, working conditions	Includes coffee, tea, cocoa, sugar, bananas, soccer balls	Primary and value added producers	Yes
International Federation of Organic Agriculture Movements (IFOAM)	1997[c]	Organic-focused farmers' organizations and extension specialists	Impacts of food production (chemicals in soil, water, human health)	Agricultural products	Farmers and processors	Yes

	Origin	Initiators	Policy problem	Market	Regulatory target	Tracking process?
Leadership in Energy and Environmental Design (LEED)	2000	US Green Building Council	Environmental impacts of construction industry	Home and business builders	Building sector	Yes
Marine Aquarium Council (MAC)	1998	Environmental groups, aquarium industry, public aquariums and hobbyist groups	Ecosystem fisheries management and fish handling	Hobby aquarium trade	Fishers	Yes
Marine Stewardship Council (MSC)	1996	World Wide Fund for Nature (WWF), Unilever	Fisheries depletion	Fish sales	Industrial fishers	Yes
Mining Certification Initiative (still in formulation phase)	2001	World Wide Fund for Nature, Placer Dome	Natural resource destruction	Mining products, including gold and jewelry	Mining companies	Emerging
Program for the Endorsement of Forest Certification (PEFC) (umbrella for a number of national schemes)	2000	European Forest Owners Association	Sustainable forestry	Forest products	Forest owners	Yes (in some countries)

	Origin	Initiators	Policy problem	Market	Regulatory target	Tracking process?
Rainforest Alliance Certification	1993	Sustainable Agriculture Network (SAN) (Environmental groups)[d]	Impacts of tropical agriculture on biodiversity, waterways, deforestation and soil erosion	Agricultural products including bananas, coffee, cocoa, citrus, flowers and foliage	Tropical farmers, especially in Central America	Yes
Social Accountability International (SAI) (originally CEPAA)	1997	Council on Economic Priorities, and handful of firms	Workers' rights, community involvement	Wide range of factory products including toys and cosmetics (excludes by design extractive operations)	Factories (manufacturing facilities)	Yes
Sustainable Forestry Initiative (SFI) Certification	1994[e]	American Forest & Paper Association	Sustaining forests	Forest products	Forest companies	Yes
Sustainable Tourism Stewardship Council	2003[f]	Rainforest Alliance, multilateral agencies and industry representatives	Impacts of tourism on biodiversity	Tourism	Tourism facilities, operators, organizers, and tourists	Emerging

[a] Year FLA established a system in which auditors verified samples of companies for compliance. In 2002, the FLA Board, rather than companies, decided which companies to monitor and assigned monitors to them.

[b] FLO united fifteen separate initiatives, the first of which was the 1988 Fair Trade Initiative based in Holland.

[c] Founded in 1972, but gradually evolved into an NSMD system. In 1997 established an arms-length body to accredit certifiers.

[d] SAN was created in 1992 to develop standards and pave the way for Rainforest Alliance certification of agricultural products, the first of which occurred in 1993. Its first coffee certification took place in 1996.

[e] 1994 was the year that the SFI provided for a third-party verification component.

[f] Effort to unify disparate eco-tourism programs operating globally.

Source: Bernstein and Cashore (2007)

PART IV

Conclusion

8

Research opportunities in the area of governance for sustainable development

MAGALI A. DELMAS

Introduction

This volume brings together perspectives from economics, business management, and political science to produce a critical assessment of the current state of knowledge regarding environmental governance, in contrast to government. In this chapter, I describe recent achievements in this field of study and identify cutting-edge questions for future research. I turn first to the challenge of providing analytic distinctions of governance and those associated with the assessment of the effectiveness of environmental governance as an alternative to government. Next, I examine the various incentive mechanisms at play within alternative environmental governance mechanisms. Finally, I discuss how we can sharpen our understanding of the conditions under which specific types of environmental governance are likely to prove effective.

Analytic distinctions of governance

Our first objective was to identify the principal types or forms of environmental governance. The aim was to develop a set of analytic distinctions that allow us to think systematically about alternative mechanisms for the supply of governance and that provide a common terminology to guide research and discussion in this area.

Actors and governance

The authors of this volume have provided several definitions of governance, which range from general definitions encompassing the entire spectrum of environmental governance to more restrictive definitions focused on specific aspects of environmental governance, or the actors involved in environmental governance. Oran Young defines governance as "a social function centered on efforts to guide or steer societies toward collectively beneficial outcomes and away from outcomes that are collectively harmful" (Young, Chapter 1, this volume). Lemos and Agrawal (Chapter 3, this volume) define environmental governance as "the use of institutionalized power to shape environmental processes and outcomes" and "synonymous with interventions aiming at changes in environment-related incentives, knowledges, institutions, decision-making behaviors, and identities." It is important to note that both of these definitions of governance are not synonymous with government. They encompass the action of state and of other actors such as businesses, nongovernmental organizations (NGOs), and supranational organizations. Within this broad definition of governance, definitions of more specific governance systems have emerged based on the type of actor involved. Environmental governance systems can be based on a single type of actor. This is the case for business self-regulation, where firms adopt corporate codes of conduct and other voluntary commitments that establish standards and principles for how firms should conduct their business (King and Toffel, Chapter 4, this volume). Environmental governance systems also include hybrid governance mechanisms based on multiple actors such as businesses and government. These include negotiated agreements, where firms and regulators negotiate pollution targets beyond compliance levels in exchange for regulatory flexibility (Delmas and Terlaak 2002). Eco-labels can also be devised in collaborations between the private sector and civil society, as well as including the public sector (Auld et al., Chapter 7, this volume; Lyon, Chapter 2, this volume).

As Haufler noted, an actor-centric perspective is useful in order to focus the analytical attention on non-state actors (Haufler, Chapter 5, this volume). While there has been considerable research on environmental governance by government, the research on environmental governance without government, or between government and other actors, is only just emerging. The main contribution of this volume is to look at these hybrid situations that emerge from the intersection of the spheres of public sector, private sector, and civil society, and to study the alternative governance mechanisms that address these hybrid situations.

However, an actor-based typology of governance systems is not without its limitations. The problem with a classification of governance systems based on the actors involved is that some governance mechanisms could be placed in several categories. Indeed, while most negotiated agreements are between firms and regulatory agencies, it is possible for NGOs to be involved in such agreements. For example, the participation of NGOs was solicited within the US EPA XL voluntary program (Delmas and Mazurek 2004). Likewise, while eco-labels are often created and managed by non-state actors, there are numerous cases where the government plays a leading role in the establishment of eco-labels. An example of this is the Energy Star program in the United States, which was established by the Department of Energy (Howarth, Haddad, and Paton 2000). In addition, an actor-based classification becomes more difficult when we get to the international level, since there is no world government. Further research should seek to precisely identity the specific mechanisms or incentives at play in each of these governance mechanisms. Understanding the different mechanisms at stake in these various programs will allow us to undertake comparative work on the motivations and effectiveness of alternative governance mechanisms; a subject I will discuss next.

Incentive mechanisms for environmental governance

As most authors acknowledge, the inadequacy of governments to resolve some environmental issues has generated the search for alternative governance mechanisms. The difficult departure point is the "tragedy of the commons," where each actor shares the benefits derived from the conservation of common resources, but also directly benefits by consuming more of the resource (G. Hardin 1968). In this setting, any cooperation could potentially lead to free-riding on the efforts of actors who try to reduce the use of common-pool resources. However, empirical evidence shows that governance mechanisms can be devised, outside traditional regulation, in an attempt to overcome such problems (Ostrom 2000). These alternative governance mechanisms rely on various incentive mechanisms that can be divided into two main types of behavioral action (March and Olsen 1998). The first refers to the logic of consequences, which addresses the likely consequences for personal or collective objectives. The second refers to the logic of appropriateness, which involves cognitive, ethical dimensions. In this case, the pursuit of purpose is associated with identities more than with interests (March and Olsen 1988). These two different logics are at the root of collective-action models and social-practice models (Young 2002b). In collective-action models, decision-makers base their choice on utilitarian calculation, while, in social-practice models, actors are influenced by culture norms and habits (Young 2002b).

In the first type of logic, related to the consequences of actions, we find incentives that relate to regulatory flexibility, provided by regulators to corporations. For example, voluntary agreements between firms and regulatory agencies provide firms with regulatory relief (or the hope for firms to forestall regulation) in exchange for higher environmental performance (Khanna 2001; Delmas and Terlaak 2002; Lyon and Maxwell 2004b; King and Toffel, Chapter 4, this volume). Another potential incentive mechanism relates to disclosing information aimed at market actors and civil society (Cashore, Auld, and Newsom 2004). In this case, alternative governance systems provide information to consumers, investors, or NGOs about the environmental attributes of products or processes that will help such actors to make choices about products or processes.

In the second type of logic, related to appropriateness, actors can respond to cognitive and normative pressures. In such cases, organizations adopt alternative governance mechanisms because others do so or because they perceive that they will gain legitimacy by adopting such mechanisms (Hoffman 2001). In all of these cases, the programs can involve the same actors (firms and regulatory agencies, for example), but operate with different mechanisms that will likely impact on their effectiveness. Focusing on the incentives to participate in these alternative governance mechanisms allows us to understand the conditions that facilitate or hamper the provision of such incentives and the likelihood of the success of such mechanisms. I describe below, in more detail, the challenges related to studying the incentives and effectiveness related to alternative governance mechanisms and, more specifically, to voluntary agreements and information disclosure programs.

Challenges associated with the assessment of the effectiveness of environmental governance

The most difficult task ahead is to understand the drivers of effective environmental governance. As described by Khanna and Brouhle (Chapter 6, this volume), the empirical literature on the effectiveness of voluntary programs has reported mixed results. Likewise, the effectiveness of information disclosure programs is still largely undetermined (Delmas, Montes-Sancho, and Shimshack 2009). This may be due, in part, to the empirical and analytical challenges related to the study of effectiveness (Khanna and Brouhle, Chapter 6, this volume). First, effectiveness is a complex concept that requires further definition. Second, alternative governance mechanisms are often embedded in their institutional environment and it is not easy to isolate them. Third, we often lack the available information to conduct empirical studies.

The first difficulty in assessing the effectiveness of alternative governance mechanisms relates to the complexity of defining effectiveness. There can be various levels of effectiveness. The first level is related to the observed change in the adoption and diffusion of alternative governance mechanisms. The second level is related to changes in behavior associated with the adoption of the governance mechanism. Indeed, it is possible that organizations adopt alternative governance mechanisms merely as symbolic strategies without actually making any structural change (Meyer and Rowan 1977). For example, corporations can participate in some voluntary programs without changing their organizational procedures in order to reduce emissions. This behavior has been identified in the case of Responsible Care (King and Lenox 2000) and the US DOE Climate Challenge program (Delmas and Montes-Sancho 2007). The third level corresponds to progress in solving the original environmental problem that had been identified. For example, does the adoption of an eco-label help the recovery of an endangered species? Beyond these three levels, one can also seek to identify additional consequences related to the adoption of alternative governance mechanisms. As Young noted, environmental governance mechanisms can, and often do, produce consequences whose effects are felt beyond their own issue areas, independently from their success at solving the problems that motivate their creation (Underdal and Young 2004). For example, there could be some cross-regime effects where the adoption of specific alternative governance mechanisms impacts on the adoption of other mechanisms (Delmas and Montiel 2008). The adoption of alternative governance mechanisms can also impact on society at large, by changing the way that citizens look at a specific problem and how it can be solved.

Furthermore, there is an empirical challenge related to the lack of data available to identify improved environmental performance (Khanna and Brouhle, Chapter 6, this volume). So, it is difficult to compare the performance of organizations participating in environmental governance with that of those who did not participate. This can be explained because of the lack of consensus on what should be a measure of environmental performance, but also because of the reluctance of organizations to disclose environmental performance data. The related point suggests that it is possible that the lack of data and transparency about environmental performance is not only a problem when studying the effectiveness of environmental governance, but also hampers the effectiveness of environmental governance. As described below, most of these governance mechanisms function under the assumption that information on environmental performance is available.

In addition, as Oran Young noted, another difficulty in analyzing the effectiveness of governance systems relates to the fact that governance systems regularly interact with other factors, including demographic, technological, and cultural forces, so that the collective outcomes are products of clusters of factors that interact with one another to produce a stream of outcomes (Young 2002b). More important, it is difficult to estimate the effectiveness of programs without a counterfactual. What would have happened in the absence of the program? It is, indeed, possible that a program impacted on both participants and nonparticipants.

Additionally, as Khanna and Brouhle have noted, since the decision to participate in an alternative governance mechanism is unlikely to be made randomly by firms, studies analyzing the impact of such governance mechanisms on environmental performance must include not only participants in the governance mechanism but also nonparticipants, in order to avoid sample selection bias. This condition arises when performance is evaluated for only a restricted, nonrandom sample (Khanna and Brouhle, Chapter 6, this volume). The evaluation of the effectiveness of alternative governance mechanisms involves isolating the causal impact of the governance mechanism on performance. However, this requires controlling for the unobserved factors, such as management support, that could influence both participation in a governance mechanism and its environmental outcome. Since the participation decision is made endogenously (jointly) by a firm together with its performance decisions, disregarding that decision in an empirical analysis results in biased estimates of the impact of alternative governance mechanisms. In conclusion, we need first to be able to understand the motivations that drive organizations to participate in alternative governance mechanisms, in order to evaluate the outcomes of such governance mechanisms. As Khanna and Brouhle suggested, models that combine both motivations and outcomes will have more explanatory power.

In summary, the challenges of assessing the effectiveness of alternative governance mechanisms are multiple. We need to better identify what we mean by effectiveness, but also to understand its meaning according to the context in which alternative governance mechanisms are implemented. This relates not only to the institutional context, but also to the motivations of the actors involved in alternative governance mechanisms. Below, I suggest further areas of research related to studying the motivation of organizations to participate in voluntary environment and information disclosure programs, as well as the effectiveness of these alternative governance mechanisms.

Institutional factors and environmental voluntary agreements

Most of the contributors to this volume recognize the fact that alternative environmental governance mechanisms do not operate in isolation, but within the context of larger cultures or national regulations, and in concert with other private or semi-private environmental governance. While the focus of this volume is on "non-state" governance mechanisms, it is clear that environmental governance mechanisms do not operate in a political vacuum and that government plays an important role, directly or indirectly, in facilitating the emergence of alternative governance mechanisms. This is particularly true for voluntary agreements (VAs) between firms and regulatory agencies. Lyon (Chapter 2, this volume) notes that corporate environmental behavior is strongly influenced by political forces, perhaps mainly by the perceived threat of regulation. King and Toffel (Chapter 4, this volume) also argue that collective action is encouraged by shared fate, and that firms seek collective improvements that may forestall government regulation. As Khanna and Brouhle (Chapter 6, this volume) recognize, there is fairly consistent evidence across the various public voluntary programs that regulatory pressures are important in motivating participation (Segerson and Miceli 1998; Maxwell, Lyon, and Hackett 2000; Delmas and Terlaak 2001; Rivera 2004). Because of the importance of the relationship between voluntary programs and regulatory incentives, we need to better understand the elements of the political and regulatory environments that facilitate or hamper the emergence and success of alternative governance mechanisms. For example, Prakash and Potoski (2006) have shown that the value of the ISO 14001 International Environmental Management System standard brand reputation varies across policy and economic contexts. We need to identify the conditions where the government can provide effective regulatory incentives. Furthermore, voluntary initiatives can be marked by high transaction costs and can be significantly affected by free-riding behavior (King and Lenox 2000; Marcus, Geffen, and Sexton 2002; Delmas and Mazurek 2004; Rivera and de Leon 2004; Delmas and Keller 2005; Delmas and Montes-Sancho 2007). It is important to understand how these challenges vary across institutional contexts, and whether they may be serious enough to make these initiatives unattractive to policymakers and corporations (Delmas and Terlaak 2002). Some empirical research has shown how the ability of the government to commit to the objectives of voluntary agreements impacted on the likelihood of success of the diffusion of such schemes. For example, the US EPA's Project XL (eXcellence and Leadership) helped firms define site-specific performance standards that were more stringent than the de facto standards implied by current regulation and, in return, provided firms with flexibility concerning how to meet these standards for a specified period of time (Marcus, Geffen, and Sexton 2002; Delmas and Mazurek 2004). However, this program was hampered by high transaction costs due to the difficulty experienced by the US EPA in actually coordinating the negotiation and providing regulatory flexibility to firms. In this case, firms had to negotiate not only with community stakeholders and NGOs, but also with state and local government, as well as the regional and the various federal offices of the EPA. The costs of negotiation incurred in Project XL were estimated to be $320,000, with an average negotiation time of twenty-six months per firm (Delmas and Mazurek 2004). Likewise, the uncertainty of US regulatory behavior directed toward firms seeking ISO 14001 certification impacted on the level of transaction costs between the firm and the certification body (Delmas 2000). Citing the case of Mexico and the United States, Husted (2004) highlighted the importance of avoiding voluntary environmental programs that ignore the stark discrepancies in political support and administrative capacity enjoyed by environmental agencies on both sides of the border.

While the regulatory context is important, cultural realities are also likely to play a significant role in facilitating or hampering the diffusion of alternative governance mechanisms (Rivera 2004). Delmas and Terlaak (2002) have identified some elements of the legal, social, and cultural aspects of the institutional environment that facilitate or hamper the implementation of negotiated agreements and public voluntary programs in Europe and in the United States.

While this type of research is helpful in understanding the emergence of voluntary agreements between firms and regulatory agencies, we need a better understanding of the elements of the institutional context that are driving the demand for voluntary agreements, and also that will make these environmental governances more likely to succeed. Using international comparisons, further research could seek to identify how the characteristics of national institutional environments facilitate the adoption of successful alternative governance mechanisms. This question is particularly important when dealing with less-developed countries. Are voluntary programs appropriate in these countries (Rivera 2004), and could these be used as substitutes for traditional command-and-control regulations? Or, would such voluntary programs be marked by more free-riding behavior than in more developed countries because of weaker monitoring systems? In addition, further research should examine the link between the politics leading to the creation of these alternative governance mechanisms and their actual success or effectiveness.

In this section, we used the case of voluntary agreements between firms and regulatory agencies to exemplify the importance of the regulatory and cultural context, as driving the demand and success of governance. Similar questions could be raised for other governance mechanisms that have been identified in this volume.

Information-based governance mechanisms

Governance mechanisms based on information provisions may also be particularly useful for solving environmental problems that are difficult to enforce in a regulatory context. The main mechanism that drives information disclosure policies is the ability to deal with asymmetric information between corporations and stakeholders. Theory suggests that information-based programs can lead to improved environmental performance by increasing: (1) consumer demand for a reporting firm's environmental performance, (2) a reporting firm's susceptibility to liability under legal statutes, (3) investor and/or employee pressure for the reporting firm's pollution abatement, and (4) community coercion (Arora and Gangopadhyay 1995; Kirchhoff 2000; Maxwell, Lyon, and Hackett 2000).

Despite the theoretical findings reported in the literature, the empirical effects of disclosure programs remain inconclusive (Delmas, Montes-Sancho and Shimshack 2009). We still know little about how investors or consumers value improved environmental performance and how they react to the provision of information on environmental performance.

Investors

Socially responsible investing (SRI) represents strategies by investors to screen corporations based on their corporate social and environmental performance. The idea is to reward best performers by including them in investment portfolios based on social and environmental criteria. While there is a rapid development of SRI, studies of the role of investors reacting to information disclosure programs and the impact of SRI on firms' environmental performance yielded mixed results. One prominent information disclosure program in the United States is the Environmental Protection Agency's Toxic Release Inventory (TRI). This requires that certain firms report their toxic releases and make this information available to the public. Konar and Cohen (1997) and Khanna, Quimio, and Bojilova (1998) found that stock movements associated with the USA's (TRI) announcements led to reduced emissions. However, Bui (2005) found that the declines in emissions after TRI reporting events could be attributable to regulation rather than investor pressure. Likewise, empirical studies on the link between environmental and financial performance have shown conflicting evidence (Hart and Ahuja 1996; Klassen and McLaughlin 1996; Russo and Fouts 1997; Khanna 2001; Konar and Cohen 2001; Margolis and Walsh 2001; King and Lenox 2002). This may be explained, in part, by the difficulty of measuring environmental, as well as financial, performance (Johnston and Smith 2001; Koehler and Cram 2001; Margolis and Walsh 2001; Toffel and Marshall 2004).

The difficulty in assessing the effect of investors' choice on firms' performance is due not only to the lack of standardized screening strategies and the lack of available environmental performance data, but also to the lack of information provided by SRI funds about choices made in terms of indicators and levels (Chatterji, Levine, and Toffel 2008). First, SRI fund managers have an array of social screening strategies from which to choose. Some funds will simply screen securities based on the industry in which the corporation is operating (e.g., screen out firms involved in the tobacco industry). Others will embrace much more sophisticated methods involving multi-criteria approaches. For example, investors can use (1) physical indicators related to the material and energy output, (2) management indicators concerned with efforts toward environmental management within a firm, and/or (3) impact indicators that relate to physical output data (on emissions for instance) or to potential environmental impact (global warming potential) (Lober 1996; Ilinitch, Soderstrom, and Thomas 1998). Without agreement on what a green corporation is, or agreement on how to evaluate corporations, it will be difficult for investors to compare corporations and for corporations to compete on confused criteria.

Second, little information on environmental performance is publicly available. The main exception is the US TRI, which has been studied extensively. The lack of available objective data requires investors to seek out their own data (mostly through surveys) using their own methodology. This hampers the diffusion of the information gathered, which remains in the hands of specific investors. Some authors have voiced the optimistic view that firms can gain sizeable profits within the context of corporate social responsibility or improved environmental performance (Henderson 2001; Vogel 2005). However, these authors do not recognize that the "green and competitive" hypothesis is based on the assumption that information about the environmental attributes of firms and products is available. Without available and agreed-upon information on the environmental performance of corporations, investors cannot make informed decisions. Research on defining criteria to define corporate environmental performance is definitely required. This research will need to highlight the categories of environmental performance measurement used, and devise methodologies to aggregate various categories. For example, should such criteria emphasize input (management practices) or output measures (environmental performance)? How can we establish the right mix between various criteria? Should statistical tools be used to assess the mix, such as component factor analysis? Or should the choice of weight between criteria be established through surveys of what investors and citizen are more likely to value? Surely a mix of these approaches will be necessary.

Consumers

Likewise, the literature on consumers' reactions to information disclosure programs, such as eco-labels, is still thin. Eco-labels aim at differentiating products with respect to the characteristics of the product's production, as opposed to non-eco labels such as food labeling, which focus on the product characteristics (Teisl, Roe, and Hicks 2002). Emerging empirical literature either identifies changes in consumer awareness after exposure to the label (Leire and Thidell 2005; Loureiro and Lotade 2005), or asks consumers how they would change their behavior if provided with additional information through eco-labels (Loureiro 2003). However, it is known that survey respondents tend to overestimate their willingness to pay for environmental attributes and that awareness does not automatically translate into changes in purchasing habits. Therefore, this literature provides limited empirical evidence as to whether information disclosure programs directed toward consumers are effective in changing their behavior (Teisl, Roe, and Hicks 2002).

With the rapid growth of eco-labels, several questions have arisen. The increased competition between eco-labels has led to some confusion for producers and consumers regarding the differences between eco-labels and what they all stand for. For example, it is unclear whether eco-labels reinforce each other in "greening" the food market, or whether the existence of competing eco-labels creates confusion that discredits eco-labels as a whole. More research is needed on the motivations for customers to seek greener products. Are these "green" consumers limited to a small fringe of the population, or are there specific attributes of green products that make them attractive to a larger population? One of the challenges associated with the study of the empirical effectiveness of information disclosure programs lies in the difficulty in attributing program-induced changes to agent preferences. Indeed, products offered under information disclosure programs may provide additional quality attributes that are related to the attributes disclosed. For example, if eco- or organic-labeled products gain market share, it is difficult to establish whether consumers are expressing a preference for environmental improvement or whether they perceive other differences in product quality (such as health, safety, and taste). Are consumers valuing the public good related to green products (i.e., reducing the environmental impact) or simply the private benefit associated with these products (improved health or superior quality of the product)?

We will also need to understand the limitations of information-based policies. Are these only used to capture a marginal share of consumers, or can they be effective in reaching a broader set of consumers? The recent adoption of organic products by large retailers (e.g., Wal-Mart) calls into question the idea that organic food is limited in appeal to a small number of educated people with higher incomes. In addition, would it be possible to use information-based policies to influence other actors such as governments? Breitmeier, Young, and Zürn (2006b) have shown that activities designed to produce consensual knowledge about the causes and effects of environmental problems within international organizations can have an influence on the behavior of the actors involved in a given issue area. Further research could identify the conditions under which such a mechanism is applicable to influencing actors within the public sector.

Opening the organizational black box

Firms or corporations are another essential actor involved in the creation and implementation of alternative governance mechanisms. Similarly to customers and investors, a better understanding of a firm's motivation to participate in alternative governance mechanisms will facilitate the analysis of the effectiveness of these governance mechanisms. Why do some firms participate in alternative environmental governance mechanisms, while others do not? Is the participation in alternative governance mechanisms driven by potential performance outcomes or by pressures from various stakeholders? Are there other factors related to the internal organization of the firms which drive these decisions and possibly influence the effectiveness of firms' participation in these governance mechanisms?

Business behavior with respect to the environment, like any other aspect of strategy or management, can be considered in light of the basic economic situation of the firm: the structure of the industry in which it competes, its own position within that industry, and its internal organizational capabilities (Reinhardtl 1998). Some firms can respond to social pressure for improved environmental conditions while simultaneously delivering increased value to shareholders. However, this will be possible for some firms and not others, depending on the particular market imperfections that each confronts. Basically, each individual organization may respond differently to the same set of incentives that are related to alternative governance mechanisms.

Several basic strategies have been identified to reconcile shareholder value and environmental performance (Porter and van der Linde 1995a; Reinhardt 1998, 2000). Cost reduction is one strategy that firms can pursue. Some firms invest in environmental quality as a way of reducing the probability (or the cost) of uncertain, but adverse, outcomes (accidents or other environmental insults, for example), or as a way to realize significant savings in production costs by preventing pollution (Hart and Ahuja 1996; Klassen and Whybark 1999). Indeed, pollution prevention may not only save the cost of installing and operating end-of-pipe pollution-control devices, but also increase productivity and efficiency (Smart 1992). Besides objectives of cost reduction such as those just discussed, firms can pursue value-creation strategies. A firm can provide environmentally sound goods and then capture the extra costs from consumers. As an alternative, it can try to influence government regulation so that its rivals are disadvantaged. All attempts to use the environment as a way of creating additional value for shareholders are permutations of these basic strategies (Reinhardt 2000).

However, as with any strategy within a firm, the success of these strategies will depend on the characteristics of industry structure, business-government relations, and organizational capability, which determine corporate success more generally (Reinhardt 2000). Some firms have a profitable option to differentiate products or processes along environmental lines; for others, any time spent pursuing such strategies is squandered. Some other firms should not spend time reducing their energy input, if this is a minor element of their costs. That is to say, these strategies will depend on the firm's main corporate strategy.

In addition, some firms may resist participation in these schemes, while "similar" firms, operating in comparable environments, may seem keen to participate. Studies opening the organizational black box could help explain these differences (Delmas and Toffel 2008). Some research has looked at the role of the characteristics of the firm to explain the adoption of "beyond-compliance" strategies. This includes the influence of organizational context and design (Sharma, Pablo, and Vredenburg 1999; Christmann, 2000; Ramus and Steger 2000; Sharma 2000; Darnall and Edwards 2006) and organizational learning (Marcus and Nichols 1999). Other analyses have focused on the individual or managerial level, examining the role of leadership values (Egri and Herman 2000) and managerial attitudes (Sharma, Pablo, and Vredenburg 1999; Cordano and Frieze 2000; Sharma 2000; Rivera and de Leon 2005). While each has provided a piece of the puzzle, there is still a lack of understanding of the conditions under which these various rationales matter. As others have recently pointed out, "our understanding of factors that foster the adoption of voluntary management practices beyond compliance within a firm, particularly with operations at the plant level, still remains limited" (Klassen 2001, p. 257). We need research that not only evaluates the relative influences of external stakeholders – such as investors and customers – exerting pressures on firms to participate in alternative governance mechanisms (Henriques and Sadorsky 1999), but also depicts how a firm's characteristics moderate these pressures. For example, Delmas and Toffel (2008) propose a model where managers of different plants are subject to the same level of pressures from stakeholders, but they are expected to perceive these pressures differently due to disparities in their companies' organizational structure, strategic position, and financial and environmental performance. This difference between "objective" and "perceived" pressure leads to different calculations and responses. The adoption of environmental management practices by firms varies, therefore, not only due to different levels of stakeholder pressure, but also because of the process that transforms objective pressure into perceived pressure.

To be tested empirically, this comprehensive framework of the drivers of the adoption of environmental management practices necessitates a multi-source empirical approach that combines both existing publicly available databases, as well as original data from interviews and surveys at the facility level. Indeed, publicly available databases can provide information on "objective pressures," while interviews and surveys can give information about the perception of the pressure and the actions taken in response to the perceived pressure. The combination of these sources of information could allow the evaluation of the difference between objective and perceived pressure and the resulting adoption of environmental management practices (Delmas and Toffel 2008).

Another interesting avenue, which is not the focus of this chapter, is related to understanding how environmental NGOs operate. NGOs play an important role in creating the supply and demand for governance. While political scientists, sociologists, and some economists have started to study NGOs, we still know little about the internal functioning of these organizations and the rationale for their strategies related to environmental governance mechanisms (Haufler, Chapter 5, this volume; Lyon, Chapter 2, this volume). This creates interesting research opportunities. In addition, the same line of questioning and analysis would apply in looking at other organizations, such as political parties, policy think tanks, or voters. In conclusion, while the emerging literature has identified some of the motivations for corporations to participate in alternative governance mechanisms, we need more focused research that opens the black box of organizations and also analyzes the interaction between factors related to the external environment of organizations, as well as factors related to the internal workings of organizations.

"Compare and combine" governance mechanisms

Research in the area of governance needs to provide prescriptive tools to design and implement governance systems that fit the circumstances prevailing in specific situations. Academic research assessing the costs and benefits of such instruments, and how they compare with more traditional policy instruments, remains limited. Indeed, governance mechanisms need to be compared based on their effectiveness, but also based on their costs. For example, research has shown that the comparative efficiency of voluntary agreements, command-and-control regulations, and market-based mechanisms varies with the transaction attributes of the firm and its market opportunities (Delmas and Marcus 2004).

We also need to understand the limitations of alternative governance mechanisms. Can these replace traditional governance? Or are they complementary tools? As the contributors to this volume have noted, there are often opportunities for creating complex or compound governance systems and using adaptive management to encourage social learning regarding the pros and cons of different ways to configure these systems (Young, Chapter 1, this volume). We still know little about whether governance mechanisms are competing with each other or whether they can complement each other. Some studies show that alternative governance mechanisms can enhance each other, while others argue that there could be information overload and that competition between alternative governance mechanisms could hamper their effectiveness (Delmas and Montiel 2008). The issue here concerns the identification of effective combinations of forms of governance.

Alternative governance mechanisms are usually treated as alternatives to one another, rather than as complementary. Gunningham, Grabosky, and Sinclair (1998) have developed a theory of regulatory pluralism, demonstrating how *combinations* of public and private orderings can be integrated into an overall optimal regulatory mix, and how third parties can be harnessed in the furtherance of environmental policy. We need more studies that show how the design of complementary combinations of policy instruments, tailored to particular environmental goals and circumstances, will produce more effective and efficient policy outcomes.

Furthermore, we still know little about the dynamic evolution of governance mechanisms (Auld et al., Chapter 7, this volume). Are there salient differences between the various phases of diffusion of a governance mechanism?

Conclusions

The emerging area of study of alternative governance mechanisms is particularly fascinating, with many challenges ahead of us. An important goal in this connection is to enlarge the current debate in this field by expanding the tool kit available to those seeking to enhance their understanding of the effectiveness of alternative governance mechanisms. In this chapter, I have described the challenges associated with such an endeavor and proposed several areas of research.

Emerging from this exercise is not only the need to identify more precisely the incentive mechanisms at stake within alternative governance mechanisms, but also the specific context in which these incentive mechanisms are implemented. Table 8.1 describes the various elements of a context-oriented analysis of the incentives and effectiveness of

Table 8.1 *The elements of a context-oriented analysis of the effectiveness of alternative governance mechanisms*

Actors involved	Incentive mechanisms	Institutional environment	Organizational characteristics	Effectiveness measurement
• Corporations • Investors • Customers • Trade associations • Government • Political parties • Policy think tanks • Voters • Environmental NGOs • Other	• Regulatory flexibility • Information-based mechanisms • Normative and cognitive mechanisms • Other	• Regulatory environment • Cultural and cognitive environment	• Governance structure • Organizational structure • Leadership and employee characteristics • Other	• Adoption of the practice • Impact on environmental problems • Broader consequences for other governance mechanisms and for society at large

alternative governance mechanisms. First, it requires attention to the actors involved: investors, consumers, and corporations all differ in their objectives and organization. Second, it directs attention to the incentive mechanisms at stake within alternative governance mechanisms. Several incentive mechanisms are identified, including regulatory incentives and information disclosure mechanisms. Third, we need to understand how these mechanisms and actors vary according to the external environment in which they operate. Fourth, it is important to open the black box of organizations, in order to understand differences in behavior related to the participation and implementation of alternative governance mechanisms. Finally, an analysis of effectiveness may not be one-dimensional, but would benefit by integrating broader views of the effectiveness of alternative governance mechanisms, including the diffusion of these mechanisms, their impact on environmental problems, and their broader consequences on other governance mechanisms and on society at large. Efforts to contribute to our understanding of the effectiveness of alternative governance mechanisms may proceed by focusing either on specific rows for specific actors, or on the columns of this table. We hope that such a framework can direct scholars to study the effectiveness of alternative governance mechanisms and further help them develop prescriptive tools to design and implement governance systems that fit the circumstances prevailing in specific situations.

REFERENCES

Abreu, D. 1988. "On the theory of infinitely repeated games with discounting," *Econometrica* 56(2): 383–96.

Adger, W. N. 2001. "Scales of governance and environmental justice for adaptation and mitigation of climate change," *Journal of International Development* 13(7): 921–31.

Adger, W. N., N. W. Arnell, and E. L. Tompkins. 2005. "Successful adaptation to climate change across scales," *Global Environmental Change* 15: 77–86.

Agrawal, A. 2005. *Environmentality: Technologies of Government and the Making of Subjects.* Durham, NC: Duke University Press.

Agrawal, A. and E. Ostrom. 2006. "Political science and conservation biology: The dialog of the deaf?" *Conservation Biology* 20(3): 681–2.

Akerlof, G. A. 1970. "Market for lemons: Quality uncertainty and market mechanism," *Quarterly Journal of Economics* 84(3): 488–500.

Alberini, A. and K. Segerson. 2002. "Assessing voluntary programs to improve environmental quality," *Environmental and Resource Economics* 22: 157–84.

Alchian, A. and H. Demsetz. 1972. "Production, information costs, and economic organization," *American Economic Review* 62(5): 777–95.

Alexy, O. and J. Henkel. 2007. "Promoting the penguin: Who is advocating open source software in commercial settings?" Paper presented at the Second Annual Conference on Institutional Foundations for Industry Self-Regulation, Harvard Business School, Boston, MA.

Allott, P. 1990. *Eunomia: New Order for a New World.* Oxford University Press.

Anderson, K. 2000. "The Ottawa Convention banning landmines, the role of international nongovernmental organizations and the idea of international civil society," *European Journal of International Law* 11(1): 91–120.

Anderson, S. W., J. Daly and M. Johnson. 1999. "Why firms seek ISO 9000 certification: Regulatory compliance or competitive advantage?" *Production and Operations Management* 8(1): 28–43.

Andonova, L. B. and M. A. Levy. 2003. "Franchising global governance: Making sense of the Johannesburg Type II partnerships," in O. Schram Stokke and O. B. Thommessen (eds.) *Yearbook of International Co-operation and Development 2003/2004*, pp. 19–31. London: Earthscan.

Anheier, H.K. and N. Themudo. 2004. "Governance and management of international membership organizations," *Brown Journal of World Affairs* 11(2): 185–98.

Anton, W.R., G. Deltas, and M. Khanna. 2004. "Incentives for environmental self-regulation and implications for environmental performance," *Journal of Environmental Economics and Management* 48(1): 632–54.

Antweiler, W. and K. Harrison. 2007. "Canada's voluntary ARET program: Limited success despite industry cooperation," *Journal of Policy Analysis and Management* 26(4): 755–73.

Arimura, T.H., A. Hibiki, and H. Katayama. 2008. "Is a voluntary approach an effective environmental policy instrument? A case for environmental management systems," *Journal of Environmental Economics and Management* 55(3): 281–95.

Aristotle. 1962/1992. *The Politics [written 350 BC].* London: Penguin Classics.

Arora, S. and T.N. Cason. 1995. "An experiment in voluntary environmental regulation: Participation in EPA's 33/50 program," *Journal of Environmental Economics and Management* 28(3): 271–86.

1996. "Why do firms volunteer to exceed environmental regulations? Understanding participation in EPA's 33/50 program," *Land Economics* 72(4): 413–32.

Arora, S. and S. Gangopadhyay. 1995. "Toward a theoretical model of voluntary overcompliance," *Journal of Economic Behavior and Organization* 28: 289–309.

Ashford, N.A. 2002. "Government and environmental innovation in Europe and North America," *American Behavioral Scientist* 45(9): 1417–34.

Backstrand, K. 2003. "Civic science for sustainability: Reframing the role of experts, policy-makers and citizens in environmental governance," *Global Environmental Politics* 3(4): 24–41.

Baden, J.A. and D.S. Noonan (eds.) 1998. *Managing the Commons.* Bloomington, IN: Indiana University Press.

Bagchi, A. 2003. "Rethinking federalism: Changing power relations between the center and the states," *Publius: The Journal of Federalism* 33(4): 21–42.

Balboa, C.M. 2001. "The consumption of marine ornamental fish in the United States," in J.C. Cato and C.L. Brown (eds.) *Marine Ornamental Species: Collection, Culture and Conservation.* Ames, IA: Iowa State Press/Blackwell Publishing.

Baquero, J. 1999. "The trade of ornamental fish from the Philippines," *Reefs.org,* February 21, 7.

Barber, J. 1998. "Responsible action or public relations? NGO perspectives on voluntary initiatives," *Industry and Environment* 21(1–2): 9.

Barber, C. and V. Pratt. 1997. *Sullied Seas.* Washington, DC: World Resources Institute.

Barnett, M. N. and M. Finnemore. 2004. *Rules for the World: International Organizations in Global Politics*. Ithaca, NY: Cornell University Press.

Barnett, M. L. and A. A. King. 2006. "Good fences make good neighbors: An institutional explanation of industry self-regulation," Paper presented at the Academy of Management Best Paper Proceedings, Atlanta, GA.

Baron, D. P. 1985. "Non-cooperative regulation of a nonlocalized externality," *RAND Journal of Economics* 16(4): 553–68.

2004a. "Competing for the public through the news media," *Journal of Economics and Management Strategy* 14: 339–76.

2004b. "Persistent media bias," Working Paper, Stanford University, CA.

2009. *Business and Its Environment*, 6th edn. Upper Saddle River, NJ: Prentice Hall.

Baron, D. P. and D. Diermeier. 2007. "Strategic activism and non-market strategy," *Journal of Economics and Management Strategy* 16: 599–634.

Barrett, S. 1994. "Self-enforcing international environmental agreements," *Oxford Economic Papers – New Series* 46: 878–94.

2003. *Environment and Statecraft*. New York: Oxford University Press.

Bartel, A. and L. Thomas. 1985 "Direct and indirect effects of regulation," *Journal of Law and Economics* 28: 1–25.

Bartley, T. 2003. "Certifying forests and factories: States, social movements, and the rise of private regulation in the apparel and forest products fields," *Politics and Society* 31(3): 433–64.

2007. "Institutional emergence in an era of globalization: The rise of transnational private regulation of labor and environmental conditions," *American Journal of Sociology* 113(2): 297–351.

Bates, R. H. 1989. *Beyond the Miracle of the Market: The Political Economy of Agrarian Development in Africa*. New York: Cambridge University Press.

Beaver, W. 1997. "What to do about alcohol advertising," *Business Horizons* 40(4): 87–91.

Becker, G. S. 1968. "Crime and punishment: An economic approach," *Journal of Political Economy* 76: 169–217.

1978. *The Economic Approach to Human Behavior*. University of Chicago Press.

Bell, R. G. and C. Russell. 2002. "Environmental policy for developing countries," *Issues in Science and Technology* 18: 63–70.

Bennear, L. S. and C. Coglianese. 2006. "Program evaluation of environmental policies: Toward evidence-based decision making," in C. Coglianese and J. Nash (eds.) *Beyond Compliance: Business Decision Making and the US EPA's Performance Track Program*, pp. 115–30. Cambridge, MA: Harvard University John F. Kennedy School of Government.

Bennett, P. I. 2000. "Environmental governance and private actors: Enrolling insurers and international maritime regulation," *Political Geography* 19: 875–99.

Berger, P. and T. Luckmann. 1966. *The Social Construction of Reality*. New York: Doubleday.

Bernheim, D. and M. Whinston. 1986. "Common agency," *Econometrica* 54: 923–42.

Bernstein, S. and B. Cashore. 2004. "Non-state global governance: Is forest certification a legitimate alternative to a global forest convention?" in J. Kirton and M. Trebilcock (eds.) *Hard Choices, Soft Law: Combining Trade, Environment, and Social Cohesion in Global Governance*. Aldershot, UK: Ashgate Press.

  2007. "Can non-state global governance be legitimate? An analytical framework," *Regulation and Governance* 1(4): 347–71.

Best, B. 2002. "International trade in coral reef animals, algae and products: An overview," in B. A. Best, R. S. Pomeroy, and C. M. Balboa (eds.) *Implications for Coral Reef Management and Policy: Relevant Findings from the 9th International Coral Reef Symposium*. Washington, DC: USAID.

Betsill, M. M. and H. Bulkeley. 2004. "Transnational networks and global environmental governance: The Cities for Climate Protection program," *International Studies Quarterly* 48(20): 471–93.

Bird, K. and D. R. Hughes. 1997. "Ethical consumerism: The case of 'fairly traded' coffee," *Business Ethics* 6(3): 159–68.

Blacconiere, W. G. and D. M. Patten. 1994. "Environmental disclosures, regulatory costs, and changes in firm value," *Journal of Accounting and Economics* 18(3): 357–77.

Blackman, A., S. Afsah, and D. Ratunanda. 2004. "How does public disclosure work? Evidence from Indonesia's PROPER program," *Human Ecology Review* 11: 235–46.

Blackman, A., T. P. Lyon, and N. Sisto. 2006. "Voluntary environmental agreements when regulatory capacity is weak," *Comparative Economic Studies* 48: 682–702.

Blumentritt, T. and D. Nigh. 2002. "The integration of subsidiary political activities in multinational corporations," *Journal of International Business Studies* 33(1): 57–77.

Bob, C. 2005. *The Marketing of Rebellion: Insurgents, Media, and International Activism*. Cambridge Studies in Contentious Politics. Cambridge University Press.

  2007. "Boomerang or market? Theorizing transnational contention in small arms and beyond," Paper presented at Contentious Politics Workshop/ International Relations Workshop, University of Maryland.

Boli, J. and G. M. Thomas. 1997. "World culture in the world polity: A century of international non-governmental organization," *American Sociological Review* 62(2): 171–90.

Bose, P. 1995. "Regulatory errors, optimal fines and the level of compliance," *Journal of Public Economics* 56: 475–84.

Bosso, C. J. 2005. *Environment Inc.: From Grassroots to Beltway.* Lawrence, KS: University Press of Kansas.

Bourgeois, B. 2002. "Letter to FSC Canada and FSC BC Regional Initiative," Vancouver: Economic Chamber Member, Forest Stewardship Council – British Columbia Steering Committee.

Boyd, J., A. J. Krupnick, and J. Mazurek. 1998. "Intel's XL permit: A framework for evaluation," Discussion Paper 98–11. Washington, DC: Resources for the Future.

Boyer, M. and J. Laffont. 1999. "Toward a political theory of environmental policy," *RAND Journal of Economics* 30: 137–57.

Braithwaite, J. 2006. "Responsive regulation and developing economies," *World Development* 34(5): 884–98.

Braithwaite, J. and P. Drahos. 2000. *Global Business Regulation.* Cambridge University Press.

Breitmeier, H., O. R. Young, and M. Zürn. 2006a. *International Environmental Regimes: From Case Study to Database.* Cambridge, MA: The MIT Press.

2006b. "Programmatic activities, knowledge, and environmental problem-solving," in H. Breitmeier, O. Young and M. Zürn (eds.) *Analyzing International Environmental Regimes.* Cambridge, MA: The MIT Press.

Brooks, N. 2003. "Vulnerability, risk and adaptation: A conceptual framework," *Tyndall Centre Working Paper No. 38.* Norwich, UK: Tyndall Centre for Climate Change Research and Centre for Social and Economic Research on the Global Environment (CSERGE).

Brooks, N. and W. N. Adger. 2004. "Assessing and enhancing adaptive capacity," in B. Lim (ed.) *Adaptation Policy Framework.* New York: United Nations Development Programme.

Brooks, N., W. N. Adger, and M. Kelly. 2005. "The determinants of vulnerability and adaptive capacity at the national level and the implications for adaptation," *Global Environmental Change* 15: 151–63.

Brown, D. J., S. C. Brown, and S. W. Desposato. 2007. "Promoting and preventing political change through internationally funded NGO activity," *Latin American Research Review* 42(1): 126–40.

Brouhle, K., C. Griffiths, and A. Wolverton. 2009. "Evaluating the role of EPA policy levers: An examination of a voluntary program and regulatory threat in the metal finishing industry," *Journal of Environmental Economics and Management* 57(2): 166–181.

Brown, L. D. and M. H. Moore. 2001. "Accountability, strategy, and international nongovernmental organizations," *Nonprofit and Voluntary Sector Quarterly* 30(3): 569–87.

Bruch, C. and J. Prendergrass. 2003. "Type II partnerships, international law, and the commons," *Georgetown International Environmental Law Review* Summer.

Buchanan, J. M. and G. Tullock. 1962. *The Calculus of Consent: Logical Foundations of Constitutional Democracy*. Ann Arbor, MI: University of Michigan Press.
___. 1975. "Polluters' profits and political response: Direct control versus taxes," *American Economic Review* 65: 139–47.

Bui, L. 2005. "Public disclosure of private information as a tool for regulating environmental emissions: Firm-level responses by petroleum refineries to the toxics release inventory," Working Paper, Brandeis University, Waltham, MA.

Bullard, R. D. 1990. *Dumping in Dixie: Race, Class, and Environmental Quality*. Boulder, CO: Westview Press.

Bunting, B. 2001. *"Buy a Fish, Buy a Coral, Save a Reef: The Importance of Economic Incentives to Sustain Conservation,"* Presented at the Marine Ornamentals 2001 Conference, Lake Buena Vista, Florida, 26 November to 1 December 2001.

Burchell, G., C. Gordon, and P. Miller (eds.) 1991. *The Foucault Effect: Studies in Governmentality*. University of Chicago Press.

Busch, P.-O., H. Jorgens, and K. Tews. 2005. "The global diffusion of regulatory instruments: The making of a new international environmental regime," *Annals of the American Academy of Political and Social Sciences* 598: 146–67.

Buthe, T. 2002. "Taking temporality seriously: Modeling history and the use of narratives as evidence," *American Political Science Review* 96(3): 481–94.

Calfee, J. E. and R. Craswell. 1984. "Some effects of uncertainty on compliance with legal standards," *Virginia Law Review* 70(5): 965–1003.

Cardoso, F. H. and E. Faletto. 1979. *Dependency and Development*. Berkeley, CA: University of California Press.

Carmin, J., N. Darnall, and J. Mil-Homens. 2003. "Stakeholder involvement in the design of U.S. voluntary environmental initiatives: Does sponsorship matter?" *Policy Studies Journal* 31(4): 527–43.

Carpenter, C. 2005. "International agenda-setting in world politics: Issue emergence and non-emergence around children and armed conflict," *Human Rights and Human Welfare Working Paper No. 30*. Pittsburgh, PA. July 2005: 1–27.

Carpio, I. 1993. *"The Netherlands: Dutch promote alternative coffee trade"* [news wire]. IPS – Inter Press Service / Global Information Network, July 2, 1993 [accessed August 31, 2005, available at www.lexis-nexis.com].

Cashore, B. 2002. "Legitimacy and the privatization of environmental governance: How non-state market driven (NSMD) governance systems gain rule-making authority," *Governance: An International Journal of Policy, Administration and Institutions* 15(4): 503–29.

Cashore, B., G. Auld, and D. Newsom. 2004. *Governing Through Markets: Forest Certification and the Emergence of Non-State Authority*. New Haven, CT: Yale University Press.

Cashore, B., G. Auld, S. Bernstein, and C. McDermott. 2007. "Can non-state governance 'ratchet up' global environmental standards? Lessons from the forest sector," *Review of European Community and International Environmental Law* 16(2): 158–72.

Cashore, B., F. Gale, E. Meidinger, and D. Newsom. 2006a. "Introduction: Forest certification in analytical and historical perspective," in B. Cashore, F. Gale, E. Meidinger and D. Newsom (eds.) *Confronting Sustainability: Forest Certification in Developing and Transitioning Societies*. New Haven, CT: Yale School of Forestry and Environmental Studies Publication Series.

Cashore, B., C. McDermott, K. Levin, G. Auld, and D. Newsom. 2006b. *The Shaping and Reshaping of British Columbia Forest Policy in the Global Era: A Review of Governmental and Non-governmental Strategic Initiatives*. New Haven, CT: Yale Program on Forest Policy and Governance.

Caswell, J. A. 1998. "How labeling of safety and process attributes affects markets for food," *Agricultural and Resource Economics Review* 27: 151–8.

Chalmers, D. A., S. B. Martins, and K. Piester. 1997. "Associative networks: New structures of representation for the popular sectors," in D. Chalmers, C. Vilas, K. Hite, S. B. Martin, K. Piester and M. Segarra (eds.) *The New Politics of Inequality in Latin America*. New York: Oxford University Press.

Chan, E. S.W. and S.C. K. Wong. 2006. "Motivations for ISO 14001 in the hotel industry," *Tourism Management* 27(3): 481–92.

Chapin, M. 2004. "A challenge to conservationists," *Worldwatch* 17(6): 17–31.

Charnovitz, S. 2006. "Nongovernmental organizations and international law," *American Journal of International Law* 100(2): 348–72.

Chatterji, A. K., D. I. Levine, and M. W. Toffel. 2008. "How well do social ratings actually measure corporate social responsibility?" *Journal of Economics and Management Strategy* 18(1): 125–69.

Christmann, P. 2000. "Effects of 'best practices' of environmental management on cost advantage: The role of complementary assets," *Academy of Management Journal* 43(4): 663–80.

Christmann, P. and G. Taylor. 2001. "Globalization and the environment: Determinants of firm self-regulation in China," *Journal of International Business Studies* 32(3): 439–58.

Clapp, J. 1998. "The privatization of global environmental governance: ISO 14000 and the developing world," *Global Governance* 4(3): 295–316.

Clark, A. M. 1995. "Non-governmental organizations and their influence on international society," *Journal of International Affairs* 48(2): 507–25.

Clark, W. 2000. "Environmental globalization," in J. S. Nye and J. D. Donahue (eds.) *Governance in a Globalizing World*, pp. 86–108. Washington, DC: Brookings Institution Press.

Coase, R. H. 1937. "The nature of the firm," *Economica* 4(16): 386–405.

1960. "The problem of social cost," *Journal of Law and Economics* 3: 1–44.

Cochran, P. L. and R. A. Wood. 1984. "Corporate social responsibility and financial performance," *Academy of Management Journal* 27: 42–56.

Cohen, M. 1999. "Monitoring and enforcement of environmental policy," in T. Tietenberg and H. Follmer (eds.) *International Yearbook of Environmental and Resource Economics*, vol. III. Cheltenham, UK: Edward Elgar Publishers.

Collier, R.B. and D. Collier. 1991. *Shaping the Political Arena*. Princeton, NJ: Princeton University Press.

Conca, K. 2006. *Governing Water: Contentious Transnational Politics and Global Institution Building*. Cambridge, MA and London: The MIT Press.

Cooley, A. and J. Ron. 2002. "The NGO scramble: Organizational insecurity and the political economy of transnational action," *International Security* 27(1): 5–39.

Corbett, C.J., and D.A. Kirsch. 2004. "Response to 'Revisiting ISO 14000 diffusion: A new 'look' at the drivers of certification'," *Production and Operations Management* 13(3): 268–71.

Corbett, C.J., M.J. Montes-Sancho, and D.A. Kirsch. 2005. "The financial impact of ISO 9000 certification in the United States: An empirical analysis," *Management Science* 51(7): 1046–59.

Cordano, M. and I. Frieze. 2000. "Pollution reduction preferences of US environmental managers: Applying Ajzen's theory of planned behavior," *Academy of Management Journal* 43(4): 627–41.

Corell, E. and M.M. Betsill. 2001. "A comparative look at NGO influence in international environmental negotiations: Desertification and climate change," *Global Environmental Politics* 1(4): 86–107.

Cowen, T. (ed.) 1988. *The Theory of Market Failure: A Critical Examination*. Fairfax, VA: George Mason University Press.

Cowles, M.G. 1998. "The changing architecture of big business," in J. Greenwood and M. Aspinwall (eds.) *Collective Action in the European Union: Interests and the New Politics of Associability*. Abingdon, UK: Routledge.

Cropper, M. and W. Oates. 1992. "Environmental economics: A survey," *Journal of Economic Literature* 30(2): 675–740.

Cross, J.G. and M.J. Guyer. 1980. *Social Traps*. Ann Arbor, MI: University of Michigan Press.

Crystal, J. 2000. "Policy preferences and political strategies: Explaining why producers want what they want," Paper presented at International Studies Association Annual Meeting, Los Angeles, March 15–18.

Cutler, A.C., V. Haufler, and T. Porter (eds.) 1999. *Private Authority and International Affairs*. Albany, NY: SUNY Press.

Dales, J.H. 1968. "Land, water and ownership," *Canadian Journal of Economics* 1(4): 791–804.

Dankers, C. and P. Liu. 2003. *Environmental and Social Standards, Certification and Labelling for Cash Crops*. Rome: Food and Agriculture Organization of the United Nations.

Darnall, N. and J. Carmin. 2005. "Greener and cleaner? The signaling accuracy of US voluntary environmental programs," *Policy Sciences* 38(2–3): 71–90.

Darnall, N. and D. Edwards. 2006. "Predicting the cost of environmental management system adoption: The role of capabilities, resources and ownership structure," *Strategic Management Journal* 27(4): 301–20.

Dasgupta, S., H. Hettige, and D. Wheeler. 2000. "What improves environmental compliance? Evidence from Mexican industry," *Journal of Environmental Economics and Management* 39(1): 39–66.

Dawson, N. L. and K. Segerson. 2005. "Voluntary environmental agreements with industries: Participation incentives with industry-wide targets," Working Paper, University of Connecticut.

Dean, M. 1999. *Governmentality: Power and Rule in Modern Society*. London: Sage Publications.

Decker, C. 2003. "Corporate environmentalism and environmental statutory permitting," *Journal of Law and Economics* 46: 103–29.

Decker, C. and C. R. Pope. 2005. "Adherence to environmental law: The strategic complementarities of compliance decisions," *Quarterly Review of Economics and Finance* 45: 641–61.

Delmas, M. 2000. "Barriers and incentives to the adoption of ISO 14001 in the United States," *Duke Environmental Law and Policy Forum* Fall: 1–38.

2002. "The diffusion of environmental management standards in Europe and in the United States: An institutional perspective," *Policy Sciences* 35(1): 91–119.

2005. "An institutional perspective on the diffusion of international management standards: The case of the environmental management standard ISO 14001," Working Paper. Donald Bren School of Environmental Science and Management, Santa Barbara, CA.

Delmas, M. and A. Keller. 2005. "Strategic free riding in voluntary environmental programs: The case of the U.S. E.P.A. WasteWise program," *Policy Sciences* 38: 91–106.

Delmas, M. and A. Marcus. 2004. "Firms' choice of regulatory instruments to reduce pollution: A transaction cost approach," *Business and Politics* 6(3), Article 3.

Delmas, M. and J. Mazurek. 2004. "A transaction cost perspective on negotiated agreements: The case of the U.S. EPA XL program," in A. Baranzini and P. Thalmann (eds.) *Voluntary Approaches to Climate Protection: An Economic Assessment of Private-Public Partnerships*. Cheltenham, UK: Edward Elgar Publishing.

Delmas, M.A. and M. J. Montes-Sancho. 2007. "Voluntary agreements to improve environmental quality: Are late joiners the free riders?" Working Paper. Institute for Social, Behavioral, and Economic Research, University of California, Santa Barbara [available at http://repositories.cdlib.org/isber/publications/07].

Delmas, M., M. Montes-Sancho, and J. Shimshack. 2009. "Information disclosure policies: Evidence from the electricity industry," *Economic Inquiry*.

Delmas, M. and I. Montiel. 2008. "The diffusion of voluntary international management standards: responsible care, ISO 9000 and ISO 14001 in the chemical industry," *Policy Studies Journal* 36(1): 65–93.

Delmas, M. and A. Terlaak. 2001. "A framework for analyzing environmental voluntary agreements," *California Management Review* 43(3): 44–63.

2002. "Regulatory commitment to negotiated agreements: Evidence from the United States, Germany, the Netherlands, and France," *Journal of Comparative Policy Analysis* 4: 5–29.

Delmas, M. and M. W. Toffel. 2008. "Organizational responses to environmental demands: Opening the black box," *Strategic Management Journal* 29(10): 1027–55.

Dicum, G. and N. Luttinger. 1999. *The Coffee Book : Anatomy of an Industry from Crop to the Last Drop*. New York: New Press (distributed by W.W. Norton).

Dietz, T., E. Ostrom, and P. Stern. 2003. "The struggle to govern the commons," *Science* 302: 1907–12.

DiMaggio, P. J. 1988. "Interest and agency in institutional theory," in L. G. Zucker (ed.) *Institutional Patterns and Organizations: Culture and Environment*, pp. 3–21. Cambridge, MA: Ballinger.

Dingwerth, K. 2007. *The New Transnationalism: Transnational Governance and Democratic Legitimacy*. New York: Palgrave Macmillan.

Domask, J. 2003. "From boycotts to partnership: NGOs, the private sector, and the world's forests," Chapter 8 in J. P. Doh and H. Teegen (eds.) *Globalization and NGOs: Transforming Business, Governments, and Society*. New York: Praeger.

Donaldson, T. and L. Preston. 1995. "The stakeholder theory of the corporation: Concepts, evidence, and implications," *Academy of Management Review* 29(1): 65–91.

Dunning, J. 1993. *The Globalization of Business*. New York: Routledge.

Durant, R. F., Y. P. Chun, B. Kim, and S. Lee. 2004. "Toward a new governance paradigm for environmental and natural resource management in the 21st century?" *Administration and Society* 35: 643–82.

Dutta, P. K. and R. Radner. 2004. "Self-enforcing climate change treaties," *Proceedings of the National Academy of Sciences of the USA* 101(14): 5174–9.

Dyck, A. and L. Zingales. 2002. "The corporate governance role of the media," Working Paper. Harvard Business School, Cambridge, MA.

Eakin, H. and M. C. Lemos. 2006. "Adaptation and the state: Latin America and the challenge of capacity-building under globalization," *Global Environmental Change* 16(1): 7–18.

Eesley, C. and M. Lenox. 2006. "Secondary stakeholder actions and the selection of firm targets," Working Paper. Duke University, Durham, NC.

Eggertsson, T. 2005. *Imperfect Institutions: Possibilities and Limits of Reform*. Ann Arbor, MI: University of Michigan Press.

Egri, C. and S. Herman. 2000. "Leadership in the North American environmental sector: Values, leadership styles, and contexts of environmental leaders and their organizations," *Academy of Management Journal* 43: 571–604.

Engel, S., R. Lopez and C. Palmer. 2006. "Community-industry contracting over natural resource use in a context of weak property rights: The case of Indonesia," *Environmental and Resource Economics* 33: 73–93.

Environmental Protection Agency. 2001. *The United States Experience with Economic Incentives for Protecting the Environment*, EPA-240-R-01-001. Washington, DC: US EPA.

Erdmann, M., C. Pet-Soede, and A. Cabanban. 2002. "Destructive fishing practices," in B. A. Best, R. S. Pomeroy and C. M. Balboa (eds.) *Implications for Coral Reef Management and Policy: Relevant Findings from the 9th International Coral Reef Symposium*. Washington, DC: USAID.

EurepGAP. 2006. *About EurepGAP* [web page, accessed March 19, 2006, available at www.eurepgap.org/Languages/English/about.html].

Evans, P. 1996. "Government action, social capital and development: Reviewing the evidence on synergy," *World Development* 24(6): 1119–32.

Falkner, R. 2003. "Private environmental governance and international relations: Exploring the links," *Global Environmental Politics* 3(2): 72–87.

Farrell, J. and T. Simcoe. 2007. "Choosing the rules for formal standardization," Paper presented at the Second Annual Conference on Institutional Foundations for Industry Self-Regulation, Harvard Business School, Boston, MA.

Fenn, P. and C. G. Veljanovski. 1988. "A positive economic theory of regulatory enforcement," *Economic Journal* 98: 1055–70.

Fienup-Riordan, A. 1990. *Eskimo Essays: Yu'pik Lives and How We See Them*. New Brunswick, NJ: Rutgers University Press.

Financial Times. 1985. *"Coffee deal greeted with scepticism"* [newspaper article, section IV, Commodities and Agriculture, page 38], *Financial Times* April 23, 1985 [accessed March 13, 2006, available at www.lexis-nexis.com].

  1989. *"Collapse of the coffee pact"* [newspaper article, section I, Editorial, page 16], *Financial Times* July 18, 1989 [accessed March 13, 2006, available at www.lexis-nexis.com].

Finger, M. and T. Princen. 1994. *Environmental NGOs in World Politics: Linking the Local and the Global*. London and New York: Routledge.

Finnemore, M. and K. Sikkink. 1998. "International norm dynamics and political change," *International Organization* 52(4): 887–917.

Fischer, C. and T. P. Lyon. 2008. "Competing environmental labels," Working Paper. Ross School of Business, University of Michigan, Ann Arbor, MI.

Ford, L. H. 2003. "Challenging global environmental governance: Social movement agency and global civil society," *Global Environmental Politics* 3(2): 120–34.

Forest Stewardship Council. 1999. *FSC Principles and Criteria*. Forest Stewardship Council.

Fort, T. L. and C. A. Schipani. 2004. *The Role of Business in Fostering Peaceful Societies*. Cambridge University Press.

Foucault, M. 1978/1991. "Governmentality," in G. Burchell, C. Gordon and P. Miller (eds.) *The Foucault Effect: Studies in Governmentality*. University of Chicago Press.

Fox, J. (ed.) 1998. *The Struggle for Accountability: The World Bank, NGOs and Grassroots Movements*. Cambridge, MA: The MIT Press.

Friedman, M. 1970. "The Social responsibility of business," *New York Times Magazine*, 30 September.

Furger, F. 1997. "Accountability and systems of self-governance: The case of the maritime industry," *Law and Policy* 19(4): 445–76.

Furman, J. and S. Stern. 2006. "Climbing atop the shoulders of giants: The impact of institutions on cumulative research," Working Paper. Boston University/Kellogg School of Management.

Gale, F. P. 1998. *The Tropical Timber Trade Regime*. International Political Economy Series. New York: St. Martin's Press.

Gamper-Rabindran, S. 2006. "Did the EPA's voluntary industrial toxics program reduce emissions? A GIS analysis of distributional impacts and by-media analysis of substitution," *Journal of Environmental Economics and Management* 52: 391–410.

GAO (United States General Accounting Office). 1994. "Toxic substances: EPA needs more reliable source reduction data and progress measures," GAO/RCED-94-93. Washington, DC: US GAO.

Garvie, D. and A. Keeler. 1994. "Incomplete enforcement with endogenous regulatory choice," *Journal of Public Economics* 55: 141–62.

Gereffi, G., R. Garcia-Johnson, and E. Sasser. 2001. "The NGO-industrial complex," *Foreign Policy* 125: 56–65.

Gereffi, G. and M. Korzeniewicz. 1994. *Commodity Chains and Global Capitalism*. Contributions in Economics and Economic History. Westport, CT: Greenwood.

Gibson, C. C. 1999. *Politicians and Poachers: The Political Economy of Wildlife Policy in Africa*. New York: Cambridge University Press.

Gilpin, R. 1975. *U.S. Power and the Multinational Corporation*. New York: Basic Books.

Giovannucci, D. 2001. *Sustainable Coffee Survey of the North American Specialty Coffee Industry*. Report conducted for The Summit Foundation, The Nature Conservancy, The North American Commission for Environmental Cooperation, Specialty Coffee Association of America, and The World Bank, July 2001 [accessed March 13, 2006, available at www.cec.org/files/PDF/ECONOMY/CoffeeSurvey_EN.pdf].

Giovannucci, D. and F. J. Koekoek. 2003. *The State of Sustainable Coffee: A Study of Twelve Major Markets.* Report for ICO, UNCTAD and IISD 2003 [accessed March 13, 2006, available at www.iisd.org/publications/pub. aspx?pno=579].

Glachant, M. 2003. "Voluntary agreements under endogenous legislative threats," FEEM Working Paper No. 36.2003.

Gordon, P. 2005. *Lean and Green: Profit for Your Business and the Environment.* San Francisco, CA: Berrett-Koehler Publishers.

Gough, C. and S. Shackley. 2001. "The respectable politics of climate change: The epistemic communities and NGOs," *International Affairs* 77(2): 329–45.

Gourevitch, G. and J. Shinn. 2005. *Political Power and Corporate Control: The New Global Politics of Corporate Governance.* Princeton, NJ: Princeton University Press.

Gowers, A. 1985. *"The strains begin to tell: International coffee agreement"* [newspaper article, section I, page 16], *Financial Times,* September 16, 1985 [accessed March 13, 2006, available at www.lexis-nexis.com].

Grant, R. and R. Keohane. 2005. "Accountability and abuses of power in world politics," *American Political Science Review* 99(1): 29–44.

Gray, W. B. and M. E. Deily. 1996. "Compliance and enforcement: air pollution regulation in the U.S. steel industry," *Journal of Environmental Economics and Management* 31(1): 96–111.

Gresser, C. and S. Tickell. 2002. *"Mugged: Poverty in your coffee cup"* [online report], *Oxfam International* 2002 [accessed March 13, 2006, available at www.maketradefair.com/assets/english/mugged.pdf].

Grossman, G. and E. Helpman. 2001. *Special Interest Politics.* Cambridge, MA: The MIT Press.

Gulbrandsen, L. H. and S. Andresen. 2004. "NGO influence in the implementation of the Kyoto Protocol: Compliance, flexibility mechanisms, and sinks," *Global Environmental Politics* 4: 54–75.

Gunderson, L. H. and C. S. Holling (eds.) 2002. *Panarchy: Understanding Transformations in Human and Nature Systems.* Washington, DC: Island Press.

Gunningham, N. 1995. "Environment, self-regulation, and the chemical industry: Assessing Responsible Care," *Law and Policy* 17(1): 57–108.

Gunningham N., P. Grabosky, and D. Sinclair. 1998. *Smart Regulation: Designing Environmental Policy.* Oxford, UK: Clarendon Press.

Gunningham, N., R. A. Kagan, and D. Thornton. 2003. *Shades of Green: Business, Regulation, and Environment.* Stanford, CA: Stanford University Press.

Guthman, J. 2004. *Agrarian Dreams: The Paradox of Organic Farming in California.* California Studies in Critical Human Geography 11. Berkeley, CA: University of California Press.

Gutner, T. 2005. "Explaining the gaps between mandate and performance: Agency theory and world bank environmental reform," *Global Environmental Politics* 5(2): 10–37.

Haas, P. M. 1989. "Do regimes matter? Epistemic communities and Mediterranean pollution control," *International Organization* 43: 377–403.

(ed.) 1992. Knowledge, Power, and International Policy. Special issue of *International Organization* 46(1).

1999. "Social constructivism and the evolution of multilateral environmental governance," in A. Prakash and J. A. Hart (eds.) *Globalization and Governance*. London and New York: Routledge.

2004. "Addressing the global governance deficit," *Global Environmental Politics* 4: 1–15.

Haas, P. M., M. A. Levy, and R. O. Keohane. 1993. *Institutions for the Earth: Sources of Effective International Environmental Protection*. Cambridge, MA: The MIT Press.

Hahn, R. W. 1990. "The political economy of environmental regulation: Towards a unifying framework," *Public Choice* 65: 21–47.

Hall, P. 2003. "Aligning ontology and methodology in comparative politics," in J. Mahoney and D. Rueschemeyer (eds.) *Comparative Historical Analysis in the Social Sciences*. Cambridge University Press.

Hall, R. B. and T. J. Biersteker (eds.) 2002. *The Emergence of Private Authority in Global Governance*. Cambridge University Press.

Hamilton, J. T. 1995. "Pollution as news: Media and stock market reactions to the Toxics Release Inventory data," *Journal of Environmental Economics and Management* 28: 98–113.

Hansen, E. and H. Juslin. 1999. *The Status of Forest Certification in the ECE Region*. New York and Geneva: United Nations, Timber Section, Trade Division, UN-Economic Commission for Europe.

Hardin, G. 1968. "The tragedy of the commons," *Science* 162: 1243–8.

1978. "Political requirements for preserving our common heritage," in H. P. Brokaw (ed.) *Wildlife and America*, pp. 310–7. Washington, DC: Council on Environmental Quality.

Hardin, R. 1982. *Collective Action*. Baltimore, MD: Johns Hopkins University Press.

2002. "Concessionary politics in the western Congo Basin: History and culture in forest use governance and institutions," *Working Paper* 44. Washington, DC: World Resources Institute.

2006. *Concessionary Politics*. Berkeley, CA: University of California Press.

Harford, J. D. 1991. "Measurement error and state-dependent pollution control enforcement," *Journal of Environmental Economics and Management* 21: 67–81.

Harford, J. D. and W. Harrington. 1991. "A reconsideration of enforcement leverage when penalties are restricted," *Journal of Public Economics* 45: 391–5.

Harhoff, D. and P. Mayrhofer. 2007. "User communities and hybrid innovation processes: Theoretical foundations and implications for policy and research," Paper presented at the Second Annual Conference on Institutional Foundations for Industry Self-Regulation, Harvard Business School, Boston, MA.

Harrington, W. 1988. "Enforcement leverage when penalties are restricted," *Journal of Public Economics* 37(1): 29–53.

Harrison, K. 1998. "Talking with the donkey: Cooperative approaches to environmental protection," *Journal of Industrial Ecology* 2: 51–72.

2001. "Voluntarism and environmental governance," in E. A. Parson (ed.) *Governing the Environment: Persistent Challenges, Uncertain Innovations.* University of Toronto Press.

2002. "Challenges in evaluating voluntary environmental programs," in T. Dietz and P. Stern (eds.) *New Tools for Environmental Protection: Education, Information, and Voluntary Measures*, pp. 263–82. Washington, DC: National Academy Press.

Harrison, K. and W. Antweiler. 2003. "Incentives for pollution abatement: Regulation, regulatory threats, and non-governmental pressures," *Journal of Policy Analysis and Management* 22: 361–82.

Hart, S. 1995. "A natural resource-based view of the firm," *Academy of Management Review* 20: 986–1014.

Hart S. L. and G. Ahuja. 1996. "Does it pay to be green? An empirical examination of the relationship between emission reduction and firm performance," *Business Strategy and Environment* 5(1): 30–7.

Haufler, V. 1999. "Negotiating international standards for environmental management systems: The ISO 14000 standards," Report to the United Nations Secretary-General. Washington, DC: Global Public Policy Network.

2001. *A Public Role for the Private Sector: Industry Self-Regulation in the Global Economy.* Washington, DC: Carnegie Endowment for International Peace.

2003. "Globalization and industry self-regulation," in M. Kahler and D. Lake (eds.) *Governance in a Global Economy.* Princeton, NJ: Princeton University Press.

Hawkins, D. G. 2006. *Delegation and Agency in International Organizations.* Cambridge and New York: Cambridge University Press.

Hay, B. L, R. N. Stavins, and R. H. K. Victor (eds.) 2005. *Environmental Protection and the Social Responsibility of Firms: Perspectives from Law, Economics, and Business.* Washington, DC: Resources for the Future.

Hayek, F. A. 1973. *Rules and Order*, vol. 1 of *Law, Legislation, and Liberty.* University of Chicago Press.

Heijden, H. A. v. d. 2006. "Globalization, environmental movements, and international political opportunity structures," *Organization and Environment* 1: 28–45.

Helland, E. and A. Whitford. 2003. "Pollution incidence and political jurisdiction: Evidence from the TRI," *Journal of Environmental Economics and Management* 46: 406–24.

Hempel, L. C. 1996. *Environmental Governance: The Global Challenge.* Washington, DC: Island Press.

Henderson, D. 2001. *Misguided Virtue.* London: Institute of Economic Affairs.

Henriques. I. and P. Sadorsky. 1999. "The relationship between environmental commitment and managerial perceptions of stakeholder importance," *Academy of Management Journal* 42(1): 87–99.

Hill, J. and T. Schneeweis. 1983. "The effect of Three Mile Island on electric utility stock-prices: A note," *Journal of Finance* 38(4): 1285–92.

Hirst, P. and G. Thompson. 2002. "The future of globalization," *Cooperation and Conflict* 37(3): 247–65.

Hiscox, M. J. 2001. "Class versus industry cleavages: Inter-industry factor mobility and the politics of trade," *International Organization* 55(1): 1–46.

Hobbes, T. 1660/1999. *Leviathan.* Hamilton, ON: McMaster University

Hocking, B. 2004. "Privatizing diplomacy," *International Studies Perspectives* 5(2): 147–52.

Hoffman, A.J. 1999. "Institutional evolution and change: Environmentalism and the US chemical industry," *Academy of Management Journal* 42(4): 351–71.

2001. "Linking organizational and field-level analyses: The diffusion of corporate environmental practice," *Organization and Environment* 14(2): 133–56.

2005. "Climate change strategy: The business logic behind voluntary greenhouse gas reductions," *California Management Review* 47: 21–46.

Hoffman, A. J. and W. Ocasio. 2001. "Not all events are attended equally: Toward a middle-range theory of industry attention to external events," *Organization Science* 12(4): 414–34.

Holmstrom, B. 1982. "Moral hazard in teams," *Bell Journal of Economics* 13(2): 324–40.

Holmstrom, B. and J. Tirole. 1989. "The theory of the firm," in R. Schmalensee and R. Willig (eds.) *Handbook of Industrial Organization*, vol. 1. Amsterdam: North Holland.

Holthus, P. 2002. "Marine ornamental trade," in B. Best, R. Pomeroy and C. M. Balboa (eds.) *Implications for Coral Reef Management and Policy: Relevant Findings from the 9th International Coral Reef Symposium.* Washington DC: USAID.

Howard, J., J. Nash, and J. Ehrenfeld. 2000. "Standard or smokescreen? Implementation of a voluntary environmental code," *California Management Review* 42(2): 63–82.

Howarth, R. B., B. M. Haddad, and B. Paton. 2000. "The economics of energy efficiency: Insights from voluntary participation programs," *Energy Policy* 28(6,7): 477–86.

Howlett, M. 2000. "Managing the 'hollow state': Procedural policy instruments and modern governance," *Canadian Public Administration* 43(4): 412–31.

Humphreys, D. 1996. *Forest Politics: The Evolution of International Cooperation.* London: Earthscan.

Husted, B. 2004. "A comparative institutional approach to environmental regulation: The case of environmental degradation along the U.S.A-Mexico border," *Human Ecology Review,* Special issue on Business and Environmental Policy.

Hutchcroft, P. D. 2001. "Centralization and decentralization in administration and politics: Assessing territorial dimensions of authority and power," *Governance: An International Journal of Policy, Administration and Institutions* 14: 23–53.

Ilinitch, A. Y., N. S. Soderstrom, and T. E. Thomas. 1998. "Measuring corporate environmental performance," *Journal of Accounting and Public Policy* 17: 383–408.

Ingram, P. and K. Clay. 2000. "The choice-within-constraints: New institutionalism and implications for sociology," *Annual Review of Sociology* 26: 525–46.

Innes, R. and A. G. Sam. 2008. "Voluntary pollution reductions and the enforcement of environmental law: An empirical study of the 33/50 program," *Journal of Law and Economics* 51(2): 271–96.

Intergovernmental Panel on Climate Change (IPCC). 2001. *Climate Change 2001: Impacts, Adaptation and Vulnerability.* Geneva: Intergovernmental Panel on Climate Change.

——— 2007. *Climate Change 2007: Synthesis Report.* Geneva: WMO/UNEP.

International Coffee Organization. 1997. *"Agriculture and economic analysis of organically grown or 'organic' coffee"* [case study], August 6, 1997 [accessed March 14, 2006, available at www.ico.org/documents/eb3639.pdf].

International Federation of Organic Agriculture Movements. 2006. *"Organic standards and certification"* [web page], March 8, 2006 [accessed March 15, 2006, available at www.ifoam.org/about_ifoam/standards/index.html].

International Marinelife Alliance. 1999. *Response to the Review of the IMA Cyanide Testing Standard Operating Procedures, Prepared by the Marine Aquarium Council.* Pasig City, The Philippines: IMA.

Jagers, S. C. and J. Stripple. 2003. "Climate governance beyond the state," *Global Governance* 9: 385–99.

Jarrell, G. and S. Peltzman. 1985. "The impact of product recalls on the wealth of sellers," *Journal of Political Economy* 93(3): 512–36.

Jayasuriya, K. 2005. "Capacity beyond the boundary: New regulatory state," in M. P. a. J. Pierre (ed.) *Challenges to State Policy Capacity,* pp. 19–37. New York: Palgrave MacMillan.

Jessop, B. 2002. "Globalization and the national state," in S. Aronowitz and P. Bratsis (eds.) *Paradigm Lost: State Theory Reconsidered*, pp. 185–220. Minneapolis, MN: University of Minnesota Press.

Jiang, R. H. J. and P. Bansal. 2003. "Seeing the need for ISO 14001," *Journal of Management Studies* 40(4): 1047–67.

Johnson, C. and T. Forsyth. 2002. "In the eyes of the state: Negotiating a 'rights-based approach' to forest conservation in Thailand," *World Development* 30: 1591–605.

Johnston, A. and A. Smith. 2001. "The characteristics and features of corporate environmental performance indicators: A case study of the water industry of England and Wales," *Eco-Management and Auditing* 8(1): 1–11.

Johnstone, N., P. Scapecchi, B. Yiterhus, and R. Wolff. 2004. "The firm, environmental management and environmental measures: Lessons from a survey of European manufacturing firms," *Journal of Environmental Planning and Management* 47(5): 685–702.

Jordan, A., R. Wurtzel, and A. R. Zito. 2003. "'New' environmental policy instruments: An evolution or a revolution in environmental policy?" *Environmental Politics* 12: 201–24.

Joskow, P. and R. Schmalensee. 1998. "The political economy of market-based environmental policy: The US Acid Rain program," *Journal of Law and Economics* 41: 37–84.

Kaldor, M. 2003. *Global Civil Society: An Answer to War.* Cambridge, UK: Polity Press.

Kalt, J. P. and M. A. Zupan. 1984. "Capture and ideology in the economic theory of politics," *American Economic Review* 74: 279–300.

Kates, R. W. 2004. "Beyond Kyoto," *Environment* 10: 2.

Keane, J. 2003. *Global Civil Society.* Cambridge University Press.

Keck, M. E. and K. Sikkink. 1998. *Activists Beyond Borders: Advocacy Networks in International Politics.* Ithaca, NY: Cornell University Press.

Keohane, R. and E. Ostrom (eds.) 1995. *Local Commons and Global Interdependence: Heterogeneity and Cooperation in Two Domains.* London: Sage.

Khagram, S., J. V. Riker, and K. Sikkink. 2002. "From Santiago to Seattle: Transnational advocacy groups restructuring world politics," in S. Khagram, J. V. Riker and K. Sikkink (eds.) *Restructuring World Politics.* Minneapolis, MN: University of Minnesota Press.

Khanna, M. 2001. "Non-mandatory approaches to environmental protection," *Journal of Economic Surveys* 15: 291–324.

Khanna, M. and W. R. Anton. 2002. "Corporate environmental management: Regulatory and market-based incentives," *Land Economics* 78(4): 539–58.

Khanna, M. and L. Damon. 1999. "EPA's voluntary 33/50 program: Impact on toxic releases and economic performance of firms," *Journal of Environmental Economics and Management* 37: 1–25.

Khanna, M., W. Quimio, and D. Bojilova. 1998. "Toxic release information: A policy tool for environmental information," *Journal of Environmental Economics and Management* 36: 243–66.

Khanna, M. and D. T. Ramirez. 2004. "Effectiveness of voluntary approaches: Implications for climate change mitigation," in A. Baranzini and P. Thalmann (eds.) *Voluntary Agreements in Climate Policy*, pp. 31–66. Cheltenham, UK: Edward Elgar Publishers.

King, A. A. and M. J. Lenox. 2000. "Industry self-regulation without sanctions: The chemical industry's Responsible Care program," *Academy of Management Journal* 43(4): 698–716.

2001. "Lean and green? An empirical examination of the relationship between lean production and environmental performance," *Production and Operations Management* 10(3): 244–56.

2002. "Exploring the locus of profitable pollution reduction," *Management Science* 48(2): 289–300.

King, A. A., M. J. Lenox, and M. Barnett. 2002. "Strategic responses to the reputation commons problem," in A. J. Hoffman and M. J. Ventresca (eds.) *Organizations, Policy and the Natural Environment: Institutional and Strategic Perspectives*, pp. 393–406. Stanford, CA: Stanford University Press.

King, A. A., M. J. Lenox, and A. K. Terlaak. 2005. "The strategic use of decentralized institutions: Exploring certification with the ISO 14001 management standard," *Academy of Management Journal* 48(6): 1091–106.

Kinnaird, M. F., E. W. Sanderson, T. G. O'Brien, H. T. Wibisono, and G. Woolmer. 2003. "Deforestation trends in a tropical landscape and implications for endangered large mammals," *Conservation Biology* 17(1): 245–57.

Kirchhoff, S. 2000. "Green business and blue angels," *Environmental and Resource Economics* 15: 403–20.

Klassen, R. D. 2001. "Plant-level environmental management orientation: The influence of management views and plant characteristics," *Production and Operations Management* 10: 257–75.

Klassen, R. D. and D. C. Whybark. 1999. "The impact of environmental technologies on manufacturing performance," *Academy of Management Journal* 42(6): 599–615.

Klassen, R. and C. P. McLaughlin. 1996. "The impact of environmental management on firm performance," *Management Science* 42(8): 1199–214.

Klooster, D. and O. Masera. 2000. "Community forest management in Mexico: Carbon mitigation and biodiversity conservation through rural development," *Global Environmental Change* 10: 259–72.

Kochen, M. 2003. *History of Fair Trade*. Report of the International Federation of Alternative Trade, December 2003 [accessed March 13, 2006, available at www.fair-trade-hub.com/history-of-fair-trade.html].

Koehler, D. and D. Cram. 2001. "The financial impact of corporate environmental performance: A review of the evidence of the link between environmental and financial performance," Working Paper, Harvard School of Public Health, Boston MA.

Kolk, A. 1998. "From conflict to cooperation: International policies to protect the Brazilian Amazon," *World Development* 26(8): 1481–93.

Konar, S. and M. A. Cohen. 1997. "Information as regulation: The effect of community right to know laws on toxic emissions," *Journal of Environmental Economics and Management* 32: 109–24.

2001. "Does the market value environmental performance?" *The Review of Economics and Statistics* 83(2): 281–9.

Kooiman, J. 2003. *Governing as Governance*. London: Sage Publications.

Kotchen, M. and M. R. Moore. 2007. "Private provision of environmental public goods: Household participation in green electricity programs," *Journal of Environmental Economics and Management* 53: 1–16.

Krasner, S. D. 1978. *Defending the National Interest: Raw Materials Investments and U.S. Foreign Policy*. Princeton, NJ: Princeton University Press.

Krech, S. III. 1999. *The Ecological Indian: Myth and History*. New York: W.W. Norton.

Krier, J. 2005. *Fair Trade in Europe 2005: Facts and Figures on Fair Trade in 25 European Countries* [online report]. Fair Trade Advocacy Office, December 2005 [accessed March 13, 2006, available at http://www.fairtrade-advocacy. org/documents/FairTradeinEurope2005_001.pdf].

Kropotkin, P. 1902/1986. *Mutual Aid: A Factor of Evolution*. London: Freedom Press.

Kuhre, W.L. 1995. *ISO 14001 Certification: Environmental Management Systems*. Upper Saddle River, NJ: Prentice Hall.

Langman, M. 1999. "Memories and notes on the beginning and early history of IFOAM" [PDF on IFOAM web site]. International Federation of Organic Agriculture Movements 1999 [accessed October 30, 2005, available at www. ifoam.org/about_ifoam/inside_ifoam/pdfs/Early_History_IFOAM.pdf].

Laplante, B. and P. Rilstone. 1996. "Environmental inspections and emissions of the pulp and paper industry in Quebec," *Journal of Environmental Economics and Management* 31: 19–36.

Lapointe, G. 1998. "Sustainable forest management certification: The Canadian programme," *Forestry Chronicle* 74(2): 227–30.

Lasswell, H. 1936. *Politics: Who Gets What, When, and How?* New York: Whittlesey House.

Leakey, R. and R. Lewin. 1995. *The Sixth Extinction: Biodiversity and its Survival*. New York: Doubleday.

Lee, K. N. 1993. *Compass and Gyroscope: Integrating Science and Politics for the Environment*. Washington, DC: Island Press.

Leire, C. and A. Thidell. 2005. "Product-related environmental information to guide consumer purchases: A review and analysis of research on perceptions, understanding and use among Nordic consumers," *Journal of Cleaner Production* 13(10–11): 1061–70.

Lemos, M. C. 2008. "Whose water is it anyway? Water management, knowledge, and equity in NE Brazil," in J. Whiteley, R. Perry and Helen Ingram (eds.) *Water, Place and Equity.* Cambridge, MA: MIT Press, pp. 249–70.

Lemos, M. C. and J. L. F. Oliveira. 2004. "Can water reform survive politics? Institutional change and river basin management in Ceará, northeast Brazil," *World Development* 32(12): 2121–37.

Lenox, M. 2006. "The role of private, decentralized institutions in sustaining industry self-regulation," *Organization Science* 17(6): 677–90.

Lenox, M. and J. Nash. 2003. "Industry self-regulation and adverse selection: A comparison across four trade association programs," *Business Strategy and Environment* 12(6): 343–56.

Lewin, B., D. Giovannucci, and P. Varangis. 2004. *Coffee Markets: New Paradigms in Global Supply and Demand,* Agriculture and Rural Development Discussion Paper 3. International Bank for Reconstruction and Development, Agriculture and Rural Development Department, March 2004 [accessed September 1, 2005, available at http://papers.ssrn.com/sol3/papers.cfm?abstract_id=996111].

Lindblom, C. 1997. *Politics and Markets: The World's Political-Economic Systems.* New York: Basic Books.

Lipschutz, R. D. 1996. *Global Civil Society and Global Environmental Governance: The Politics of Nature From Place to Planet.* Albany, NY: State University of New York Press.

Lipschutz, R. D. and C. Fogel. 2002. "The emergence of private authority in global governance," in R. B. Hall and T. J. Biersteker (eds.) *The Emergence of Private Authority in Global Governance.* Cambridge University Press.

Litfin, K. T. 1994. *Ozone Discourses: Science and Politics in Global Environmental Cooperation.* New York: Columbia University Press.

Liverman, D. 2004. "Who governs, at what scale, and at what price? Geography, environmental governance, and the commodification of nature," *Annals of the Association of American Geographers* 94(4): 734–8.

2005. "Equity, justice and climate change," in *Climate Change: The Greatest Threat We Face? Report of the Liberal Summer School,* pp. 20–5. London: Centre for Reform.

Livernois, J. and C. J. McKenna. 1999. "Truth or consequences: Enforcing pollution standards with self-reporting," *Journal of Public Economics* 71: 415–40.

Lloyd, W. F. 1833. *Two Lectures on the Checks to Population.* Oxford University Press. (Reprinted in Hardin, G. (ed.) 1964. *Population, Evolution, and Birth Control: A Collage of Controversial Readings.* San Francisco, CA: W.H. Freeman.)

Lober, D. 1996. "Evaluating the environmental performance of corporations," *Journal of Managerial Issues* 8(2): 184–205.

Lohmann, S. 1993. "A signaling model of informative and manipulative political action," *The American Political Science Review* 87: 319–33.

Loureiro, M. L. 2003. "Rethinking new wines: Implications of local and environmentally friendly labels," *Food Policy* 28(5–6): 547–60.

Loureiro, M. L. and J. Lotade. 2005. "Do fair trade and eco-labels in coffee wake up the consumer conscience?" *Ecological Economics* 53(1): 129–38.

Lowi, T. 2002. "Progress and poverty revisited: Toward construction of a statist third way," in J. S. Tulchin and A. Brown (eds.) *Democratic Governance and Social Inequality*, pp. 41–74. Boulder, CO: Lynne Rienner.

Lutz, S., T. P. Lyon, and J. W. Maxwell. 2000. "Quality leadership when regulatory standards are forthcoming," *Journal of Industrial Economics* 48: 331–48.

Luxner, L. 1996. "Zoo hosts sustainable coffee congress," *Tea and Coffee Trade Journal* November 1996 [accessed March 14, 2006, available at www.luxner.com/cgi-bin/view_article.cgi?articleID=81].

Lyon, T. P. and E. H. Kim. 2006. "Greenhouse gas reductions or greenwash? The DOE's 1605b program," Working Paper. Ann Arbor, MI: University of Michigan.

Lyon, T. P. and J. W. Maxwell. 2002. "Voluntary approaches to environmental regulation: A survey," in M. Franzini and A. Nicita (eds.) *Economic Institutions and Environmental Policy: Past, Present and Future*. Aldershot, UK: Ashgate Publishing.

2003. "Self-regulation, taxation, and public voluntary environmental agreements," *Journal of Public Economics* 87: 1453–86.

2004a. "Astroturf: Interest group lobbying and corporate strategy," *Journal of Economics and Management Strategy* 13: 561–98.

2004b. *Corporate Environmentalism and Public Policy*. Cambridge University Press.

2005. "Preempting uncertain regulation," Working Paper. Ann Arbor, MI: University of Michigan.

2006. "Greenwash: Corporate environmental disclosure under threat of audit," Working Paper. Ann Arbor, MI: University of Michigan.

2007. "Environmental Public Voluntary Programs Reconsidered," *Policy Studies Journal* 35: 723–50.

Macdonald, D. 2007. *Business and Environmental Politics in Canada*. Peterborough, ON: Broadview Press.

Magat, W. and W. K. Viscusi. 1990. "Effectiveness of the EPA's regulatory enforcement: The case of industrial effluent standards," *Journal of Law and Economics* 33: 331–60.

Maitland, I. 1985. "The limits of self-regulation," *California Management Review* 27(3): 132–47.

Maloney, M. and R. McCormick. 1982. "A positive theory of environmental quality regulation," *Journal of Law and Economics* 35: 99–123.

Manor, J. 2005. "User committees: A potentiality damaging second wave of decentralization?" in J. C. Ribot and A. M. Larson (eds.) *Democratic Decentralization through a Natural Resources Lens*, pp. 193–213. New York: Routledge.

March, J. G. and J. P. Olsen. 1998. "The institutional dynamics of international political orders," *International Organization* 52: 943–69.

Marcus, A., D. Geffen, and K. Sexton. 2002. *Reinventing Environmental Regulation: Lessons from Project XL*. Washington, DC: Resources for the Future.

Marcus, A. A. and M. L. Nichols. 1999. "On the edge: Heeding the warnings of unusual events," *Organization Science* 10: 482–99.

Margolis, J. D. and J. P. Walsh. 2001. *People and Profits? The Search for a Link Between a Company's Social and Financial Performance*. Mahwah, NJ: Lawrence Erlbaum Associates.

2003. "Misery loves companies: Rethinking social initiatives by business," *Administrative Science Quarterly* 48: 268–305.

Marimon Viadiu, F., M. Casadesús Fa, and M. Heras Saizarbitoria. 2006. "ISO 9000 and ISO 14000 standards: An international diffusion model," *International Journal of Operations and Production Management* 26(1–2): 141–65.

Marine Aquarium Council. 2001a. *Core Collection, Fishing, and Holding International Performance Standard for the Marine Aquarium Trade*. Honolulu, HI: Marine Aquarium Council.

2001b. *Core Ecosystem and Fishery Management International Performance Standard for the Marine Aquarium Trade*. Honolulu, HI: Marine Aquarium Council.

2001c. *Core Handling, Husbandry, and Transport International Performance Standard for the Marine Aquarium Trade*. Honolulu, HI: Marine Aquarium Council.

2002. *How Standards were Developed*. Honolulu, HI: Marine Aquarium Council.

Marx, K. and F. Engels. 1848/1968. *The Communist Manifesto*. New York: Monthly Press.

Mas, A. H. and T. V. Dietsch. 2004. "Linking shade coffee certification to biodiversity conservation: Butterflies and birds in Chiapas, Mexico," *Ecological Applications* 14(3): 642–54.

Massimiliano, A., L. Mosca, H. Reiter, and D. Della Porta. 2006. *Globalization from Below: Transnational Activists and Protest Networks*. Minneapolis, MN: University of Minnesota Press.

Mattoo, A. and H. V. Singh. 1994. "Eco-labeling: Policy considerations," *Kyklos* 47: 53–65.

Maxwell, J. and C. Decker. 2006. "Voluntary environmental investments and regulatory responsiveness," *Environmental and Resource Economics* 33: 425–39.

Maxwell, J., T. P. Lyon, and S. C. Hackett. 2000. "Self-regulation and social welfare: The political economy of corporate environmentalism," *Journal of Law and Economics* 43: 583–617.

McAdam, D., S. Tarrow, and C. Tilly (eds.) 2001. *Dynamics of Contention*. Cambridge University Press.

McCarthy, J. J. 2004. "Privatizing conditions of production: Trade agreements as neoliberal environmental governance," *Geoforum* 35: 327–41.

McCubbins, R., R. Noll, and B. Weingast. 1987. "Administrative procedures as instruments of political control," *Journal of Law, Economics, and Organization* 3: 243–77.

    1989. "Structure and process, politics and policy: Administration arrangements and the political control of agencies," *Virginia Law Review* 75: 431–82.

Mearsheimer, J. J. 1994/1995. "The false promise of international institutions," *International Security* 19: 5–49.

Meidinger, E. 1997. "Look who's making the rules: International environmental standard setting by non-governmental organizations," *Human Ecology Review* 4(1): 52–4.

    2000. *Incorporating Environmental Certification Systems in North American Legal Systems*. Buffalo, NY: University at Buffalo (SUNY).

Melnyk, S. A., R. P. Sroufe, and R. J. Calantone. 2003. "A model of site-specific antecedents of ISO 14001 certification," *Production and Operations Management* 12(3): 369–85.

Meyer, J. W. and B. Rowan. 1977. "Institutionalized organizations: Formal structure as myth and ceremony," *American Journal of Sociology* 83: 340–63.

Micheletti, M., A. Føllesdal, and D. Stolle (eds.) 2003. *Politics, Products, and Markets: Exploring Political Consumerism Past and Present*. New Brunswick, NJ: R. U. Transaction Press.

Miles, E. L., A. Underdal, S. Andresen, J. Wettestad, J. B. Skjærseth, and E. M. Carlin. 2002. *Environmental Regime Effectiveness: Confronting Theory with Evidence*. Cambridge, MA: The MIT Press.

Millennium Ecosystem Assessment (MEA). 2005. *Millennium Ecosystem Assessment: Ecosystems and Human Well Being – Synthesis*. Washington, DC: Island Press.

Miller, G. 1992. *Managerial Dilemmas: The Political Economy of Hierarchy*. New York: Cambridge University Press.

Miller, S. K. 1994. "Birds lose place in the shade" [This Week, page 99], *New Scientist*, July 23, 1994 [accessed October 19, 2005, available at www.lexis-nexis.com].

Mills, C. W. 2000. *The Power Elite*. New York: Oxford University Press.

Milner, H. V. 1997. *Interests, Institutions, and Information: Domestic Politics and International Relations*. Princeton, NJ: Princeton University Press.

    2005. "Globalization, development, and international institutions: Normative and positive perspectives," *Perspectives on Politics* 3: 833–54.

Milner, H.V and R. Keohane (eds.) 1997. *Internationalization and Domestic Politics*. Cambridge University Press.

Milner, H. V. and D. B. Yoffie. 1989. "Between free trade and protectionism: Strategic trade policy and a theory of corporate trade demands," *International Organization* 43(2): 238–72.

Moffat, A. C. 1998. *Forest Certification: An Examination of the Compatibility of the Canadian Standards Association and Forest Stewardship Council Systems in the Maritime Region.* MES Environmental Studies, Dalhousie University, Halifax, NS.

Montgomery, W. E. 1972. "Markets in licenses and efficient pollution control," *Journal of Economic Theory* 5: 395–418.

Morgenstern, R. D., W. A. Pizer, and J.-S. Shih. 2007. "Evaluating voluntary U.S. climate programs: The case of Climate Wise," in R. D. Morgenstern and W. A. Pizer (eds.) *Reality Check: The Nature and Performance of Voluntary Environmental Programs in the United States, Europe, and Japan*, pp. 119–37. Washington, DC: Resources for the Future.

Mueller, D. 1989. *Public Choice II.* Cambridge University Press.

Muhll, G. E. v. d. 2003. "Ancient empires, modern states, and the study of government," *Annual Review of Political Science* 6: 354–76.

Murphy, C. 1994. *International Organization and Industrial Change.* New York: Oxford University Press.

Nadeau, L. W. 1997. "EPA effectiveness at reducing the duration of plant-level noncompliance," *Journal of Environmental Economics and Management* 34: 54–78.

Naim, M. 2007. "What is a GONGO?" *Foreign Policy* 160: 96–5.

Nash, J. 1951. "Non-cooperative games," *Annals of Mathematics* 54: 286–95.

Nash, J. and J. Ehrenfeld. 1997. "Codes of environmental management practice: Assessing their potential as a tool for change," *Annual Review of Energy and the Environment* 22: 487–535.

Nelson, P. 1997. "Deliberation, leverage or coercion? The World Bank, NGOs, and global environmental politics," *Journal of Peace Research* 34(4): 467–70.

Nelson, K. and B.J.H. d. Jong. 2003. "Making global initiatives local realities: Carbon mitigation projects in Chiapas, Mexico," *Global Environmental Change* 13: 19–30.

Neumayer, E. and R. Perkins. 2004. "What explains the uneven take-up of ISO 14001 at the global level? A panel-data analysis," *Environment and Planning* 36(5): 823–39.

Newell, P. and D. Levy (eds.) 2005. *The Business of Global Environmental Governance.* Cambridge, MA: The MIT Press.

New York Times. 1991. "The nation's polluters: Who emits, what and where," *New York Times* October 13, F10.

Niebuhr, R. 1944. *The Children of Light and the Children of Darkness.* New York: Charles Scribner's Sons.

Nielson, D. L. and M. J. Tierney. 2003. "Delegation to international organizations: Agency theory and World Bank environmental reform," *International Organization* 57(2): 241–76.

Noll, R. G. 1985. "Government regulatory behavior: A multidisciplinary survey and synthesis," in R. G. Noll (ed.) *Regulatory Policy and the Social Sciences.* Berkeley, CA: University of California Press.

North, D. C. 1981. *Structure and Change in Economic History.* New York: Norton.

1990. *Institutions, Institutional Change and Economic Performance.* Cambridge University Press.

1991. "Institutions," *Journal of Economic Perspectives* 5(1): 97–112.

North, D. C. and R. P. Thomas. 1973. *The Rise of the Western World: A New Economic History.* Cambridge University Press.

Nye, J. S. 2001. "Globalization's democratic deficit: How to make international institutions more accountable," *Foreign Affairs* 4: 2–6.

O'Brien, K. L., R. Leichenko, U. Kelkarc, H. Venemad, G. Aandahl, H. Tompkins, A. Javed, S. Bhadwal, S. Barg, L. Nygaard, and J. West. 2004. "Mapping vulnerability to multiple stressors: Climate change and globalization in India," *Global Environmental Change* 14: 303–13.

Olson, M. Jr. 1965. *The Logic of Collective Action.* Cambridge, MA: Harvard University Press.

1982. *The Rise and Decline of Nations.* New Haven, NJ: Yale University Press.

O'Neill, K., J. Balsiger, and S. D. VanDeveer. 2004. "Actors, norms, and impact: Recent international cooperation theory and the influence of the agent-structure debate," *Annual Review of Political Science* 7(1): 149–75.

Ostrom, E. 1990. *Governing the Commons: The Evolution of Institutions for Collective Action.* Cambridge University Press.

1998. "A behavioral approach to the rational choice theory of collective action," *American Political Science Review* 92(1): 1–22.

2000. "Collective action and the evolution of social norms," *Journal of Economic Perspectives* 14: 137–58.

2007. "A diagnostic approach for going beyond panaceas," *Proceedings of the National Academy of Sciences of the United States of America* 104: 15181–7.

Ostrom, E., R. Gardner, and J. Walker. 1994. *Rules, Games, and Common-Pool Resources.* Ann Arbor, MI: University of Michigan Press.

Ostrom, E., L. Schroeder, and S. Wynne. 1993. *Institutional Incentives and Sustainable Development: Infrastructure Policies in Perspective.* Boulder, CO: Westview.

Ostrom, E., T. Dietz, N. Dolšak, P. C. Stern, S. Stonich, and E. U. Weber (eds.) 2002. *The Drama of the Commons.* Washington, DC: National Academy Press.

Ozinga, S. 2001. "Behind the logo: An environmental and social assessment of forest certification schemes," Moreton-in-Marsh, UK: FERN, based on case studies by WWF France, Taiga Consulting, Taiga Rescue Network, Natural Resource Defense Council (NRDC), FERN, Finnish Nature League, and Greenpeace.

Painter, M. and J. Pierre. 2005. "Unpacking policy capacity: Issues and themes," in M. Painter and J. Pierre (eds.) *Challenges to State Policy Capacity*, pp. 1–18. New York: Palgrave MacMillan.

Papadopoulos, Y. 2003. "Cooperative forms of governance: Problems of democratic accountability in complex environments," *European Journal of Political Research* 42: 473–501.

Pargal, S. and D. Wheeler. 1996. "Informal regulation of industrial pollution in developing countries: Evidence from Indonesia," *Journal of Political Economy* 104(6): 1314–27.

Parris, T. M. and R. W. Kates. 2003. "Characterizing and measuring sustainable development," *Annual Review of Environment and Resources* 28: 559–86.

Parson, E. A. 2003. *Protecting the Ozone Layer: Science and Strategy*. Oxford University Press.

Pashigian, P. 1985. "Environmental regulation: Whose self-interests are being protected?" *Economic Inquiry* 28: 551–84.

Paterson, M., D. Humphreys, and L. Pettiford. 2003. "Conceptualizing global environmental governance: From interstate regimes to counter-hegemonic struggles," *Global Environmental Politics* 3: 1–10.

Pattberg, P. 2007. *Private Institutions and Global Governance: The New Ethics of Environmental Sustainability*. Cheltenham, UK: Edward Elgar.

Patton, P. 1989. "Taylor and Foucault on power and freedom," *Political Studies* 37: 260–76.

PEFC International. 2001. "PEFC is the world's largest forest certification organisation" [web site, accessed 2001, available at www.pefc.org/internet/html/].

Pegg, S. 2003. "Corporations, conscience and conflict: Assessing NGO reports on the private sector role in African resource conflicts," *Third World Quarterly* 24(6): 1179–89.

Pelkonen, A. 2005. "State restructuring, urban competitiveness policies and technopole building in Finland: A critical view on the glocal state thesis," *European Planning Studies* 13(5): 687–705.

Peltzman, S. 1976. "Toward a more general theory of regulation," *Journal of Law and Economics* 19: 211–40.

1991. "The Handbook of Industrial Organization: A review article," *Journal of Political Economy* 99: 201–17.

Philippine Headline News Online. 1998. "Padlocked: Puerto Princesa exporter of cyanide-caught fish," *Philippine Headline News Online* December 6, 1998.

Pimm, S. L. and T. M. Brooks. 2000. "The sixth extinction: How large, how soon, and where?" in P. Raven (ed.) *Nature and Human Society: The Quest for a Sustainable World*. Washington, DC: National Academy Press.

Ponte, S. 2004. *Standards and Sustainability in the Coffee Sector*. Winnipeg, MB: International Institute for Sustainable Development.

Popp, D. 2004. "R&D subsidies and climate policy: Is there a free lunch?" NBER Working Paper No, 10880. Cambridge, MA: National Bureau of Economic Research.

Porter, M. E. and C. van der Linde. 1995a. "Green and competitive: Ending the stalemate," *Harvard Business Review* 73(5): 120–3.

1995b. "Toward a new conception of the environment-competitiveness relationship," *Journal of Economic Perspectives* 9: 97–118.

Potoski, M. and A. Prakash. 2005a. "Covenants with weak swords: ISO 14001 and facilities' environmental performance," *Journal of Policy Analysis and Management* 24(4): 745–69.

2005b. "Green clubs and voluntary governance: ISO 14001 and firms' regulatory compliance," *American Journal of Political Science* 49(2): 235–48.

Powers, N., A. Blackman, T. P. Lyon, and U. Narain. 2008. "Does disclosure reduce pollution? Evidence from India's Green Rating project," Working Paper. Ross School of Business, University of Michigan.

Prakash, A. 2000. *Greening the Firm: The Politics of Corporate Environmentalism.* Cambridge University Press.

Prakash, A. and M. Potoski. 2006. *The Voluntary Environmentalists: Green Clubs, ISO14001, and Voluntary Environmental Regulation.* Cambridge University Press.

Pretty, J. 2003. "Social capital and the collective management of resources," *Science* 302: 1912–14.

Princen, T. and M. Finger (eds.) 1994. *Environmental NGOs in World Politics: Linking the Local and the Global.* London: Routledge.

Putnam, R. 1988. "Diplomacy and domestic politics: The logic of two-level games," *International Organization* 42(3): 427–60.

2000. *Bowling Alone: The Collapse and Revival of American Community.* New York: Simon and Schuster.

Rametsteiner, E. 1999. "The attitude of European consumers toward forests and forestry," *Unasylva* 50(196): 42–8.

Ramus, C. and U. Steger. 2000. "The roles of supervisory support behaviors and environmental policy in employee 'ecoinitiatives' at leading-edge European companies," *Academy of Management Journal* 43: 605–26.

Raustiala, K. 1997. "States, NGOs, and international environmental institutions," *International Studies Quarterly* 41(4): 719–40.

2002. "The architecture of international cooperation: Transgovernmental networks and the future of international law," *Virginia Journal of International Law* 43(1): 1–92.

Raynolds, L. T. 2000. "Re-embedding global agriculture: The international organic and fair trade movements," *Agriculture and Human Values* 17(3): 297–309.

Rees, J. 1994. *Hostages of Each Other: The Transformation of Nuclear Safety Since Three Mile Island.* University of Chicago Press.

1997. "Development of communitarian regulation in the chemical industry," *Law and Policy* 19: 477–528.

Reinicke, W. 1998a. "Global public policy," *Foreign Affairs* 76(6): 127–38.

1998b. *Global Public Policy: Governing without Government?* Washington, DC: Brookings Institution.

Reinicke, W., T. Benner, and J. M. Witte. 2003. "Innovating global governance through global public policy networks: Lessons learned and challenges ahead," *Brookings Review* 1.

Reinicke, W. and F. Deng. 2000. *Critical Choices: The United Nations, Networks, and the Future of Global Governance.* Ottawa, ON: International Development Research Centre.

Reinhardt, F. L. 1998. "Environmental product differentiation: Implications for corporate strategy," *California Management Review* 40(4): 43–73.

2000. *Down to Earth: Applying Business Principles to Environmental Management.* Boston, MA: Harvard Business School Press.

Reinhardt, F. L. and R. H. K. Vietor. 1996. *Business Management and the Natural Environment: Cases and Text.* Cincinnati, OH: Southwestern Publishing Company.

Reisch, M. 1998. "Industry ponders future of Responsible Care," *Chemical and Engineering News* May 5: 13.

Rhodes, R. A. W. 1996. "The new governance: Governing without government," *Political Studies* 55: 652–67.

Ribot, J. C. and N. L. Peluso. 2003. "A theory of access," *Rural Sociology* 68(2): 153–81.

Rice, R. A. and J. McLean. 1999. *Sustainable Coffee at the Crossroads.* White Paper Prepared for the Consumer's Choice Council, October 15, 1999 [accessed March 14, 2006, available at www.greenbeanery.ca/bean/documents/sustainableCoffee.pdf].

Rice, R. A. and J. R. Ward. 1996. "Coffee, conservation, and commerce in the Western Hemisphere: How individuals and institutions can promote ecologically sound farming and forest management in northern Latin America" [online report]. Smithsonian Migratory Bird Center, June 1996 [accessed March 13, 2006, available at www.nrdc.org/health/farming/ccc/chap4.asp].

Rivera, J. 2004. "Institutional pressures and voluntary environmental behavior in developing countries: Evidence from the Costa Rican hotel industry," *Society and Natural Resources* 17(9): 779–97.

Rivera, J. and P. de Leon. 2004. "Is greener whiter? Voluntary environmental performance of Western ski areas," *Policy Studies Journal* 32(3): 417–37.

2005. "Chief Executive Officers and voluntary environmental performance: Costa Rica's certification for sustainable tourism," *Policy Sciences* 38(2–3): 107–27.

Rivera, J., P. de Leon, and C. Koerber. 2006. "Is greener whiter yet? The Sustainable Slopes program after five years," *Policy Studies Journal* 34(2): 195–221.

Roberts, M. J. and M. Spence. 1976. "Effluent charges and licenses under uncertainty," *Journal of Public Economics* 5: 193–208.

Roberts, P.W. and R. Greenwood. 1997. "Integrating transaction cost and institutional theories: Toward a constrained-efficiency framework for understanding organizational design adoption," *Academy of Management Review* 22(2): 346–73.

Robertson, M. 2004. "The neoliberalization of ecosystem services: Wetland mitigation banking and problems in environmental governance," *Geoforum* 35 (3): 361–73.

Rogowski, R. 1989. *Commerce and Coalitions: How Trade Affects Domestic Political Alignments.* Princeton, NJ: Princeton University Press.

Rosenau, J. 1997. *Along the Domestic-Foreign Frontier: Exploring Governance in a Turbulent World.* Cambridge University Press.

2000. "Change, complexity and governance in a globalizing space," in J. Pierre (ed.) *Debating Governance: Authority, Steering and Democracy.* Oxford University Press.

Rosenau, J. N. and E. Czempiel (eds.) 1992. *Governance without Government: Order and Change in World Politics.* Cambridge University Press.

Rosenau, P. 2000. *Public-Private Policy Partnerships.* Cambridge, MA: The MIT Press.

Rosenbaum, P. and D. Rubin. 1983. "The central role of the propensity score in observational studies for causal effects," *Biometrica* 70(1): 41–55.

Rubec, P. J., F. Cruz, V. Pratt, R. Oellers, and F. Lallo. 2001. "Cyanide-free, net-caught fish for the marine aquarium trade," *Aquarium Sciences and Conservation* 3(1–3): 37–51.

Ruggie, J. G. 2003. "Taking embedded liberalism global: The corporate connection," in D. Held and M. Koenig-Archibugi (eds.) *Taming Globalization*, pp. 93–129. Cambridge, UK: Polity Press.

2004. "Reconstituting the global public domain: Issues, actors, and practices," *European Journal of International Relations* 10(4): 499–531.

Russell, C. S. 1990. "Monitoring and enforcement," in P. R. Portney (ed.) *Public Policies for Environmental Protection*, pp. 243–74. Washington, DC: Resources for the Future.

Russo, M. V. and P. A. Fouts. 1997. "A resource-based perspective on corporate environmental performance and profitability," *Academy of Management Journal* 40: 534–59.

Sam, A. G., M. Khanna, and R. Innes. 2009. "Voluntary pollution reduction programs, environmental management, and environmental performance: an empirical study," *Land Economics* 85(4) (in press).

Sanderson, S. 2002. "The Future of conservation," *Foreign Affairs* 81(5): 162–82.

Sandler, T. 1992. *Collective Action: Theory and Applications.* Ann Arbor, MI: University of Michigan Press.

Sasser, E. N. 2002. "The certification solution: NGO promotion of private, voluntary self-regulation," Paper read at 74th Annual Meeting of the Canadian Political Science Association, May 29–31, 2002, at Toronto, ON.

Schelling, T. C. 1978. *Micromotives and Macrobehavior.* New York: W.W. Norton.

Schlager, E. 2002. "Rationality, cooperation, and common-pool resources," *American Behavioral Scientist* 45(5): 801–21.

Schlager, E. and E. Ostrom. 1992. "Property-rights regimes and natural resources: A conceptual analysis," *Land Economics* 68(3): 249–62.

Schmitter, P. C. 1971. *Interest Conflict and Political Change in Brazil.* Stanford, CA: Stanford University Press.

Schofield, N. and I. Sened. 2006. *Multiparty Democracy: Elections and Legislative Politics.* New York: Cambridge University Press.

Scholte, J. A. 2000. *Globalization: A Critical Introduction.* Basingstoke, UK: Palgrave Macmillan.

Schreurs, M. A. 2002. *Environmental Politics in Japan, Germany, and the United States.* Cambridge University Press.

Segerson, K. and T. Miceli. 1998. "Voluntary environmental agreements: Good or bad news for environmental protection?" *Journal of Environmental Economics and Management* 36: 109–30.

Sell, S. and A. Prakash. 2004. "Using ideas strategically: The contest between business and NGO networks in intellectual property," *International Studies Quarterly* 48(1): 143–75.

Shalaway, S. 1996. "The environmentally correct coffee has it in the shade" [newspaper article: On nature, D-17], *Pittsburgh Post-Gazette*, November 17, 1996 [accessed October 19, 2005, available at www.lexis-nexis.com].

Sharma, S. 2000. "Managerial interpretations and organizational context as predictors of corporate choice of environmental strategy," *Academy of Management Journal* 43: 681–97.

Sharma, S., A. L. Pablo, and H. Vredenburg. 1999. "Corporate environmental responsiveness strategies: The importance of issue interpretation and organizational context," *Journal of Applied Behavioural Science* 35: 87–108.

Sharma, S. and H. Vredenburg. 1998. "Proactive corporate environmental strategy and the development of competitively valuable organizational capabilities," *Strategic Management Journal* 19: 729–53.

Shin, S. 2005. "The role of the government in voluntary environmental protection schemes: The case of ISO 14001 in China," *Issues and Studies* 41(4): 141–73.

Short, J. L. and M. W. Toffel. 2008. "Coerced confessions: Self-policing in the shadow of the regulator," *Journal of Law, Economics and Organization* 24: 45–71.

Shuman, C. S., G. Hodgson, and R. F. Ambrose. 2004. "Managing the marine aquarium trade: Is eco-certification the answer?" *Environmental Conservation* 31(4): 339–48.

Silver, S. 1998. "Scientists push for shade-grown coffee" [business news], *Associated Press Business Extra*, December 15, 1998 [accessed October 19, 2005, available at www.lexis.nexis.com].

Simmons, B., F. Dobbin, and G. Garret. 2006. "Introduction: The international diffusion of liberalism," *International Organization* 60: 781–810.

Sinclair, A. R. E., D. S. Hik, O. J. Schmitz, and G.G. E. Scudder. 1995. "Biodiversity and the need for habitat renewal," *Ecological Applications* 5(3): 579–87.

Skjaerseth, J. B. 1992. "The 'successful' ozone-layer negotiations: Are there any lessons to be learned?" *Global Environmental Change* 4: 292–300.

Slaughter, A. 2004. *A New World Order.* Princeton, NJ: Princeton University Press.

Smart, B. (ed.) 1992. *Beyond Compliance: A New Industry View of the Environment.* Washington, DC: World Resources Institute.

Smith, A. 1776/1937. *The Wealth of Nations.* New York: Modern Library.

Smith, V. 1962. "An experimental study of competitive market behavior," *Journal of Political Economy* 70: 111–37.

    1982. "Microeconomic systems as an experimental science," *American Economic Review* 72: 923–55.

Sobel, J. 2002. "Can we trust social capital?" *Journal of Economic Literature* 40: 139–54.

Socolow, R., R. Hotinsky, J. Greenblatt, and S. Pacala. 2004. "Solving the climate change problem," *Environment* 46(10): 8–19.

Sonnenfeld, D. A. and A. P. J. Mol. 2002. "Ecological modernization, governance, and globalization," *American Behavioral Scientist* 45(9): 1456–61.

Spar, D. L. and L. T. La Mure. 2003. "The power of activism: Assessing the impact of NGOs on global business," *California Management Review* 45(3): 78–92.

Spruyt, H. 2002. "The origins, development, and possible decline of the modern state," *Annual Review of Political Science* 5: 127–49.

Stanbridge, K. 2005. "Review: Sidney Tarrow, the new transnational activism," *Canadian Journal of Sociology Online.*

Stavins, R. 2004. *The Political Economy of Environmental Regulation.* Cheltenham, UK: Edward Elgar.

Steffen, W., A. Sanderson, P.D. Tyson, J. Jäger, P.A. Matson, B. Moore III, F. Oldfield, K. Richardson, H.-J. Schellnhuber, B.L. Turner II, and R.J. Wasson. 2004. *Global Change and the Earth System: A Planet under Pressure.* Berlin: Springer.

Stern, S. and E. Seligmann (eds.) 2004. *The Partnership Principle: New Forms of Governance in the 21st Century.* London: Archetype Publications.

Sterner, T. 2003. *Policy Instruments for Environmental and Natural Resource Management.* Washington, DC: RFF Press.

Stigler, G. J. 1989. "Two notes on the Coase theorem," *Yale Law Journal* 99(3): 631–3.

Stiglitz, J. E. 2002. *Globalization and Its Discontents.* New York: W.W. Norton.

Stokke, O. S. 2004. "Boolean analysis, mechanisms, and the study of regime effectiveness," in A. Underdal and O.R. Young (eds.) *Regime Consequences: Methodological Challenges and Research Strategies*, pp. 87–119. Dordrecht, The Netherlands: Kluwer Academic Publishers.

Strange, S. 1983. "Cave! Hic dragones: A critique of regime analysis," in S. D. Krasner (ed.) *International Regimes*, pp. 337–54. Ithaca, NY: Cornell University Press.

Streck, C. 2004. "New partnerships in global environmental policy: The Clean Development Mechanism," *Journal of Environment and Development* 13(3): 295–322.

Streeten, P. 1997. "Nongovernmental organizations and development," *Annals of the American Academy of Political and Social Science* 554: 193–210.

Tarrow, S. 2002. "Transnational contention: Organizations, coalitions, mechanisms," Paper read at American Political Science Association Annual Meeting, August 31–September 1, 2002, at Boston, MA.

2005. *The New Transnational Activism*. Cambridge Studies in Contentious Politics, J. A. Goldstone, D. McAdam, S. Tarrow, C. Tilly and E. J. Wood (eds.). Cambridge University Press.

Teegen, H., J. P. Doh, and S. Vachani. 2004. "The importance of non-governmental organizations (NGOs) in global governance and value creation: An international business research agenda," *Journal of International Business Studies* 35(6): 463–83.

Teisl, M. F., B. Roe, and R. L. Hicks. 2002. "Can eco-labels tune a market? Evidence from dolphin-safe labeling," *Journal of Environmental Economics and Management* 43(3): 339–59.

Tejeda-Cruz, C. and W. J. Sutherland. 2004. "Bird responses to shade coffee production," *Animal Conservation* 7: 169–79.

Terlaak, A. K. 2007. "Order without law: The role of certified management standards in shaping socially desired firm behaviors," *Academy of Management Review* 32: 968–85.

Terlaak, A. K. and A. A King. 2006. "The effect of certification with the ISO 9000 quality management standard: A signaling approach," *Journal of Economic Behavior and Organization* 60(4): 579–602.

Tetlock, P. E. and A. Belkin (eds.) 1996. *Counterfactual Thought Experiments in World Politics: Logical, Methodological, and Psychological Perspectives*. Princeton, NJ: Princeton University Press.

Tilly, C. 2007. *Democracy*. New York: Cambridge University Press.

Tirole, J. 1988. *The Theory of Industrial Organization*. Cambridge, MA: The MIT Press.

Toffel, M. W. 2004. "Strategic management of product recovery," *California Management Review* 46(2): 120–41.

2006. "Resolving information asymmetries in markets: The role of certified management programs," Working Paper, Harvard Business School, Boston, MA.

Toffel, M. and J. Marshall. 2004. "Comparative analysis of weighting methods used to evaluate chemical release inventories, with Julian Marshall," *Journal of Industrial Ecology* 8(1–2): 143–72.

Townsend, J. G. and A. R. Townsend. 2004. "Accountability, motivation and practice: NGOs North and South," *Social and Cultural Geography* 5(2): 271–84.

Tully, S. R. 2004. "Corporate-NGO partnerships and the regulatory impact of the energy and biodiversity initiative," *Non-State Actors and International Law* 4(2): 111.

Underdal, A. and O. R. Young (eds.) 2004. *Regime Consequences: Methodological Challenges and Research Strategies.* Dordrecht, The Netherlands: Kluwer Academic Publishers.

UNEP (United Nations Environment Programme). 2002. *GEO: Global Environment Outlook 3.* London: Earthscan.

United Nations. 2007. *The Millennium Development Goals Report.* New York: United Nations.

US DOE (United States Department of Energy). 2002. *Climate Challenge Program Report.* DOE/FE-0355. Office of Energy Efficiency and Renewable Energy, Office of Utility Technology, United States Department of Energy.

US EPA (United States Environmental Protection Agency). 2000. *Taking Toxics Out of the Air.* EPA-452/K-00-002. United States Environmental Protection Agency, Office of Air Quality, Planning and Standards, Research Triangle Park, NC [available at www.epa.gov/air].

2005. *Everyday Choices: Opportunities for Environmental Stewardship. Technical Report by the EPA Environmental Stewardship Staff Committee for the EPA Innovation Council.* Washington, DC: US EPA.

Utz Kapeh. 2005. *Year Report 2004,* June 13, 2005 [accessed March 15, 2006, available at www.utzkapeh.org/serve_attachment.php?file=archive/downloads/annual_report_utz_kapeh2004.pdf],

VanDeveer, S. D. and H. Selin (eds.) 2009. *Changing Climates in North American Politics: Institutions, Policymaking and Multilevel Governance.* Cambridge, MA: The MIT Press.

Various. 2001–6. "MAC needs new leadership," *Reefs.org* 2001–2006 [accessed March 12, 2006].

Viana, V., J. Ervin, R. Donovan, C. Elliott, and H. Gholz. 1996. *Certification of Forest Products: Issues and Perspectives.* Washington, DC: Island Press.

Videras, J. and A. Alberini. 2000. "The appeal of voluntary environmental programs: Which firms participate and why?" *Contemporary Economic Policy* 18: 449–60.

Vidovic, M. and N. Khanna. 2007. "Can voluntary pollution prevention programs fulfill their promises? Further evidence from the EPA's 33/50 program," *Journal of Environmental Economics and Management* 53: 180–95.

Vitousek, P., H. A. Mooney, J. Lubchenco, and J. M. Melillo. 1997. "Human domination of Earth's ecosystems," *Science* 277: 494–9.

Vlosky, R. P. 2000. *Certification: Perceptions of Non-Industrial Private Forestland Owners in Louisiana.* Baton Rouge, LA: Louisiana Forest Products Laboratory, Louisiana State University Agricultural Center.

Vogel, D. 1995. *Trading Up: Consumer and Environmental Regulation in a Global Economy*. Cambridge, MA: Harvard University Press.

——— 2005. *The Market for Virtue: The Potential and Limits of Corporate Social Responsibility*. Washington, DC: Brookings Institution.

Wallerstein, I. 1974. *The Modern World System*. Orlando, FL: Academic Press.

Waltz, K. 1979. *Theory of International Politics*. Reading, MA: Addison-Wesley.

Wapner, P. 1996. *Environmental Activism and World Civic Politics*. New York: State University of New York.

——— 1997. "Governance in global civil society," in O. R. Young (ed.) *Global Governance*, pp. 65–84. Cambridge, MA: The MIT Press.

Watts, M. J. 2005. "Righteous oil: Human rights, the oil complex, and corporate social responsibility," *Annual Review of Environment and Resources* 30: 373–407.

Weaver, R. K. and B. A. Rockman (eds.) 1993. *Do Institutions Matter? Government Capabilities in the United States and Abroad*. Washington, DC: Brookings Institution.

Webb, K. (ed.) 2002. *Voluntary Codes: Private Governance, the Public Interest and Innovation*. Ottawa, ON: Carleton University Research Unit for Innovation, Science and the Environment.

Weil, D. 1996. "If OSHA is so bad, why is compliance so good?" *RAND Journal of Economics* 27: 618–40.

Weitzman, M. 1974. "Prices vs. quantities," *Review of Economic Studies* 41: 225–34.

Welch, E., A. Mazur, and S. Bretschneider. 2000. "Voluntary behavior by electric utilities: Level of adoption and contribution of the climate challenge program to the reduction of carbon dioxide," *Journal of Policy Analysis and Management* 19(3): 407–25.

Welch, E. W., Y. Mori, and M. Aoyagi-Usui. 2002. "Voluntary adoption of ISO 14001 in Japan: Mechanisms, stages, and effects," *Business Strategy and the Environment* 10(1): 43–62.

Wendt, A. 1999. *Social Theory of International Politics*. Cambridge University Press.

West, P., J. Igoe, and D. Brockington. 2006. "Parks and peoples: The social impact of protected areas," *Annual Review of Anthropology* 35: 251–77.

Wilks, S. 2005. "Agency escape: Decentralization or dominance of the European Commission in the modernization of competition policy," *Governance: An International Journal of Policy and Administration* 18(3): 431–52.

Williams, O. F. (ed.) 2004. *Global Codes of Conduct: An Idea Whose Time Has Come*. Notre Dame, IN: University of Notre Dame Press.

Williamson, O. 1985. *The Economic Institutions of Capitalism*. New York: Free Press.

Winston, C. 2006. *Government Failure vs. Market Failure: Microeconomic Policy Research and Government Performance*. Washington, DC: Brookings Institution.

Wolf, C. Jr. 1988. *Markets or Government: Choosing between Imperfect Alternatives.* Cambridge, MA: The MIT Press.

Woolcock, M. 1998. "Social capital and economic development: Toward a theoretical synthesis and policy framework," *Theory and Society* 27: 151–208.

World Commission on Environment and Sustainable Development. 1987. *Our Common Future.* New York: Oxford University Press.

World Commodity Report. 1989. *Demise of Coffee Pact Brings Uncertainty.* Informa Publishing Group [accessed March 13, 2006, available at www.lexis-nexis.com].

World Trade Organization (WTO). 2003. *Trade Statistics by Sector.* Geneva: WTO.

Worldwatch Institute. 2006. *Vital Signs 2006–2007: The Trends that are Shaping Our Future.* New York: W.W. Norton.

Young, O. R. 1989. *International Cooperation: Building Regimes for Natural Resources and the Environment.* Ithaca, NY: Cornell University Press.

 1994. *International Governance: Protecting the Environment in a Stateless Society.* Ithaca, NY: Cornell University Press.

 1999a. *Governance in World Affairs.* Ithaca, NY: Cornell University Press.

 (ed.) 1999b. *The Effectiveness of International Environmental Regimes: Causal Connections and Behavioral Mechanisms.* Cambridge, MA: The MIT Press.

 2002a. "Are institutions intervening variables or basic causal forces? Causal clusters versus causal chains in international society," in M. Brecher and F. Harvey (eds.) *Millennium Reflections on International Studies,* pp. 176–91. Ann Arbor, MI: University of Michigan Press.

 2002b. *The Environmental Dimensions of Environmental Change: Fit, Interplay, and Scale.* Cambridge, MA: The MIT Press.

 2005. "Why is there no unified theory of environmental governance?" in P. Dauverge (ed.) *Handbook of Global Environmental Politics,* pp. 170–84. Cheltenham, UK: Edward Elgar.

 2008. "Building regimes for socio-ecological systems: The diagnostic method," Chapter 5 in O. R. Young, L. A. King, and H. Schroeder (eds.) *Institutions and Environmental Change: Principal Findings, Applications, and Future Directions.* Cambridge, MA: The MIT Press.

Young, O. R., E. F. Lambin, F. Alcock, H. Haberl, S. I. Karlsson, W. J. McConnell, T. Myint, C. Pahl-Wostl, C. Polsky, P. S. Ramakrishnan, H. Schroeder, M. Scouvart, and P. H. Verburg. 2006. "A portfolio approach to analyzing complex human–environment interactions: Institutions and land change," *Ecology and Society* 11(2): art. 31.

Zammit, A. 2003. *Development at Risk: Rethinking UN-Business Partnerships.* Geneva: South Centre and UNRISD.

INDEX